A History of Korea

PALGRAVE ESSENTIAL HISTORIES

General Editor: Jeremy Black

This series of compact, readable and informative national histories is designed to appeal to anyone wishing to gain a broad understanding of a country's history.

Published

A History of the Low Countries (2nd edn) *Paul Arblaster*
A History of Italy *Claudia Baldoli*
A History of Russia *Roger Bartlett*
A History of Spain (2nd edn) *Simon Barton*
A History of the British Isles (4th edn) *Jeremy Black*
A History of France *Joseph Bergin*
A History of Israel *Ahron Bregman*
A History of Ireland (2nd edn) *Mike Cronin & Liam O'Callaghan*
A History of Greece *Nicholas Doumanis*
A History of the Pacific Islands (2nd edn) *Steven Roger Fischer*
A History of Korea (2nd edn) *Kyung Moon Hwang*
A History of the United States (4th edn) *Philip Jenkins*
A History of Denmark (2nd edn) *Knud J. V. Jespersen*
A History of the Baltic States *Andres Kasekamp*
A History of Australia *Mark Peel and Christina Twomey*
A History of Poland (2nd edn) *Anita J. Prazmowska*
A History of India (2nd edn) *Peter Robb*
A History of China (3rd edn) *J. A. G. Roberts*
A History of Germany *Peter Wende*

Series Standing Order
ISBN 978-1-4039-3811-4 hardback
ISBN 978-1-4039-3812-1 paperback

If you would like to receive future titles in this series as they are published, you can make use of our standing order facility. To place a standing order please contact your bookseller or, in case of difficulty, write to us at the address below with your name and address and the name of the series. Please state with which title you wish to begin your standing order. (If you live outside the United Kingdom we may not have the rights for your area, in which case we will forward your order to the publisher concerned.) Customer Services Department, Macmillan Distribution Ltd, Houndmills, Basingstoke, Hampshire, RG21 6XS, UK

A HISTORY OF KOREA
AN EPISODIC NARRATIVE

2nd Edition

Kyung Moon Hwang

macmillan education   palgrave

First edition 2010
Published 2017 by
PALGRAVE

Palgrave in the UK is an imprint of Macmillan Publishers Limited, registered in England, company number 785998, of 4 Crinan Street, London, N1 9XW.

Palgrave Macmillan in the US is a division of St Martin's Press LLC, 175 Fifth Avenue, New York, NY 10010.

Palgrave is a global imprint of the above companies and is represented throughout the world.

Palgrave® and Macmillan® are registered trademarks in the United States, the United Kingdom, Europe and other countries.

ISBN 978–1–137–57357–5 hardback
ISBN 978–1–137–57356–8 paperback

This book is printed on paper suitable for recycling and made from fully managed and sustained forest sources. Logging, pulping and manufacturing processes are expected to conform to the environmental regulations of the country of origin.

A catalogue record for this book is available from the British Library.

A catalog record for this book is available from the Library of Congress.

Printed in China

Contents

List of Images and Boxes

Preface to the Second Edition

I have benefited considerably from feedback to the first edition of *A History of Korea*, whether from colleagues or through the review process for this second edition. I wish to thank them all for their criticisms and suggestions.

This second edition has undergone an extensive makeover, with almost every paragraph revised to improve readability and correct errors or oversights from the first edition. Among the chapters most revamped were: Chapter 1, in order to insert an introduction to Korea's environmental and geographical features as they might have affected the development of Korean civilization; Chapters 22 and 25, in order to further account for both internal and external factors in early North Korean history, as well as for the extraordinary changes in North Korea over the past two decades; and Chapters 24, 26, and 27, in order to incorporate the most recent developments in South Korea as well as new scholarship demonstrating the ongoing interaction between South Koreans' present circumstances and their turbulent history of industrialization and democratization.

This consciousness of historiography, a point of emphasis in the first edition, becomes even stronger in this second edition, as every chapter now includes extensive discussion of how the events and themes under consideration have been viewed up to the present day. The kingdom of Balhae as a catalyst of recent efforts to reconceptualize ancient Korean history (Chapter 3), for example, or the place of late-Joseon popular culture in the modern construction of tradition (Chapter 12), prompts further thinking of how historical perception reflects contemporary political or cultural concerns. Another example comes from the intriguing differences in the way the East Asian War of the 1590s (Chapter 9) or the Korean War of the 1950s (Chapter 21) is viewed across national boundaries today. In general, this international dimension of Korean history has been further accentuated, as has been the role of women, if not quite gender, as a consistent point of insight in understanding the Korean past. Thus, even without comprehensive arguments, the author's general approach and perspective should become apparent. As for the rest, it is a matter of more open-ended inquiry, the spirit and basis for which, I hope, this second edition further strengthens.

Note on Romanization

Korean terms will be rendered with the Revised Romanization System of Korean, with the exceptions of "Pyongyang" and the names of certain well-known individuals.

Maps of Korea and East Asia

Map 1 Korea, ca. 1905. (Courtesy of Lohnes+Wright)

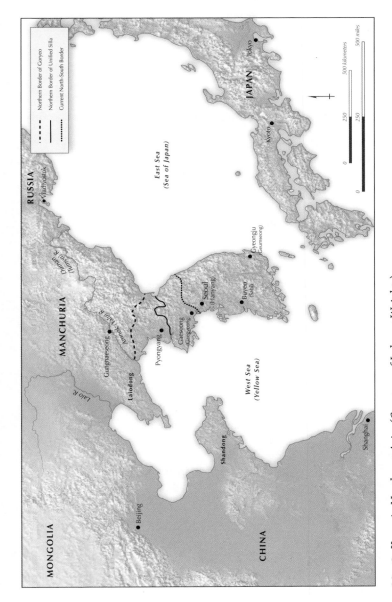

Map 2 Korea in Northeast Asia. (Courtesy of Lohnes+Wright.)

Brief Chronology of Korean History

4th–7th centuries	Three Kingdoms Period (Goguryeo, Baekje, Silla)
668–935	Unified Silla
918–1392	Goryeo Dynasty
1170–1270	Military Rule
1270–1356	Mongol Overlord Period
1392–1897	Joseon Dynasty
1446	Promulgation of the Korean Alphabet
1592–98	Japanese Invasions
1627–36	Manchu Invasions
1894	Donghak Rebellion, Sino-Japanese War, Gabo Reforms
1897–1910	Great Korean Empire (*Daehan jeguk*)
1905–10	Japanese Protectorate
1910–45	Japanese Colonial Rule
1910–19	"Military Rule"
1919	March First Uprisings
1920s	"Cultural Rule"
1938–45	Wartime Mobilization
1945	Liberation and Occupation by Allied Forces
1948	Establishment of the Republic of Korea (South) and Democratic People's Republic of Korea (North)
1950–3	Korean War
1987	Democratization in South Korea

Introduction

This book assumes no prior knowledge of Korean history, but it does ask that the reader remain open to an uncommon narrative structure for presenting the richness and distinctiveness, as well as the universality, of one of the world's oldest cultures. The sweep of Korean civilization, furthermore, is matched by the scope of its modern transformation. This book attempts to make this complex history more accessible by dividing its coverage into short chapters, each of which uses a representative event, or "episode," as a window into the chapter's broader topic and themes. The order of the chapters is chronological as well as thematic. Not everything important that happened in Korean history is highlighted, but the hope is that a focus on particular moments, people, and patterns will provide ample understanding of the major historical connections and issues.

This is, then, a somewhat idiosyncratic narrative. Some professional historians of Korea will undoubtedly find major topics either being neglected or given short shrift, while others will disagree with the author's choices. This book contains, for example, relatively little coverage of the mythological era of ancient Korea, King Yeongjo's reign in the eighteenth century, or the independence movements during the Japanese colonial period of the early twentieth century. The rationale for these decisions will either be explained or strongly implied in the respective chapters. Still other observers will of course object to the author's own biases, however veiled, in interpretation, analysis, and even periodization. This book remains mindful of the legendary accounts of earliest times, for example, but its coverage of Korean history starts much later than in most narratives—with the Goguryeo kingdom around the fourth century CE. Approximately half of the book is devoted to the premodern era, and half to the modern, with Chapter 14, covering the momentous events of 1894, functioning as a narrative fulcrum just as the year 1894 served as a historical turning point.

Readers might also wonder how to make sense of all the details, particularly about a culture that for many will be completely unfamiliar. The following themes can act as narrative anchors that ground the information to a comprehensible structure: Korean character and identity, forms of political authority, religion, economy and daily life, women and family, social hierarchy, and external relations. These themes will allow the reader to draw connections over vast temporal distances through the perception of recurrent patterns, such as Korea's complicated relationship with China and Japan, the ties between social hierarchy and political power, or the bursts of major change inspired by religion. Some chapters will tackle multiple themes, some just a couple, but all the information is designed to illuminate either a theme or a specific argument. No content is presented just for the sake of transmitting facts. Interpretative statements infuse every chapter, with the hope that these claims will spur further thinking and exploration from the reader. Toward this end the back of the book contains a list of further readings, which include many primary documents published in English translation.

Historiography, or prior historical scholarship and its methods of inquiry, is thus featured prominently, with most chapters alluding to a scholarly debate, usually by connecting the topic at hand to larger perspectives on Korean history. Each chapter acts, then, as an intervention, of varying degrees, in these considerations of historical meaning. The historiographical issues are also critical because they reflect contemporary circumstances in Korea. While always a point of contention (and command), the historical consciousness of Koreans is key to understanding Korea today; in both the North and the South, Koreans are fully aware that they are the products of their past, from the ancient to most recent times. This book attempts to demonstrate how.

1 Goguryeo and Ancient Korea

CHRONOLOGY

108 BCE	Establishment of Chinese Han dynasty commanderies on the Korean peninsula
1st c. BCE	Founding of Goguryeo
3rd–4th c. CE	Emergence of Baekje and Silla kingdoms
581	Establishment of Sui dynasty in China
598	First Sui invasion of Goguryeo
612	Massive Sui dynasty campaign against Goguryeo; Great Battle of Salsu River
618	Fall of Sui, founding of Tang dynasty in China
668	Defeat of Goguryeo by joint Silla–Tang forces

THE GREAT BATTLE OF SALSU RIVER, 612

In the first half of the year 612, Sui dynasty China attempted to conquer Goguryeo, a pesky kingdom on its northeastern border, and threw at this the full might of its resources and skills. The final confrontation took place in what came to be known as the "Great Battle of Salsu River," where Goguryeo forces maneuvered the Chinese army into a death trap that left barely 3,000 survivors out of an initial invasion force of over one million soldiers. This triumphant effort can be considered a formative event for a distinctive civilization, Korea, that would go on to withstand many such threats to its existence.

The Goguryeo kingdom (first century BCE to seventh century CE), the earliest political entity on the Korean peninsula supported by substantial and reliable historical records, came to rule a vast territory extending well into Manchuria. This geographical dominion, together with historical evidence of its military prowess, its cultural achievements, and its forms of political and religious authority, has led to the widespread embrace of this kingdom as the great representative of

1

early Korean civilization. This identification of Korea with Goguryeo, from which the name "Korea" itself is derived, has grown even stronger as a backlash against recent Chinese efforts to insert this kingdom into China's own historical trajectory. Such an uneasy relationship, which undergirds a panoply of issues regarding Korean history and identity, has characterized Korea's existence since the very beginning, which most Koreans actually believe far predated Goguryeo. The earliest years of Korean civilization are shrouded in sacred myths that invoke familiar themes—heavenly descent, early trials and tribulations, and so on—but also speak to distinctive features of Korean identity, especially in relation to the dominant civilization on the continent, China.

ANCIENT KOREA AND GOGURYEO

Goguryeo as a coherent political entity appears to have materialized out of the consolidation of proto-states and statelets in the first century BCE, long after the purported origins of Korean civilization itself, according to official and conventional histories. Indeed the Korean people supposedly began with the mythical progenitor, Dangun, born on the sacred Mount Baekdu through the mating of the son of the presiding god over the universe, and a bear transformed into a woman. This legend, the earliest extant version of which dates to the thirteenth century, relates that Dangun established the state of "Joseon" in the northern reaches of the peninsula and extending well into Manchuria. The curious precision of the date of this founding, 2333 BCE (Dangun is credited with a reign over Joseon lasting over 1500 years), has given license to round up the age of Korean civilization in today's common parlance to 5000 years. Joseon, or "Old Joseon" as it is referred to today, supposedly gave way to smaller states that developed more features of higher civilization on the peninsula. Some of these earliest polities, such as Goguryeo, Buyeo, Okjeo, and the Three Han confederations (Mahan, Jinhan, and Byeonhan) on the southern half of the peninsula, made their way into descriptions of various "barbarians" in ancient Chinese histories.

Such accounts include colorful observations of these peoples' clothing, food, customs, and rituals, which today provide valuable indications of primal religion and its place in these societies' formation. The most common element in the foundation myths, including that of

Goguryeo, is the birth of the founder from an animalistic element, such as a bear or an egg. Mythologists detect in such features the influence of shamanism, which perceives the natural world as infused with spirits that affect human life and can be appeased only through a priestly *shaman*, the liaison to the spirit world. As in other early civilizations, the priest who claimed access to the spirits (or gods) enjoyed political power as well, and this appears to be reflected in these early states' mythologies. Dangun, with his parentage in the spirit world, can thus be considered symbolic of the first Great Shaman, and the same could be said for Jumong, the mythical progenitor of Goguryeo, who is said to have hatched from an egg.

Such a preponderance of natural elements in these early societies' spiritual life also likely reflected the dynamic influence of Korea's environment. Anchored by the Taebaek mountain chain on the eastern side that functions as a geographical backbone, the peninsula is filled with mountains, which drive the rush of waters, nutrients, and energies down to the valleys and the scattered expanses of flat land. Rice-based agriculture, which arose before the formation of the ancient polities described above, came to be concentrated in the southern half of the peninsula, which boasts much broader plains, while the north features more rugged peaks and formidable plateaus, as well as longer bouts of cold. But the peninsula as a whole experiences four distinctive seasons as well as summer monsoons. The waters drain through several major rivers, such as the Han, Daedong, Cheongcheon, and Nakdong, that originate in the Taebaek Mountains and flow out to the Yellow Sea in the west or to the South Sea, which separates the peninsula from Japan. In relation to the Asian mainland, since the fifteenth century the Korean peninsula has been demarcated by the Amnok (Yalu) and Duman (Tumen) Rivers, which flow southwesterly and northeasterly, respectively, from their sources on Mount Baekdu, Korea's tallest peak. The west and south coasts, which are relatively shallow, murky, and dotted with thousands of islands, contrast with the east coast, which borders the deep, expansive, and brilliant East Sea. Fishing, naturally, came to take a prominent place in Koreans' economic and cultural development, as did in general the interaction, both physical and spiritual, with flowing water. It was the mountains, however, that both dominated the landscape and shaped core features of Korean civilization, serving as boundaries between culturally distinctive regions and corresponding broadly to the borders between major polities that emerged in the ancient era.

One of the consistent dynamics throughout Korean history, indeed, was the effort to overcome this naturally induced fragmentation, manifested in distinctive customs and collective identities, through administrative penetration and centralization. But political and military conquest did eventually integrate the disparate segments of the peninsula, and the mountains came to serve as channels of amalgamation, if not quite homogenization. Just as importantly, the geographical, topographical, and environmental features of the peninsula, which bleed into Manchuria, eventually came to be recognized as organically distinctive from that of China, especially the central plain where Chinese civilization was rooted. This also reinforced the sense of separation based on the customary, culinary, sartorial, and linguistic differences with the Middle Kingdom.

The legends of the early period, too, suggest a strong consciousness of China, though not necessarily one of opposition. The best-known version of the Dangun story, for example, recites that Dangun introduced administrative capacities to govern his realm. This suggests the need to legitimate this civilization as worthy of both Chinese-derived recognition, on the one hand, and autonomy from China, on the other. Indeed, the ability to resist absorption into China while benefiting from its cultural influence proved critical since the earliest times. This theme was exemplified by the well-known story, eventually integrated into the "Old Joseon" narrative, that Dangun was succeeded by a sage named Gija, an aristocratic refugee from Zhou dynasty China, a millennium before Goguryeo came into being. Gija, then, represented the authenticating presence of Chinese civilization, and until the twentieth century Koreans tended to believe that Dangun bestowed upon Korea its people and basic culture, while Gija gave Korea its high culture— and, presumably, its standing as a legitimate civilization. Nationalist sentiment in the modern era has nearly obliterated Gija, but unquestionably, whether real or fictitious, he symbolized the powerful self-consciousness vis-à-vis China from the earliest times of Korean civilization.

More historically tenable is the struggle Goguryeo waged, in its formative years, against the Chinese military presence on the Korean peninsula. In the corridors connecting the peninsula to the mainland, the Chinese Han dynasty established four commanderies over the surrounding territories, much as modern imperial powers governed their colonies. Like their contemporary Roman counterparts, these Chinese colonies transmitted the fruits of a more advanced culture and technology to the "barbarians," but they also had an uneasy relationship with these tribes, whom they both nominally ruled over and kept a wary distance from. Eventually the Lelang (Korean: Nangnang) Commandery, around present-day Pyongyang, would establish itself as the most formidable and durable of these colonial administrations. While Lelang survived the fall of the Han dynasty itself, Goguryeo, which had offered the most consistent peninsular resistance to Chinese dominion, overran it in the early fourth century. But soon Goguryeo itself had to contend with competing kingdoms on the peninsula that had undergone much the same process of consolidation from tribal confederations. All these early kingdoms, from their adoption of Buddhism and Chinese writing to their embrace of Confucian administrative models, reflected the blend of Chinese cultural influence and long-standing peninsular cultural behaviors. Among these polities, Goguryeo, thanks to its geographical proximity to China, remained the most wary of, even hostile to, Chinese influence.

THE RISE AND FALL OF GOGURYEO

Goguryeo seems not to have taken well to the notion of "eastern barbarians" (*dongi*), the original Chinese moniker for the peninsular tribes that eventually became a self-deprecating term of prestige for Koreans, who considered themselves "first among seconds" among the peoples surrounding China. After the fall of the Han dynasty in the early third century CE, China underwent centuries of fragmentation, and Goguryeo took advantage of this situation to grow increasingly powerful in northeast Asia and dominant on the peninsula. The martial vigor, economic vitality, and cultural advancement of this kingdom, so visible in the numerous extant tomb paintings (see text box), reflected well the impressive political and military power that Goguryeo amassed. The neighboring kingdoms were much younger and, until the latter part of the sixth century, left to contend for the southern half of the peninsula, while Goguryeo's authority stretched to the far reaches of Manchuria.

An early peak in power came at the turn of the fifth century under the reign of King Gwanggaeto, whose exploits in pushing the boundaries of Goguryeo's dominion in all directions befit his name, which means "extender of territory." Goguryeo, however, did not trample over the entire peninsula, despite the chronic condition of competition and struggle among the kingdoms. And the balance of power was maintained when Baekje and Silla, by the fifth century the other two remaining kingdoms, entered into a semi-formal alliance to check Goguryeo. Henceforth the borders between these three ebbed and flowed. Even Baekje, better known for its cultural achievements than for its martial prowess, managed to gain territorial victories. By the middle of the sixth century, however, it was the prickly, relatively late-blooming kingdom of Silla that began to ascend in this tripartite rivalry, which would not have endangered Goguryeo had it not been for the simultaneously ominous circumstances brewing in China.

In the year 581, after nearly four centuries of internal division, China was reunified by the Sui dynasty. Soon thereafter Sui rulers turned to one of the most nettlesome matters that had plagued Chinese polities, namely, what to do about the feisty kingdom to their northeast, Goguryeo. The Sui's early years witnessed an effort on both sides to establish a working relationship, but soon internal developments within Goguryeo that the Sui emperor objected to led to a deterioration of relations. As with its drives to extend the Grand Canal and to fortify the Great Wall, the Sui leadership took a heavy-handed approach to the Goguryeo question. And as with these other campaigns, the efforts to conquer Goguryeo would contribute to the shortened life span of the Sui dynasty itself. In response to Goguryeo's encroachment into the western banks of the Liao River, the first Chinese invasion attempt came in 598, amassing a force of 300,000 naval and ground soldiers that became bogged down in bad weather and worse luck on their way to the peninsula.

These heavy losses suffered by the Sui forces would pale in comparison to the calamities of the next major invasion attempt in 612, which would end with defeat at the Battle of Salsu River. The Chinese force mobilized for this campaign in the early part of the year was staggering in scale: over one million soldiers alone, not counting the accompanying manpower to move and feed them. The Korean historical records, based primarily on Chinese accounts, recount that the original six divisions of fighters marching together stretched for thirty miles. These armies managed eventually to overwhelm the Goguryeo defenses in the Laiodong border area. The Chinese, however, suffered enormous casualties and other losses (through, for example, sickness and runaways), enabling Goguryeo not only to stave off conquest but also to inflict severe damage on the invaders as they made their way to the

Goguryeo capital of Pyongyang. In their siege on Pyongyang, the Sui forces penetrated the outer walls of the city, but Goguryeo held them off enough to negotiate a peace settlement. This agreement would ostensibly signal Goguryeo's capitulation and entrance into a subordinate tributary relationship with the Sui emperor, in return for Chinese withdrawal from the peninsula.

The Goguryeo commander assigned to negotiate with the Sui forces, Eulji Mundeok, would go down in Korean historical lore as one of its great heroes, not for surrendering to the Chinese—for this was but a ploy—but for destroying the Chinese army on its slow retreat back to China. As it trod northward along the western coast of the peninsula and started crossing the Salsu River (known as the Cheongcheon River today), Eulji unleashed a barrage of attacks on the rear flank, decimating the weary Chinese, who beat a frenzied retreat to the Yalu River. Legend has it that among the strategies Eulji deployed was the releasing of dammed water upriver that overwhelmed many of the Chinese soldiers as they attempted to cross the Salsu. In any case, the official Korean and Chinese histories note that the Sui army, which numbered over 300,000 soldiers laying siege to Pyongyang, had fewer than 3,000 remaining when it reached Liaodong several weeks later. This would go down as one of the monumental defeats in military history; rarely had such an enormous force—beginning with over a million combatants—suffered such devastation from a severely outmanned counterpart. For the Goguryeo, and for Koreans looking back on their history of constantly repelling foreign invaders, this episode constituted a victory of epic proportions.

The stupendous scale of this defeat did not deter the Sui emperor, however, from launching another invasion the next year, and yet another in 614, though both subsequent efforts also failed to subdue Goguryeo. The Sui dynasty began to collapse shortly thereafter, partly because of the enormous cost of these conquest attempts. The succeeding Chinese dynasty, the Tang, followed up with campaigns of its own in the 640s, but these, too, met with failure due to fierce resistance under the direction of Goguryeo's military ruler, Yeon Gaesomun. It was evident that the Chinese would not be able to defeat this kingdom on their own, and indeed it took an alliance with the peninsular kingdom of Silla, which had chafed under Goguryeo's imposing presence, for this to take place. The resolution to the intra-peninsular rivalry would finally come in 668 through the destruction of Goguryeo at the hands of the joint Silla–Tang forces.

The wall paintings of the Goguryeo tombs

The relative dearth of written documentation about Goguryeo is compensated by the wondrously vivid wall paintings found in more than a hundred tombs around the major Goguryeo settlements, in particular the Liaodong area and the capitals of Pyongyang and Gungnaeseong, on the banks of the Yalu River. These extraordinary paintings visually expound upon what the textual evidence hints at: a vigorous, sophisticated, and advanced civilization. That the images exist at all tells us that Goguryeo was a highly stratified society with a powerful and wealthy aristocracy, the highest members of whom, along with the royal families, left this world encased in elaborately decorated tombs. The paintings usually depict the buried person himself (or herself), accompanied by attendees drawn to smaller size but equally colorful in their dress. Other scenes testify to a martial vitality, with depictions of muscled strongmen, elaborately clad warriors, and immaculately dressed hunters on horseback aiming their bows at leaping deer and tigers. Great skill in archery and riding, indeed, would constitute signal features of Korean military culture thereafter.

The wall paintings also provide a strong indication of how the Goguryeo people, or at least its ruling class, viewed the greater cosmos, and of how their arts and architecture elegantly reflected this cosmology. Wondrous spirits abound, including the "four guardian deities" (*sasin*) of ancient East Asian folklore. There are also depictions of human-like figures in flowing robes representing the gods of the earth, moon, sun, and fire. Buddhist paintings tell us that this imported, systematic, and textual religion was making its presence felt in the religious order, likely melding with native folk practices and boasting an understanding of the movement of the heavens, as represented in the star charts painted onto the walls. Art was not limited just to the service of Goguryeo cosmology, though, as we see in the portrayals of musical and dance performances and other signs of a sophisticated aristocratic sensibility.

Depictions of the daily lives of the people, however, are equally revealing. We are treated to scenes of women going about their weaving activities, of fields and marketplaces with people dressed in polka-dotted clothing, and of an ancient form of *ssireum*, or Korean wrestling. We also get a strong sense of the economic advancement

→

of Goguryeo civilization, for amidst the displays of agricultural and handicraft goods are numerous appearances of wagons. Indeed, there is even a portrayal of what appears to be a "wagon goddess" wielding an oversized wheel like a magic wand. Based on the lack of such visual indicators and on the general condition of Korean roads thereafter, which were designed for walking—by both humans and horses—wagons seem to have diminished considerably in Korea's subsequent socioeconomic order. Indeed, these extraordinary wall paintings suggest that transportation technologies might have been just one of many aspects of Korean civilization for which Goguryeo had achieved an early peak.

Image 1a Scene from Goguryeo Tomb Painting, Corridor Eastern Wall, Deokheungni. (Courtesy of the Northeast Asia History Foundation.)

Image 1b Scene from Goguryeo Tomb Painting, Front Room Wall, Deokheungni. (Courtesy of the Northeast Asia History Foundation.)

GOGURYEO AND KOREAN HISTORY

Until the twentieth century, Silla's "unification" of the peninsula enjoyed the stamp of legitimacy in the prevailing Korean historical perspective, for each succeeding dynastic order traced its lineage ultimately to this seventh-century event. In the modern era, however, nationalist historical views deemed Silla's action more a betrayal of the nation than a solution to centuries of peninsular balkanization, for it destroyed what many consider the truer representative of Korea's ancient civilization, Goguryeo. Goguryeo appears to have had the most vibrant and advanced political, military, and cultural order, and, perhaps most importantly, Goguryeo was the ancient kingdom that refused to budge in the face of threats to peninsular autonomy. Goguryeo's relentless resistance to the Chinese, then, stood in stark contrast to Silla's behavior of turning to the Chinese for help.

The problem with this revisionist perspective, which is now orthodoxy in North Korea and widely accepted in South Korea, is that it overlooks the many examples of Goguryeo's close ties to China and exaggerates the dependence of Silla or Baekje on outside forces. More importantly, it imposes a modern nation-centered perspective on the ancient era. There is little evidence suggesting that the people on the peninsula from the fourth to the seventh century perceived a common bond equivalent to a collective ethnic identity. In fact, the reordering of history to make it appear as such began after Silla's conquest of the other two kingdoms in order to legitimate its dominion. The official historians of the Goryeo dynasty (918–1392)—which, despite its very telling name, proclaimed itself also the rightful heir to Silla—further cemented the notion of a "Three Kingdoms" era by bestowing upon Silla the status of national unifier. Ironically, their successors in the twentieth century would turn this imagined unity into an insistence on the centrality not of Silla, but rather of Goguryeo.

Indeed, so widely accepted has this view become in Korea today, that to consider Goguryeo an unaligned kingdom based partly in the peninsula and partly in Manchuria is to provoke outrage. What contemporary Chinese historians have done, apparently with the blessings of the Chinese government, is to go one step further and imply that Goguryeo was actually part of *Chinese* history: Just as China today is one country with many ethnicities, China in the past was one country with many groups, including the people of Goguryeo. From the Koreans' perspective, this amounts to robbing them of their own history, of the very kingdom on which the name "Korea" itself is based. Lying beneath the surface, however, is also the latent Korean belief, of which the Chinese are aware, that Goguryeo can provide a lesson on how Koreans—eventually reunified, as warranted by the official national imperative—should deal with a resurgent, dominant China: at arm's length, and with an assertiveness of Korea's autonomy and interests. Such is the power of even ancient history in Korea today.

2 Queen Seondeok and Silla's Unification of Korea

CHRONOLOGY

SILLA'S DISPATCH OF A TRIBUTE EMBASSY TO CHINA, 643

Feeling besieged, the monarch of the Silla kingdom sent a tributary embassy to the emperor of Tang dynasty China in 643 with an urgent request for Chinese assistance in fending off incursions from the other two peninsular powers, Goguryeo and Baekje. The Chinese emperor, sensing another opportunity to strike Goguryeo, vowed to attack the two adversaries and even offered thousands of Chinese army uniforms so that Silla soldiers could intimidate their opponents on the battlefield. The emperor's third suggestion, though, was startling: Silla should accept a Chinese prince as its interim ruler, whose presence would put an end to Silla's misfortune—a misfortune that, according to the emperor, was due to its monarch. It was not the Silla ruler's actions or policies that were objectionable, but rather her gender, for it was Queen Seondeok, the first of three female rulers of Silla.

Tang China would become the indispensable partner in Silla's defeat of its peninsular rivals, but the Sillan leaders' capacity to walk a diplomatic tightrope between autonomy and Chinese assistance would prove instrumental in securing the kingdom's supremacy. This process began indeed in the reign of Queen Seondeok, from 632 to 647, when the Silla state further systematized central rule and cultivated the realms of religion, culture, science, and the military.

BUDDHISM AND POWER

Queen Seondeok's most notable accomplishment might have come in developing state sponsorship of the Buddhist establishment. Buddhism, a religion preaching the path to overcoming human suffering through ritual, restraint, study, and meditation, had by the fourth century CE traversed its way eastward through northern India, Tibet, China, and the Korean peninsula, on its way eventually toward Japan. In this process Buddhism usually gained initial following among learned elites, who developed approaches and perspectives in line with their specific cultural traditions and contemporary circumstances. They then disseminated the modified forms to the laity, absorbed local religious customs, and usually persuaded the ruling groups to embrace this powerfully systematic set of teachings.

The political rulers, in turn, found Buddhism, in particular the Buddhist clergy, a useful ally in further consolidating their dominion and in strengthening their aura of authority. Eventually, political domination went hand-in-hand with patronage of Buddhism. The authoritative twelfth-century Korean historical source, *History of the Three Kingdoms* (*Samguk sagi*), relates that an especially large number of Buddhist temples were erected during Queen Seondeok's reign, a reflection of the religion's increasing dependence on the state, and vice-versa, in the early seventh century. In fact, the "Mireuk" sect of Buddhism that came to prevail on the peninsula considered the monarch the potential Maitreya, or the salvational future Buddha. The ancient Korean rulers, even those of relatively systematic states like Silla, basked in this religious eminence, which accompanied the increasing centralization of state authority in all three kingdoms.

For some leaders, like Queen Seondeok, the latter historical perception of their rule, as well, appears to have been wedded to their spiritual mystique. The *Tales of the Three Kingdoms* (*Samguk yusa*), a work from the thirteenth century that mostly recounts the legendary history of Buddhism in ancient Korea, provides glimpses of this relationship. She is said to have issued three prophecies during her reign, all coming true: one concerning a cryptic gift from the Chinese emperor, another suspecting an imminent Baekje attack, and finally a prediction of the manner of her own death. The themes of these prophecies reflect important issues that surrounded her reign, as we will see below. But the overarching impression left by these stories is of a skillful, sagacious monarch whose mystical powers reflected her illustrious status, as if she were indeed a reincarnation of the Buddha.

Buddhism's influence also came from the great standing that China enjoyed as the perceived center of high culture. The three kingdoms each sent students, scholars, and clergymen to the Middle Kingdom to gain exposure to advanced Buddhist learning. Indeed Wonhyo (617–86), a gifted monk who was a younger contemporary of Queen Seondeok, is still the most celebrated figure in Korean Buddhist history, so influential was his synthesis of Buddhist teachings into a more comprehensible form. He was among the first great Korean popularizers of this foreign religion, and his reputation extended all the way to Japan, which became a depository of continental civilization as filtered largely through the kingdoms on the Korean peninsula. Such activity was not limited to Buddhism, however; other aspects of Chinese culture were eagerly absorbed (and transmitted), including the complicated but impressively ordered set of teachings about government and politics known as Confucianism. Wonhyo's own son, Seol Chong (660–730), became one of the early eminent Confucian scholars and traditionally has been credited with developing the Korean writing system known as *idu*. This father–son tandem symbolized the momentous transitions in Korean civilization during their life spans, in particular the consolidation of the peninsula under Silla rule.

LEGENDS OF THE UNIFICATION

Queen Seondeok's reign is often associated with the beginning of the unification process, which ended in the 670s when Silla, having conquered the other two peninsular states, established a working peace with its main ally-turned-rival, Tang dynasty China. Queen Seondeok has stood as a key contributor to the unification saga, but the most prominent figures have traditionally been two officials who came of age under her reign, Gim Chunchu and Gim Yusin.

In the 630s, when Queen Seondeok ascended the throne, Silla was not in a strong position to emerge as the eventual victor on the peninsula. It was under constant attack from both of its rivals and losing territory, especially to Baekje. As the *History of the Three Kingdoms* recounts, when

Gim Chunchu, a nephew of the Queen, lost one of his daughters in a Baekje attack in 641, he turned his grief into a raging pursuit of vengeance. He received Seondeok's permission to take a small delegation to Goguryeo to ask for its assistance in the struggle against Baekje. The Goguryeo monarch demanded in return promises from Silla to return some of Goguryeo's former territory that Silla had seized earlier. When Gim rejected this demand, the Goguryeo king immediately incarcerated him. Word reached the Silla court, and soon the queen had her skilled commander, Gim Yusin, mobilize 10,000 crack troops to attack Goguryeo. Before fighting ensued, this daring move appeared sufficient to earn Chunchu's release, and the legend of the two Gims was born, eventually to climax in their respective roles in the unification.

Gim Chunchu would gain fame as the ambitious enabler of Silla's victories. He laid the diplomatic groundwork, through his status as Silla's royal envoy, for the indispensable alliance with the Tang dynasty. For this, he would also be eventually excoriated by some modern historians for setting a precedent of political dependence that would reappear repeatedly in Korean history, and a pattern of cultural subservience that robbed the Koreans of their sense of identity. Later, after being enthroned as King Muyeol in 654, Chunchu cemented this relationship with China, which paid off when, in early 660, the Tang emperor sent 130,000 Chinese troops to join Silla in its attack on Baekje forces. Baekje would fall that summer in the famous Battle of Hwangsanbeol. Chunchu died the following year, and it would be his son, the next Silla king, who would oversee the completion of peninsular conquest under the direction of Gim Yusin.

If Gim Chunchu has faced a mixed reception among modern historians, Gim Yusin has continued to enjoy a positive assessment. The military hero of the unification wars, Yusin's popular standing has as much to do with the mystique of his exploits as with his historically verifiable accomplishments, which were spectacular to begin with. First, he played a central role, as Gim Chunchu's brother-in-law, in providing the political and military support for Chunchu to ascend the throne in the first place. He served thereafter as Chunchu's right-hand man in efforts to solidify the alliance with China, consolidate and strengthen monarchical control, and carry out military campaigns against Baekje. As the leader of Silla's forces, Gim Yusin is credited with vanquishing Baekje, and with mapping out the plan to conquer Goguryeo. The defeat of Goguryeo, again in partnership with the Tang forces, came finally in 668, but not without the threat of Silla itself becoming absorbed by its erstwhile Chinese ally. When Tang forces remained in Korea to enforce the Chinese emperor's claims to dominion over the peninsula as a whole, Yusin led the resistance in what has come to be known as the Silla–Tang War of the 670s. Gim's eventual success in driving out the Chinese from the peninsula was tempered by the compromise reached for the sake of peace, namely the limitation of Silla's advance into Goguryeo's old territory. While modern historians would lament this outcome, Gim Yusin's heroic status remains unblemished. In fact it has spawned a modern romanticization of Gim and especially of the troupe of young men that had trained him, the *Hwarang*.

The *Hwarang*, literally the "Flower Youth" corps, appears to have risen to prominence during the reign of Queen Seondeok's father, King Jinpyeong. The *History of the Three Kingdoms*, which seems to have referenced a work called the *Chronicles of the Hwarang* (*Hwarang segi*), includes a few passages that portray the *Hwarang* as a youth group that inculcated the spirit of camaraderie, learning, and service. Gim Yusin was the most famous *Hwarang* graduate, but prominent also were his son, Wonsul, and Gwanchang, a brave youth who died in the decisive battle against Baekje in 660. The legendary standing of these three, and the relative absence of *Hwarang* actions in the records after the seventh century, point again to the appropriation of people, events, and legends for the historical legitimation of the Silla unification. Such an exercise was not limited to this narrative of glorification, however. Even before, but particularly after, the controversial discovery of a manuscript of *The Chronicles of the Hwarang* in the late 1980s, political and cultural leaders in South Korea pointed to this troupe as a model for traditional values, patriotism, national service, and even the martial arts.

Baekje, the third kingdom

The debate about the legitimacy of Silla's unification is itself based on the notion of the Three Kingdoms being somehow "Korean" because what later became Korea occupied the same geographical territory as the three kingdoms. Such a structuring of the past according to what happened later—what historians call the fallacy of *teleology*—overlooks the political as well as nationalistic motivations for devising such narratives of legitimation. Furthermore, this premise tends to downgrade other important elements of ancient history on the peninsula, in particular the "third kingdom" of Baekje. In addition to being a major political and cultural entity, Baekje best reflected the complex, close ties between the peninsular

→

polities and those in the islands to the south and east that, around the time of Silla's conquest, formed what we now call Japan.

At one time Baekje might have been the most dynamic and powerful of the three kingdoms. Although the mythologies of this kingdom date its founding to the first century BCE by migrants from the north, historical records more soundly place its emergence in the fourth century CE. The early Baekje state, however, was driven further southward from its original position around present-day Seoul, and for the last two centuries of its existence until 660, Baekje territory was limited mostly to the southwestern portion of the peninsula. But it occupied the peninsula's most fertile regions and developed a sophisticated political and economic system, as well as impressive achievements in religion and culture. Indeed Buddhism's paramount position in Baekje civilization appears to have inspired some of the most outstanding religious artifacts from the ancient era.

Baekje transmitted many of these cultural advances, including technologies in metallurgy and architecture, to the polities that began forming simultaneously across the strait in the Japanese islands. The archaeological and historical evidence, including from ancient Japanese sources, of consistent, active interaction between the archipelago and the states on the peninsula is overwhelming. So strong were the ties between the early Japanese state and Baekje, in particular, that when Baekje battled Silla in the unification wars, aid arrived from the islands, and after Baekje's defeat in 660, many of its people fled to Japan. These developments reinforced a connection that likely dated back several centuries. But how close was this connection? Did, for example, Baekje rulers contribute to establishing the Japanese royal line, and if so, to what extent? In 2001 the Japanese emperor himself acknowledged the Baekje contributions to his ancestry, which further complicated the historical claims on both sides. But it is difficult to assert the existence, before the seventh century, of such things as Korea and Japan, which began as political constructs, not primordial civilizations.

SILLA'S "WINNING" FEATURES

The modern appropriation of the *Hwarang* myths extended the centuries-long drive to see something spectacular in Silla's conquest of the other two kingdoms. But it can be argued that these attempts to incorporate the unification struggle into a grand narrative of national unity did a disservice. In Chapter 1 we noted that many observers have come to consider Goguryeo a truer representative of ancient Korean civilization. To them, Silla betrayed the nation by turning to the Chinese for solving an internal Korean issue and thereby setting a precedent of reliance on foreign powers that would warp the entirety of Korean history thereafter. A further problem, though having less to do with modern nationalism, is that the triumphal narratives of Silla's unification can overshadow other intriguing features of this kingdom. Two such facets of Silla and, by extension, of ancient Korea as a whole, come to mind, both highlighted by their association with Queen Seondeok.

The first theme is the impressive technological and cultural advancement of the ancient societies on the peninsula. We have noted already the Goguryeo achievements in this regard, and Baekje also demonstrated such advances (see text box). Silla, too, reached notable heights, with stunning examples still readily visible today in the "museum without walls," the city of Gyeongju, Silla's capital. These include enormous and immaculate bronze bells, the pagodas in and around Buddhist temples, the intricately crafted stone carvings of ancient spirits and legends that grace the numerous tombs and other artifacts, and the extraordinary "Seokguram" Buddhist grotto that achieved perfection in the unity of art and spirituality. Perhaps the most intriguing remnant of ancient Gyeongju is the eight-meter high Cheomseongdae astronomical observatory that visitors today can easily view up close. This observatory's precise date of origin is unclear, but all of the historical accounts about it, beginning with the *History of the Three Kingdoms*, point toward the reign of Queen Seondeok. In addition to the historical records, another feature of this observatory also seems to support this perspective: It is comprised of twenty-seven layers of stone, and Seondeok was the twenty-seventh monarch of Silla. Before dismissing this as a coincidence, one has to consider the precision in the construction of this observatory. The twenty-seven layers are divided by a square-shaped entrance mid-way up the structure, which takes up three layers. That leaves twelve layers above and twelve below the entrance, in reference to the twelve months of the lunar year. Even the number of stones is roughly 365, the number of days in the solar year. Given its role in setting the agricultural calendar, forecasting the weather, and, presumably, predicting natural disasters, astronomy (or astrology) occupied a central place in the economic life of the people and, hence, also in maintaining the aura of legitimacy surrounding the monarchs.

Image 2 *The Cheomseongdae Observatory, Gyeongju, South Korea. (Author's photo.)*

Another notable feature of the observatory's construction is its shape (see Image 2), which is very different from other astronomical observatories in traditional Korea. While one could easily regard this shape as that of a vase, one might surmise that, because it was built during the reign of Queen Seondeok and may have even functioned as an altar to her, the observatory actually is shaped to resemble a female body. Whether this is true or not, the possibility leads us to the other feature of Silla and ancient Korea evoked by Queen Seondeok, and that is the surprisingly high status of females. Textual and archaeological sources both point toward practices, such as uxorilocalism, or the custom of the husband living in his bride's household, suggesting a relatively high standing of females in these kingdoms. The Goguryeo tomb paintings discussed in Chapter 1 also feature prominent females in a way never seen again in later Korean eras. Perhaps the most convincing sign of high female standing, however, are Silla's three female monarchs, starting with Seondeok, then her successor, Jindeok, and finally Queen Jinseong, who reigned in the late ninth century toward the end of the Silla kingdom. A female ruler of Korea would not reappear thereafter until the twenty-first century.

There remain competing interpretations regarding Seondeok's background and achievements, which paved the way toward the reigns of the other two female monarchs, but the important point is that Seondeok was almost certainly more than a figurehead. Indeed, she appears to have elicited fierce pride and loyalty. The stories surrounding her mystical powers, described above, point to this, but a more convincing source is the *History of the Three Kingdoms*, which notes that, even before her reign, she had proven herself "generous, benevolent, wise, and smart." This source reveals that, upon ascending the throne, she undertook a major relief campaign on behalf of suffering commoners in the countryside, and later she coordinated efforts to beat back the barrage of attacks from the other two peninsular kingdoms.

Perhaps the most memorable episode came in 643, the twelfth year of her reign, when she dispatched a diplomatic mission to Tang emperor Taizong of China, only to be ridiculed for being a female monarch in the first place. The Tang emperor, it is recorded, put forth three proposals in response to the Silla diplomats' pleas. First, he would attack the Liaodong peninsula, between China and the Korean peninsula, in order to divert the attention of Goguryeo, China's longtime nemesis, and carry out a naval campaign on the west coast to preoccupy Baekje. Second, the emperor would provide thousands of Tang uniforms and army flags in order to help Silla soldiers disguise themselves as fearsome Chinese troops. Finally, he would send a Tang prince to serve as the new monarch of Silla, for Silla, according to the emperor, faced constant siege because its enemies felt emboldened by its female monarch. The unsettling implications of this final proposal could not have escaped the Silla ambassador, who is recorded as having simply but respectfully acknowledged the emperor's proposals.

What is equally remarkable about this account is that the twelfth-century compiler of the *History of the Three Kingdoms*, Gim Busik, was a Confucian scholar-official who also disdained the idea of a female ruler. In addition to other details suggesting that the Tang emperor's proposals provoked political intrigue among Seondeok's opponents in the Silla elite, the *History of the Three Kingdoms*' coverage of Queen Seondeok's reign concludes with commentary that supports the emperor's proposal: "According to heavenly principles, the *yang* [male] is hard while the *yin* [female] is soft; and people know that men are to be revered and women are subordinate. So how could Silla have allowed an old maid to leave her inner sanctum in order to govern the country's affairs? Silla allowed her to ascend to become the king, and sure enough chaos ensued. How fortunate that the country did not get destroyed!"

Not only did the country avoid destruction, but it might have been Seondeok's accomplishments, including her patronage of the Buddhist establishment as well as her cultivation of statecraft, that helped save the kingdom in the face of its imminent demise. That this could have even contributed to Silla's ultimate triumph on the peninsula is an irony that seems to have escaped Gim Pusik, himself a descendant of the Silla monarchy, in his critique. But these tantalizing signs of Seondeok's savvy and prowess, however scarce the reliable historical details, have worked in a way that reverses the traditional historical perspective. Today Queen Seondeok, like the Silla unification, Gim Yusin, and other venerable relics of ancient Korea, is being reevaluated and freely appropriated by Koreans in reconsidering their identity and heritage. In reimaginings reflected in popular culture, Queen Seondeok today often serves as a paragon of female virtue, a great symbol of a time when Korea stayed true to itself and held (some) women in high esteem.

3 Unified Silla

CHRONOLOGY

ASSASSINATION OF JANG BOGO, 846

The mid-ninth century witnessed the rise of Jang Bogo, a local strongman of the southwestern coast of Silla who dominated the profitable trading networks that linked the peninsula to Japan and China. But despite Jang's tremendous economic and military might, a wily assassin was able to penetrate the defenses surrounding him and end an ongoing struggle between Jang and the central elites of the Unified Silla kingdom. Jang's death demonstrated that, for all his powers, he could not evade the intrigues of court politics 200 miles away in the Silla capital of Gyeongju; indeed, Jang had willfully engaged in them, even going so far as to arrange a marriage between his daughter and the Silla monarch. When this effort turned powerful monarchical and aristocratic forces against him, he met his fate.

As it turned out, Jang's demise would mark the beginning of the end of the Unified Silla era. This appears fitting, for Jang's successes and travails also captured key facets of Silla society, from his social background and his rise as a local warlord to his activities beyond the Korean peninsula. That Jang would become known as the man most responsible for Korea's brief centrality in the regional trading system points also to the revival of interest in him in contemporary times, when (South) Korea has sought to revive this former standing. Such interest in Jang's exploits from 1200 years ago harkens back to an era, swathed in mystique, when Korea lay at the heart of northeast Asia.

JANG BOGO, CHOE CHIWON, AND UNIFIED SILLA SOCIETY

The scattered sources of information regarding Jang Bogo's early life hardly suggest a future as a historically important figure. He appears to have made his way to the Shandong Peninsula in China as a young man, where he became a local military officer and later gained experience in seafaring and trading activities as a member of the Silla expatriate community. He is also credited with establishing a Buddhist temple for the Sillans, *Beophwawon*, which served also as a kind of consulate, a base for not only religious worship and ceremonies but economic and diplomatic activities. Jang's return to his homeland is the next entrance in his sketchy biography. However, it is uncertain whether he was driven by a determination to thwart the pirates who regularly plied the shores of Korea, snatching Korean captives to sell as slaves in China, or if he became conscious of this issue upon his return. In any case in 828 Jang was able to convince the Silla government to appoint him as magistrate of a large naval fortress off the peninsula's southwest coast near the island of Wando. This fort became known as "Cheonghaejin," or Cheonghae Garrison, and it boasted 10,000 troops. From this base, Jang not only put a stop to the pirates, but he applied his Shandong formula of integrating military with economic pursuits to establish himself as the dominant figure in the trilateral maritime trade between Korea, Japan, and China.

Jang soon became enmeshed also in the politics of the Silla court, if not by his own initiative, then certainly because his prominence made him a ready target for ambitious figures looking for support. In 837, Gim Ujing, loser in the latest battle over royal succession, made his way across the southern coast and pleaded for Jang's protection, and within two years Jang found himself raising a private military force to battle the government's army on Gim's behalf. When victory allowed Gim to ascend the throne, he enfeoffed Jang and bestowed upon him the elevated title of Grand General of Cheonghae Garrison. Jang, flush with success in his political interventions, maneuvered in 845 to marry off his daughter as the monarch's second queen. This raised fervent objections from the capital's aristocratic elite, and the king relented. The *History of the Three Kingdoms* records that Jang, resentful at this slight, led a rebellion against the court, and in response the government sent a man, Yeomjang, to assassinate Jang at a private gathering in 846.

While there is no explicit evidence, the common perception among historians is that resistance to Jang's efforts to insert himself into capital politics and society likely had something to do with his social status. This in turn leads us to consider the Silla social hierarchy, which represented an early form of the stout hereditary status system that came to characterize premodern Korea as a whole. The Silla method assigned a "bone rank" (*golpum*) to people, based on their parentage, that determined their social identity and, in turn, their spheres and manner of public interaction, marriage possibilities, tax and service obligations, and eligibility for bureaucratic office (or even for royalty).

Especially striking were the limits of economic activity in generating social mobility. For social status was first and foremost determined by birth. One's occupation or primary economic activity also flowed from one's ascriptive status. Although the evidence is sketchy, there was probably a substantial group of people born into servitude, likely descended from captives or other victims of the unification wars. Above them were the majority of the population, the commoners, most of whom were engaged in agriculture, while some earned their livelihoods through artisanal crafts, fishing and hunting, or trade. The category of "merchants" in reference to the latter group included those whose scope of activity ranged from inter-village exchange to international trade, as was the case with Jang Bogo. Like Jang, merchants could amass wealth and in turn sociopolitical prestige, but this wealth ultimately could not gain entry into the highest ranks of elites who lived off the masses through rent and bound labor, or through government service. In the Silla system, even those eligible for the state bureaucracy were distributed into an intricate hierarchy, again primarily according to birth.

By the time of Unified Silla, the original highest rank of Hallowed Bone had dissipated, and the monarchy and top officials came from the True Bone ranks. Those in Head Rank Six to Head Rank Four (presumably the head ranks reached down all the way to one) comprised the hereditary elites and could attain government office, but they encountered restrictions in gaining the highest posts. Jang appears not to have belonged to any of these upper head ranks, so his attempts to ingratiate himself into the governing order likely generated gasps at such a violation of norms. He was, in other words, a prime example of both the flexibility and rigidity of the Silla social hierarchy—able to rise to prominence as a local strongman engaged in maritime commerce, but unable to overcome the barriers to social and political power at the center.

Probably the best-known example of the constraints of the Silla social hierarchy was Choe Chiwon, the most prominent intellectual of Unified Silla and archetype of the Confucian scholar-official in premodern Korea. Choe, born into Head Rank Six a decade after Jang Bogo's death, traveled to study in China at the age of twelve, following the example of other precocious Sillans. Choe's talents, however, were truly exceptional. He passed the Tang civil service examination in 874, a remarkable feat on its own, and before he turned twenty had already achieved renown, particularly as the scribe and advisor to the Chinese official in charge of putting down a major rebellion. (This uprising would eventually lead to the fall of the Tang dynasty itself.) Choe managed to return home to Silla in 885, in his late twenties, and took high office. Eventually, however, he appears to have chafed at the barriers, in both promotion possibilities and policy implementation, of the Silla governing system. And as rebellions from local strongmen began to intensify, he withdrew from the capital to take provincial posts and eventually to retire to a Buddhist temple. His works—including a famous "Ten-Point Policy Recommendation" to the final female Silla monarch, Queen Jinseong, as well as a chronicle of his observations while in the service of the Tang emperor—displayed the full range of his scholarly expertise, from Buddhist and Confucian teachings to poetry. Only a fraction of his voluminous writings remains today, but they were prized and rediscovered throughout the subsequent course of Korean history. Like those of Jang Bogo himself, Choe Chiwon's life and times offer a window into the final phase of a golden era in ancient Korea, when Silla showed both its maturity and its old age.

SILLA AND NORTHEAST ASIA

That Choe Chiwon and Jang Bogo both made their reputations and gained seminal experience in China before making an impact in their homeland illustrates the vibrant connections that Silla enjoyed at the crossroads (or cross-straits) of northeast Asia. In fact, Jang Bogo's influence extended far beyond the region, and indeed most of the sources upon which his biographical portrait has been constructed and embellished come from China and Japan. Especially influential are the writings of the great Tang poet Du Mu, whose familiarity with Jang reflects the latter's considerable fame and what appear to be strong connections to the Chinese elite, and the chronicles of the Japanese Buddhist monk Ennin.

According to Ennin's fascinating "Account of Travels in Tang for the Purpose of Seeking the Law," the Sillans in Shandong constituted a thriving community, concentrated around the Korean Buddhist temples, that dominated the regional maritime trading system. Indeed Ennin witnessed a major Korean Buddhist festival that endured for three days, another celebration commemorating Silla's victory over Goguryeo 150 years earlier, and other expressions of Silla's collective identity. Although Ennin never recounts meeting him, Jang Bogo, not the king of Silla, is the looming authority figure to whom this community answered. So moved was Ennin by the kind treatment and protection offered to him by Jang's surrogates in the Shandong Silla society that the monk wrote the great man a letter of gratitude. To Ennin, Jang was clearly the mastermind and dominant figure behind this intricately and efficiently designed network of merchants, monks, and others who shuttled between the Korean peninsula and the east coast of China.

From this base of operations Jang's agents in turn connected to a trading network that stretched all the way to eastern Africa and the Arabian peninsula, whose merchants, it appears, also visited Silla. What flowed through these channels in northeast Asia originally reflected the official commerce in tribute goods such as ginseng and silk, but by the time Jang achieved his dominant position in Cheonghae Garrison, trade items also included animal products such as horns, falcons, and sealskins, and particularly ceramics. In fact, Jang appears to have facilitated significantly the circulation of Chinese porcelain, as well as the application of Chinese technologies to further develop a Korean ceramics industry on the peninsula's south coast. The prime locations connected with Korean pottery, including Gangjin and Namhae Island, are usually associated with the subsequent Goryeo era, but this development might have begun in Jang's time. Excavations of both ceramic factories and shipwrecks from the era have added to this impression that Silla's maritime power once served as a major engine of economic vitality in the area.

Such a connection between Korea's seafaring potential and internal development has been reestablished over the past forty years in South Korea, with its export-oriented industrial growth and the preeminent global position of Korean companies in the shipbuilding industry. Indeed Jang Bogo's commanding influence over trade in northeast Asia tells us much about Silla's relationship to the region as a whole, and it prompts further thinking about Silla's standing in the longer trajectory of Korean history. In one sense, Jang Bogo's activities demonstrated Korea's capacity to take advantage of its geographical position at the center of northeast Asia instead of being victimized by these circumstances. Furthermore, Jang's story shows that, in this particular era of Korean history at least, trade and commerce could indeed exert strong influence in wider circles, enough to allow a merchant to use his wealth and power to play political mediator and, indeed, even kingmaker. Both tendencies—Korea's commercial prominence in northeast Asia and the force of economic activity in the realms of politics, society, and culture—were also pursued by South Korean leaders at the turn of the early twenty-first century. Since the 1990s, interest in, and the further mythologizing of, Jang Bogo have gone hand-in-hand with the construction of tourist-oriented memorials and museums in Shandong, site of the temple complex that Jang established, as well as with pop culture products in Korea such as the "God of the Seas" hit television series. Jang serves, then, as a symbol of expansive visions of Korean identity and influence in the context of globalization and regional integration. If it could be done before, so the thinking goes, it can be done again.

The reconsideration of Korea's regional position via a creative appropriation of Jang Bogo and his era also accompanies, ironically, a recent downgrading of Unified Silla's historical standing. A growing perspective in both popular and academic arenas has come to view "Unified Silla" as somewhat of a misnomer, given that Silla's vanquishing of Baekje and Goguryeo in the seventh century left unincorporated the majority of former Goguryeo territory. This area was claimed by a thriving kingdom, Barhae, that stretched from the northern part of the peninsula well into Manchuria. Barhae's status in conventional Korean historiography has always been somewhat ambiguous, as only its ruling elite seem to have descended from Goguryeo origins, while the masses came from an assortment of various ethnicities. More influential in excluding Barhae were official histories compiled in subsequent periods instituting the notion of a "Three Kingdoms" era of ancient Korea that came to an end through Silla's unification. Partly due to nationalist sentiment, the concept of a "Unified Silla" era has lost ground to a perception of this era as that of the "First North-South Division," with the strong implication that Barhae was a fully Korean historical entity. (In North Korea, for obvious reasons, this view is a matter of course.) Jang Bogo, then, is not the only artifact of his era to be mined for contemporary purposes; Barhae is grounds for claiming that Korea at this time was a central player in northeast Asia in more ways than one.

LOCAL STRONGMEN AND THE END OF SILLA

For all his utility as a symbol of Unified Silla's growth and achievements, in the end Jang tells us just as much about its demise. We have reason and documentation, in particular the remarkable fragments of village household registers discovered in the early twentieth century, to believe that the Unified Silla state had made notable strides in extending central control, or at least taxation authority. Cultural integration, too, appears to have proceeded apace, helped considerably by Buddhist clerics, many associated with the state, who in their evangelization and organizational efforts helped to synthesize a collective sense of religious identity as the people of the "Buddha Land" (*Bulguk*).

There were definite limits to this integration, however. Indeed Jang's great power might have reflected not the Silla state's authority but rather its lack of control in the outlying provinces. Within half a century after Jang's death, the area that had served as his base—the southwestern part of the country that used to belong to the kingdom of Baekje—would erupt in rebellion against the Silla state in the early 890s. This uprising was led by a warlord, Gyeon Hwon, who, while fanning the flames of local resentment and calling his breakaway areas "Baekje," likely envisioned himself a successor to Jang Bogo. Another local strongman, however, would prove even more effective in overturning Silla control, and he called his territory "Goguryeo."

4 Founding of the Goryeo Dynasty

CHRONOLOGY

THE ISSUANCE OF WANG GEON'S "TEN INJUNCTIONS," 943

The founding of the Goryeo dynasty was a seminal event in many ways. It pacified the peninsula after decades of civil war during what is commonly called the "Latter Three Kingdoms" period (late ninth–early tenth centuries), extended the territory of the country further northward by incorporating the southern edge of the Barhae kingdom, integrated the ruling groups of both the Barhae and Silla into a new aristocratic element that might have lasted into the twentieth century, and expressed a sense of civilizational identity based on a mixture of native religious and cultural elements. The apex figure in this process was Wang Geon, the founder of the Wang dynasty of Goryeo, and the event that binds him to these significant trends is the issuance of the "Ten Injunctions" to his royal successors.

The Ten Injunctions has come down as one of the most influential documents in Korean history and a testament to the forces that shaped Goryeo into an enduring political entity. This series of directives accentuated both the distinctiveness and heterogeneity of Korea's cultural identity, emphasized the centrality of Buddhism and geomancy as well as of Confucian statecraft, warned of the "barbarians" to the north, and institutionalized, some say, discrimination against the southwestern region of the peninsula.

This last feature, specified in the eighth injunction, has aroused considerable interest lately because of its ostensible endorsement of the bane of South Korean politics since democratization in 1987—namely, regionalism. Many scholars claim, in fact, that Injunction #8 proves that the Ten Injunctions was a forgery, that circumstantial evidence renders it highly unlikely if not impossible that Wang Geon himself actually issued such orders. The skepticism is well founded, but it does not deny the impact of this document in Goryeo and Korean history.

"GREAT FOUNDER OF KOREA"

Wang came of age as the Silla kingdom was falling apart in the final two decades of the tenth century. As noted in Chapter 3, Unified Silla experienced difficulties keeping parts of its domain under institutional control, as local strongmen who arose in the peripheries, such as Jang Bogo, posed challenges to Silla rule. Indeed the first major rebel leader, Gyeon Hwon, was a high Silla military official assigned to the same southwestern coastal zone that had served as Jang's power base. Gyeon Hwon fanned the flames of anti-Silla resentment and remnant loyalties from the Three Kingdoms era to amass a polity that he called "Baekje," which proved formidable enough at one time to ransack the Silla capital and install his own preferred monarch. His primary opposition, however, came not from the Silla court but rather from another rebel leader based in the central part of the peninsula, Gim Gungye, who referred to himself as the successor to the Goguryeo monarchs. Like Gyeon, Gungye came from the upper tiers of Silla society—he was a prince, in fact. When he was cast off from his family (perhaps because he was an illegitimate son), he retreated to the countryside and became a Buddhist monk. Before long, however, he joined the growing anti-Silla movement among local strongmen in the 890s and captured areas in the peninsula's heartland. Gungye's battles against Gyeon Hwon over peninsular supremacy at the turn of the tenth century rendered imminent the end of Silla, but this duel was not decided until Gungye was toppled, not by Gyeon, but rather by one of his own lieutenants.

The person who took Gungye's place was Wang Geon, who had for some time been Gungye's most successful commander in the struggles against other regional lords. Wang had entered Gungye's orbit in 895 when Wang's father, a court-sanctioned local leader in the west-central coastal city of Songak—today known as Gaeseong—joined the monk's expanding new kingdom, which by the year 911 had conquered vast territory. According to official historical accounts from the Goryeo dynasty, when Gungye began to show disturbing signs of cruelty and uncontrolled despotism, his top officers overthrew him and handed the crown to Wang Geon. In these sources, Wang is depicted as having displayed great reluctance to betray his loyalty to his lord, but it is likely that Wang himself led the effort to take control. Gungye perished while being chased from the throne, and Wang formally established his own reign in 918 and immediately set his sights on overcoming the lingering resistance from both Silla and Latter Baekje. His longtime nemesis, Gyeon Hwon, who had meanwhile been overthrown himself by his own son, actually joined Wang's cause to defeat his former country. By 935, Wang had gained the peaceful submission of Silla's last monarch, who, it is chronicled, led a procession to Songak from Gyeongju stretching over ten miles in length in order to formally hand over rule. Upon putting down the final bout of Baekje resistance in 936, Wang, known historically through his reign name of "Taejo," or "Great Founder," accomplished the successful political reunification of the peninsula.

Given his own beginnings as the scion of a powerful merchant family in a far-off province of Silla, Wang knew well the potential pitfalls presented by regional power holders. Hence his most urgent task in fortifying his rule was to gain the submission, or at least the consent, of the many local chiefs scattered around the peninsula. This issue of political integration would remain at the forefront of challenges faced by the Goryeo monarchy for the rest of the five-century-long dynasty. Eventually the Goryeo instituted a kind of cooperative "hostage" system, much like the one used later in Shogunal Japan, that required family members of local elites to reside for stretches of time in the capital. For the moment, however, Wang Geon turned to what many rulers around the world in similar circumstances did: use marriage alliances to consolidate political power. Wang in fact went a step further; he himself did the marrying, and to the daughters of an astounding twenty-nine different local rulers. Not all of the many sons produced from these alliances went on to become king or even play important political roles, but this step proved instrumental in securing a large pool of loyal descendants with a stake in maintaining the dynasty. To them, and more specifically to his eldest sons—three of whom would take turns in serving as the succeeding monarchs—Wang appears to have left behind a very specific blueprint for ruling the Goryeo dynasty and a personal vision for what made Goryeo, Korea.

CONTENT OF THE TEN INJUNCTIONS

The country envisioned by the Ten Injunctions reflected the many different strands of thought and religion, originating internally and externally, that had come to shape civilization on the peninsula. More impressive than the specific policy recommendations, which were significant in themselves, were the Ten Injunctions' expansive proclamations of the cultural currents that defined Korea's past, present, and future. One specific civilizational strain, however, stood out as primary: "Every great undertaking in our country depends upon the power of the Buddha's protection," begins the first of the Ten Injunctions. Indeed, the significance of regulating well the Buddhist establishment, of building temples and other places of worship, and of sponsoring the major Buddhist festivals is emphasized in three separate injunctions. Little wonder, then, that the centrality of Buddhism in Korean civilization would reach unprecedented heights during the Goryeo dynasty, reflecting the maturity, diversity, and even the decadence of Buddhism's near-millennium of dominance, especially in concert with political power. One could argue, in fact, that the Goryeo state's patronage of Buddhism represented the peak of Korean civilization itself, given the extraordinary cultural advances that arose from this relationship.

Like Buddhism, Confucian teachings also had entered the peninsula from China in the Three Kingdoms era. Although there was much overlap in the two great thought systems, particularly as they functioned to assist and legitimate political rule, by Wang Geon's time, Confucianism had become the clear purveyor of statecraft on the peninsula, with a mass of devoted scholars and officials helping to further refine it. Indeed Wang appears in the Ten Injunctions as holding a keen awareness of the importance of Confucian precepts, particularly for providing the lexicon and ideologies of administration. Four of the injunctions allude to Confucian prescriptions for royal succession and the management of state affairs, including the acceptance of admonishment by the ruler. The numerous allusions to passages in the Confucian classics, in fact, might lead one to take the Injunctions as a Confucian document in some ways.

While such cultural elements originating from abroad hold a prominent standing in the Ten Injunctions, there is also a pronounced emphasis on maintaining Korea's distinctiveness in the face of external influences, including even those from the Middle Kingdom. "In the past we have always had a deep attachment to the ways of China ... but our country occupies a different geographical location and our people's character is different from that of the Chinese," warns the fourth injunction. "Hence, there is no reason to strain ourselves unreasonably to copy the Chinese way." By this time, though, Buddhism is considered a native cultural element, as stated explicitly in the sixth injunction, which insists that the great state-sponsored Buddhist festivals retain the worship of elements of primal Korean religion. Indeed in the fifth injunction Wang credits his great achievement of peninsular reunification to the combination of geomancy and shamanism, and he implores his descendants to maintain the centrality of Pyongyang in Korean civilization. He designates this city the Western Capital, second in importance only to his home town, the Goryeo capital of Gaegyeong (formerly Songak, and later known as Gaeseong). This mixture of cultural and ideological elements that characterized the Ten Injunctions—on the one hand, native, including Buddhist, ways and, on the other, "Chinese" Confucian learning—would help shape and sustain Goryeo's distinctive identity, but also spark considerable tension.

This tension often arose from real threats from the outside world, which explains the Ten Injunctions' explicit condemnation of the people lying to Goryeo's north, the Khitan, who are referred to as "savage beasts" (more Confucian language). The periodic intrusions and skirmishes from the north—a recurring theme throughout Korean history—were not lost on the early Goryeo rulers, whose instructions, as expressed in the Ten Injunctions, were to keep a watchful eye on the northern frontier. This proved prescient, for Goryeo would suffer major invasions from various peoples originating in Manchuria and central Asia, beginning with the Khitan, and then the Jurchen, then finally the Mongols, who conquered Korea in the thirteenth century and ruled the country as semi-colonial overlords for nearly a century (Chapter 6).

Such concerns about the north were understandably inscribed into the Ten Injunctions, but what of the wariness of the southern part of the peninsula, in particular the southwestern region that had previously stood as the domain of Latter Baekje (and before then, Baekje)? The infamous eighth injunction goes into detail about the negative geomantic and cultural features of this area as a prelude to the stunning instruction not to allow people from there to become central government officials. Goryeo's recent struggles to conquer Latter Baekje are unequivocally acknowledged as the source of the suspicion of this region. Even so, as historians have pointed out, it is remarkable that Wang would issue such a pronouncement, given his general policy of appeasement of local elites around the country (he married several women from this region), and given that one of his highest officials came from the southwest. Here we encounter, then, the doubts about the authenticity of the Ten Injunctions itself as originating with its purported author, Wang Geon. There are persuasive arguments that indeed, the Ten Injunctions date to the late tenth century or early eleventh century, more than fifty years after Wang Geon's passing, and that they reflected the political circumstances and concerns of that subsequent period. The more important point, however, is that, regardless of the precise dating or even authorship of this document, it exerted a great influence in the following four centuries of the Goryeo. And for the most part, the eighth injunction did not raise doubts about Wang's authorship of the Ten Injunctions until the latter part of the twentieth century, when regional hostilities, particularly those aggravated by the South Korean dictatorships, flared into a major impairment to establishing a democratic political culture.

LEGACY

It is difficult to determine to what extent, if any, the eighth injunction had on Goryeo history itself, given the prolonged periods of political power held in the hands of military officials and Mongol overlords. The other injunctions appear more effective in forecasting future tasks and concerns, especially in regard to Goryeo's collective identity and cultural core, both of which were infused with diversity as much as uniformity. The founder's strenuous efforts to legitimize his family's dominion, for example, went far beyond his incorporation of local lords through marriage ties. In addition to proclaiming his dynasty the successor to Unified Silla, he also placed Goryeo firmly in the longer-term historical lineage of the peninsula's history through his dynasty's name, which reinforced its claims as a successor to Goguryeo as well. Indeed the overarching claims of descent extended back to the "Three Han" era (*Samhan*), in reference to the ancient confederations on the southern half of the peninsula (Chapter 1), as well as to the ensuing period of the Three Kingdoms. And the early Goryeo conspicuously integrated the former leaders of both Silla and Barhae into the country's aristocratic order. The significance of the Barhae connection, moreover, could have been another reason behind the Ten Injunctions' vitriol against the foreigners to the north, especially the Khitan, who conquered Barhae around the same time that Silla itself came to an end. Subsequent periods in the Goryeo era witnessed follow-up efforts, such as the compilation of official histories, to reinforce these historical claims to legitimacy.

Just as important but perhaps less notable were the substantial administrative advances that the Ten Injunctions appeared to endorse. The further systematization of government, both institutionally and symbolically, constituted an urgent task for the early Goryeo leaders, who endeavored to overcome the decades-long period of disintegration and local rivalries that had marked the late Unified Silla period. The pervasiveness of Confucian language when describing the general approaches to proper government paved the way for major developments during the reigns of Wang's immediate descendants on the throne. These included the increasing administrative integration of the provinces and, in 958, under the reign of King Gwangjong, one of Wang Geon's sons, the implementation of the state examination system, which had a sweeping effect on the politics, society, and culture of premodern Korea.

5 Religion and Regionalism in the Goryeo Order

CHRONOLOGY

1126   Yi Jagyeom Rebellion
1129   Construction of a new royal palace in Pyongyang
1135   Myocheong Rebellion
1136   Suppression of the Myocheong Rebellion by Gim Busik
1145   Publication of the *History of the Three Kingdoms*
1170   Takeover of government by military officials

THE OUTBREAK OF THE MYOCHEONG REBELLION, 1135

In early 1135 an uprising arose in Pyongyang and quickly spread throughout the northwest, as most of this region fell under the control of rebels under the leadership of a charismatic Buddhist monk. Before demonstrating his propensity for havoc, this man, Myocheong, had set his powers of persuasion—the official histories called it something more akin to sorcery—on the king himself, convincing the monarch that the dynastic capital of Goryeo must be moved to Pyongyang in order to avoid national disaster. When the king, under great pressure from his highest officials, changed his mind, Myocheong and his cohorts in Pyongyang broke away. The leaders of this movement proclaimed a new, paradisiacal land, but to the Goryeo court, of course, their actions constituted nothing more than a treasonous insurrection.

It took over a year to quash the uprising, which shook the foundations of Goryeo, and the reverberations would endure. Myocheong's downfall, for example, carried ample repercussions for the structures of political and social power in Goryeo, including the decline of the monk's home region and home town of Pyongyang. On the whole, the Myocheong Rebellion reflected important social, political, and cultural developments in the Goryeo dynasty, particularly the special influence and character of Korean religion.

THE INSTITUTIONALIZED INFLUENCE OF THE BUDDHIST CLERGY

Following Buddhism's inception on the Korean peninsula around the fourth century, the sociopolitical elite and the Buddhist clergy developed a mutually beneficial relationship by incorporating each other into their respective realms of influence and claims to legitimacy. But Buddhism's impact extended far beyond politics, for the centuries of steady propagation had produced a culture suffused with Buddhist sentiment. Both the central and regional elites, for example, patronized the Buddhist establishment, whether through their support of local temples or sponsorship of Buddhist festivals. A visible example of the pervasiveness of Buddhism, especially among the upper-status taste-setters, was the emergence of the remarkable style of blue-green "Goryeo celadon," prized now (as then) even beyond Korea for its ethereal beauty. These ceramics' almost indescribable sheen itself seems to evoke Buddhist spirituality, as do the many inlaid graphical motifs that refer to well-known Buddhist themes.

The state took the lead in this patronage of Buddhism in the Goryeo era. The separate spheres of influence by now had been settled: the spiritual realm, including family rituals, for the Buddhist order; and the temporal realm of political power for the state. But the state also intervened in the affairs of the Buddhist clergy by overseeing the ordination of monks and by instituting an examination system through which high officials in the religious bureaucracy and abbots of major temples were selected. The state furthermore sponsored or licensed major temples, which enjoyed tax and other benefits that allowed them to accumulate, and often abuse, immense wealth. The monarch, moreover, appointed royal and national preceptors, who served as religious advisors to the king and officials and endowed the state with the stamp of Buddhist blessings. Perhaps the most eminent monk to be named national preceptor was Jinul, a figure of the late twelfth and early thirteenth centuries. Jinul developed a unified system of thought and practice for Korean Buddhism, which had long been divided, sometimes bitterly, into the meditation (*Seon*) and textual (*Gyo*) schools. (The largest Buddhist order in South Korea today counts him as its founder.)

What proved most distinctive about Goryeo Buddhism, perhaps, was its thorough incorporation of shamanistic and geomantic elements. As the Ten Injunctions of the founding period strongly suggested (Chapter 4), Korean Buddhism by this time drew from a great mixture of

Buddhist printing advances of the Goryeo

When asked to name their nation's greatest cultural achievement, most South Koreans likely would choose the invention of the native alphabet in the fifteenth century, but they might also list two products from the Buddhist-dominated civilization of the Goryeo era: the remarkable celadon pottery, and the great advances in printing developed by the Buddhist establishment. In fact, one could argue that, taken together, the most impressive accomplishments of premodern Korean civilization came in printing technologies, dating back to the Unified Silla era (668–935), when the oldest extant printed work in the world was produced, then stored in a Buddhist altar. It was done through woodblock printing, a technique invented by the Chinese and further refined in Goryeo-era Korea, which in turn laid the groundwork for the next major breakthrough, that of moveable metal type printing, also invented by Goryeo Buddhist clergy.

Most people in the West associate the invention of moveable metal type, the holy grail of premodern techniques because of the flexibility and durability it provided to enable mass printing, with Johannes Gutenberg. Gutenberg's invention in the mid-fifteenth century ushered in the era of widespread information dissemination in Europe, which had an immediately colossal impact through the pamphlets and other rapidly produced publications that fueled the Renaissance and the Protestant Reformation. Very few people outside of Korea know that moveable metal type was actually invented two centuries earlier, around 1230, by Buddhist monks in a temple in south-central Korea. In fact the earliest extant book printed with moveable metal type, a Korean work of Buddhist scripture, dates to the 1370s. In Korea, however, this breakthrough did not lead to significant social or religious change, even after the crafting of the Korean alphabet in the fifteenth century—a major issue, given the impact of the printed vernacular on the rise of early modern Europe. What if something similar had happened in Korea?

Around the same time as this invention, the storied *Tripitika Koreana*—over 80,000 wooden blocks on which were carved nearly the entirety of the East Asian Buddhist canon—was being destroyed by the Mongol invasions that began in the 1230s. Originally

→

produced as a testament to religious devotion amid the Khitan invasions of the eleventh century, the *Tripitika's* destruction by the Mongols prompted the Koreans to reproduce it, again as an appeal to the Buddhas for protection from the carnage. The result was a project that took nearly two decades to complete the carving of the blocks, which are now preserved in Haeinsa Temple near the southern city of Daegu. This extraordinary feat demonstrated the symbiotic relationship of mutual legitimation between the Goryeo state and Buddhist establishment, which together could mobilize enormous human and material resources, and the high level of literacy and technology associated with Korean Buddhism that dated back centuries.

Image 5 Wooden blocks of the Tripitika Koreana, *Haeinsa Temple, near Daegu, South Korea. (Author's photo.)*

Buddhist doctrines, folk beliefs in local gods and spirits, and geomancy, which endowed geographical features with spiritual qualities. The great state-sponsored Buddhist celebrations, the Lantern Festival and the Eight Prohibitions Festival, for example, reflected these various strains. Through such a blend of religious influences, together with the further development of Buddhist scholarship, a distinctively hybrid form of Buddhist practice emerged. Indeed, Korean geomancy was itself systematized by a Buddhist monk in the Unified Silla era, Doseon, who developed an organic vision of the peninsula, with its particular layout of mountains and rivers, as a living entity fed by the spiritual energy of Buddhist temples and practices. Doseon's followers, including Myocheong, cultivated and popularized this perspective, to the extent that geomancy, including the notion of a geomantic unity for Korea, held an influential standing among the aristocracy and monarchy well into the twentieth century. The location of the capital of the next dynasty, Joseon—still the capital of (South) Korea today—was determined according to geomantic principles, for example. Long before then, however, geomancy played a central role in a watershed moment in the Goryeo.

MYOCHEONG'S REBELLION

Aside from the fact that he was a monk from Pyongyang, little is known about Myocheong's life before his role as protagonist in the tumult that engulfed the country in the early twelfth century. The official historical accounts excoriate him for his deceitfulness and cunning, but he clearly had considerable charisma and skill. Like Rasputin, who held an unshakable grip over the Russian royal family at the turn of the twentieth century through his seemingly magical ability to treat the Romanovs' hemophilia, Myocheong appears to have cast a spell over the Goryeo monarch, Injong. Most consequentially, the monk convinced him of a direct geomantic relationship between the ongoing misfortunes of the dynasty—especially the constant attacks and threats of invasion from the Jurchen people to the north—and the location of the dynastic capital in Gaegyeong (present-day Gaeseong). Myocheong's solution was to move the capital to Pyongyang, which held more favorable geomantic features, he claimed. He also urged the monarch to declare Goryeo an empire and launch a military campaign against the Jurchen, steps opposed by the king's ministers.

That King Injong succumbed to Myocheong's reasoning cannot be explained simply by dismissing the monarch as a dupe, for the baseline of belief tying geomancy directly to the health of the country, as explained above, had an extensive history. Furthermore, Pyongyang had long enjoyed a centrality in Korean civilization, reflected in the fact that, since the early Goryeo period, it was deemed the Western Capital (Seogyeong), the second most important city. And, as noted in Chapter 1, Pyongyang had served as the administrative center of the Lelang Chinese commandery and the capital city of the Goguryeo kingdom. Furthermore, according to the conventional understanding of Korean origins codified in the Goryeo era, this city represented the birthplace of Korean civilization itself. So said the legends of Dangun, the founder of the Korean people who established his court there, and of Gija, the Chinese official who transmitted higher civilization to the peninsula and ruled from Pyongyang. From Myocheong's perspective, and likely that of many elites from the north, the transfer of Goryeo's capital to Pyongyang represented simply the return of this city to its rightful centrality, which would in turn lead to better fortunes for a country besieged by both internal and external threats.

The capital region, in fact, was still recovering from the biggest domestic challenge to the Goryeo dynasty hitherto, the rebellion in 1126 led by Yi Jagyeom. The powerful scion of a royal consort family and the monarch's father-in-law, Yi attempted a personal takeover of the throne before his uprising was suppressed with tremendous bloodshed. The capital elites, in short, were extra wary of brewing trouble, and these sensitivities grew even more acute when, soon after the Yi Jagyeom incident, King Injong began to show signs of having fallen under the sway of the mysterious monk from Pyongyang. Injong made frequent visits to that city and eventually ordered the construction of a royal palace there. Most central officials, fearing a major shift in power to the northwestern region, implored the monarch to examine the countervailing evidence: The greater attention shown to Pyongyang, including the construction of the royal palace, not only failed to eliminate the Jurchen menace, but also failed to halt a series of natural calamities that beset this region. The monarch became convinced by these arguments and put a stop to plans for moving the capital city. Prompted by an official, Jo Gwang, and other cohorts from Pyongyang, Myocheong's response to this royal turnabout was straightforward: rebellion.

In the first month of 1135 Myocheong, Jo Gwang, and the other leaders orchestrated a swift takeover of most of the administrative centers in the north, incarcerating officials sent from the capital and cutting off the major pass that connected this region to the capital. They proclaimed their new realm the Empire of Daewi ("Great Purpose"). King Injong, meanwhile, appointed Gim Busik, one of the most powerful officials, to lead the government armies as Supreme Commander for the Pacification of Pyongyang. Gim's forces entered the breakaway region and issued ultimatums to local leaders, who for the most part quickly capitulated, and soon surrounded the rebels in Pyongyang. In fear and hope for clemency, Jo Gwang, who by now was acting as the true ringleader of the uprising, killed Myocheong and other rebel leaders and sent the heads to Gim Busik as a sign of surrender. But Gim would have none of it, and Jo Gwang in turn decided to fight to the end, which came after many more months of bloodletting—including the killing of government negotiators by Jo. Eventually, Jo's forces, holed up in Pyongyang fortress, ran out of provisions under the government siege. The defeat of the rebels came in the second month of 1136, more than a year after the eruption. It would take much longer for the region to return to normalcy, and for Pyongyang, the city would never be the same.

AFTERMATH

Myocheong's antagonist in this ordeal, Gim Busik, would have an impact on Korean history far beyond his suppression of the uprising. As the prime representative of the power elite of the Goryeo capital region, however, his later exploits can be considered an extension of his role in the Myocheong saga. Gim was a descendant of the old Silla royalty, which constituted one of the key components of the capital-based aristocracy that the Goryeo founder, Taejo, had incorporated into his ruling order. This was significant because Gim would eventually take the leading role in writing, a decade following the rebellion, the court-sanctioned historical narrative of the pre-Goryeo era, the *History of the Three Kingdoms* (*Samguk sagi*). This work serves to this day as the core source of understanding about ancient Korea. But beginning with Sin Chaeho, who called the Myocheong Rebellion the "most important event in a thousand years" of Korean history, many modern historians have condemned Gim Busik's influence. In particular, they have bemoaned Gim's attempt in the *History of the Three Kingdoms* to strengthen Goryeo's historical legitimacy by reinforcing the notion of this dynasty's historical standing as Silla's legitimate successor. This move, they claim, together with the generally lesser attention paid to non-Silla polities, downplayed the standing of Goguryeo, the kingdom conquered by Silla (with China's help), in the Three Kingdoms era and as a source of the Goryeo dynasty's own identity.

Furthermore, the capital aristocratic elite that Gim represented, which coalesced around bureaucratic domination and hence maintained itself as the official class, came to be known as the *yangban* ("two orders"), in reference to the two sets of high officials, the civilian and the military. But, as symbolized by Gim, a firm hierarchy developed between these two strains of the central officialdom, with civilians like Gim enjoying supremacy. The Myocheong Rebellion and Gim Busik's centrality in its outcome, in other words, may have strengthened such civilian domination to the point of excess, and a backlash to this ordering came relatively soon thereafter. In 1170, military officials rose in revolt and implemented a hundred-year period of military domination of the government (Chapter 6), much like the Shogunal system in Japan. But this represented merely a short hiatus in the millennium of Korean history from the tenth to the twentieth centuries, when on the whole the principle of civilian supremacy and military subordination prevailed. Gim's victory, furthermore, contributed to the permanent branding of Pyongyang, and the northern regions as a whole, as the preserve of the military, rebellious, even uncivilized underbelly of the country. This view constituted a very real prejudice in the subsequent Joseon dynasty, when the north, considered a backwater, suffered social and political discrimination, and Pyongyang fell further from Korea's civilizational core.

Little wonder, then, that in the early nineteenth century, another uprising, the Hong Gyeongnae Rebellion of 1811–12, erupted with remarkable resemblances to the Myocheong episode: a charismatic malcontent from Pyongyang, preaching the north's geomantic superiority, fought to break away from the capital-based power structure. This, too, was eventually suppressed, and not until the circumstances of the mid-twentieth century elevated yet another magnetic military leader from Pyongyang, Kim Il Sung, did finally the northern part of the country succeed in recovering its long-lost glory, but at the cost of a nation divided permanently.

6 The Mongol Overlord Period

CHRONOLOGY

1231	First Mongol invasion of Korea
1261	Assassination of the last Choe ruler; end of military rule in Goryeo
1270	Final capitulation of Goryeo court to Mongols; beginning of Mongol overlord period
1274	First of two joint Mongol-Korean invasion attempts of Japan
1320s	Lady Gi's abduction to Yuan Dynasty China as a "tribute woman"
1333	Lady Gi named an imperial concubine
1339	Birth of Lady Gi's son, the future crown prince and emperor of the Yuan dynasty
1340	Marriage of Lady Gi to the Mongol emperor as secondary imperial consort
1356	Purge of Empress Gi's family members in the Goryeo court by King Gongmin
1365	Empress Gi's ascent to primary consort
1368	Ming dynasty's conquest of China

THE MARRIAGE OF LADY GI TO THE YUAN EMPEROR, 1340

By the summer of 1340, seven decades had passed since Korea had succumbed to a long siege by invading Mongol forces. And in the intervening period Goryeo had become suffused with all things Mongol—its culture, its politics, and even its monarch bore the stamp of Mongol dominance. But soon Koreans received word of an event demonstrating that their country, in turn, could wield influence over the stupendously powerful Mongol empire based in China, the Yuan dynasty. In the previous year, Lady Gi, a Korean and favored concubine of the Yuan emperor, had given birth to the

43

likely crown prince, and now she was being crowned as an imperial consort through her marriage to the Yuan emperor. This outcome could hardly have been imagined two decades earlier, when she was delivered as a captive prize of submission to the Mongol rulers. Indeed she and hundreds of other "tribute women" sent to Mongol-controlled China had embodied the Mongols' comprehensive domination over the Goryeo kingdom, a period in Korean history normally viewed with shame.

Koreans' experience of Mongol supremacy, however, resists easy judgment. Empress Ki's story, in fact, represents a microcosm of Goryeo's complex relationship to the Mongol empire—one that produced tragedy and horror, to be sure, but also reform, opportunity, and valuable exposure to the external world. This period also highlighted key features of Goryeo civilization and its place in the annals of Korean history, especially for practices and customs concerning females. In these and other ways, the Mongol era constituted a seminal turning point in Korean history: It directly led to the fall of the Goryeo dynasty, but it also constituted a degree of integration into the world order not seen again until the twentieth century.

THE MONGOL CONQUEST

The first Mongol invasion, in 1231, led by the son of the founder of the Mongol empire, Genghis Khan, came six decades after the institution of military rule in Goryeo had turned the Korean monarch into a mere puppet. Notwithstanding the many incursions across the northern border, the administrative reforms over the Goryeo dynasty's first century had helped establish the principle of civilian rule. Hence military officials gradually experienced a decline in authority over the next 150 years, even to the point of humiliating deference to their civilian counterparts. This, apparently, led to the military coup of 1170, which purged top civil officials and gave military officers control over the government. By the turn of the thirteenth century, the Choe family emerged to constitute a mini-dynasty of martial strongmen, who ruled a land racked by bouts of unrest, including a large-scale slave rebellion. The devastating Mongol invasions, beginning in 1231, eventually forced the house of Choe to flee to Ganghwa Island, just to the south of the capital. There the Goryeo court under Choe control resisted final capitulation, even as the rest of the country suffered. The final Choe generalissimo, however, was assassinated in 1261, and this opened the door for the court to enter negotiations of surrender. Given the continuing decimation of the countryside, including the destruction of countless cultural artifacts, the Goryeo monarchy had little choice but to accept Mongol overlordship. Despite the lingering resistance to the Mongols on Jeju Island, which was eventually put down, for all intents and purposes Korea was now part of the Mongol empire.

That Goryeo maintained a semblance of independence by holding onto its monarchy and government might be considered a fortunate outcome of its defeat, given that the Mongols could have easily wiped out the entire leadership. But such autonomy was severely curtailed, as the Mongols dictated the general direction of the government. This was soon made apparent when Goryeo was forced to provide manpower and expertise for the next stage of Mongol expansion, into Japan, in 1274. Koreans, long known as master seafarers, built and guided the ships loaded with thousands of soldiers from the joint Mongol-Korean force. This armada twice attempted, and failed in, the invasion of Japan. The military organ devised to oversee these campaigns, the Eastern Expedition Field Headquarters, remained intact even after its original purpose expired, however, serving as the institutional representative of Mongol domination in Korea. The Korean king nominally headed the agency, but in reality this and other major institutions were controlled mostly by Mongol overseers whose interference in Korea extended to internal Korean affairs as well. The Mongols, in fact, established commanderies in various parts of Goryeo to reinforce their suzerainty, and this does not even count the northern quarter of Goryeo territory that came under direct Mongol control.

Needless to say, politics in the Goryeo court often hinged on tendencies and sentiments regarding the Mongols, as the monarch found himself severely weakened. The Mongols dictated everything from the kings' reign names, which humiliatingly bore the word "Loyal" (*Chung*), to their clothing and even their consorts. The Yuan court also controlled who would be king, on several occasions returning a Goryeo monarch to the throne not long after deposing him. But on another level, these signs of subservience might have been moot, for within a few decades the Goryeo king himself was barely Korean. Under the arrangements of Korea's surrender, Goryeo's crown prince had to spend his childhood in the Yuan dynasty capital, where he would marry a Mongol princess, and then return to Korea when it was his turn on the throne. The first such monarch, King Chungnyeol, married a daughter of the third Mongol emperor, Kublai Khan (of Marco Polo fame), and hence thereafter all the Goryeo kings, except the final one, were direct descendants of not only Wang Geon but Genghis Khan himself. One could argue that the Goryeo court had to submit in order to prevent mass slaughter and hence pre-serve Korean nationhood, or even in order to escape domination by Korean military officials. But one also has to wonder whether the Goryeo kings under Mongol rule held a meaningful identity as Koreans. Even the monarch credited with anti-Mongol policies in the mid-fourteenth century, King Gongmin—who, by twist of fate, was mostly Korean and served as the last of the Mongol-era kings—was married to a Mongol princess, whom he adored and famously mourned with obsession upon her passing.

This brings us to the larger implications of these circumstances, and here one must tread with some sensitivity. For not only was the Wang monarchy infused with Mongol ancestry, but intermarriage with the Mongols took place among other Korean groups as well, from the aristoc-racy down to the lowest status groups who had no choice in the matter. This accompanied the significant spread of Mongol influence in Korean culture in the fourteenth century, from language, food, hairstyles, and clothing to even family and marriage customs. Together, these two lev-els of Mongol influence led to what many Koreans today would consider embarrassing: a significant strain of Mongol provenance in the Korean people and culture. DNA analysis, which strongly suggests that central Asians share widespread common descent from Genghis Khan, would probably show not an insignificant number of Koreans today with the same ancestry. Such are the results, repeated countless times throughout world history, of military conquest. We can imagine the often horrific circumstances under which such a mixture of peoples took place, and we can abhor, from the Korean perspective, the shameful consequences. But whether one condemns this particular episode in Korean history or examines it with scholarly detachment, it undoubtedly complicates any sacrosanct notion of Korean homogeneity.

If we can take a difficult step back from the horrors of war and forced subjugation to forge a broader perspective, we should also consider the salutary impact of Mongol domination on the Goryeo era and on Korean history. Under the Mongol empire, Koreans had many more occasions to make their way to China as tributary officials, diplomats, scholars, traders, and others, and once in the Yuan dynasty capital (present-day Beijing), they encountered a teeming tapestry of peoples and cultures from throughout the vast Mongol empire. The exchange of books, ideas, and other artifacts of both high and low culture from these encounters integrated Koreans, for the first time in their history, into a truly global order. The Chinese civilization that Koreans had emulated always aspired to be universal, but in geographical scope and the willingness to integrate other cultures, it paled in comparison to the Mongol empire. And among the significant outcomes of these cultural currents was the introduction of both the cotton seed and Neo-Confucian philosophy to Korea, both of which would have enormous long-term consequences. But this interaction drove the flow of influence in the opposite direction as well.

GORYEO WOMEN IN THE MONGOL EMPIRE

One of the most intriguing areas of Mongol influence in Goryeo lay in marriage and family customs, particularly as they affected women. Scholars have suggested, for example, that the practice of taking multiple wives, though not uncommon in the late Goryeo aristocracy, might have expanded under Mongol rule. If so, such influence introduces interesting complexities, given native Korean customs characterized by a relatively high social and familial position of females. This is not to suggest that the Goryeo era featured something approaching equality between the sexes. It is now commonly accepted, however, that Korean women enjoyed far greater standing in marriage, inheritance, and social status in the Goryeo than in the succeeding Joseon era (Chapter 8).

Whatever benefits that Korean women might have enjoyed, the Mongol period also reinforced the subordination of females through the demand for "tribute women" exacted upon the vanquished Goryeo. Government records indicate that, between 1275 and 1355, there were approximately fifty instances of the Goryeo court sending tribute women to the Mongol court, which took almost two hundred girls. But this is likely a gross underestimation, for the officially recorded instances only counted the mostly higher-status females sent to become concubines for the Mongol royalty and aristocracy, and did not include the hundreds, perhaps thousands, of those sent under more wretched circumstances. Like the other major group of Koreans sent to China—males bound to serve as eunuchs for the Yuan court—the tribute women represented little more than human booty, in effect slaves handed over as a sign of submission. Out of these terrible conditions, however, a fraction of both the eunuchs and tribute women managed to ascend to the highest levels of court life in the Mongol capital. And among these examples, the most fascinating figure was Lady Gi.

Lady Gi, daughter of a lower-level official's family, was sent as a tribute woman to the Mongol capital sometime in the 1320s. Little is known about how she came to catch the emperor's attention, but as noted in her official biography, it is likely that her beauty and her artistic talents were extraordinary. She was formally named an imperial concubine in 1333. The Mongol emperor, who as a boy had fallen victim to political strife and spent over a year in exile on an island off Korea's west coast, might have had a favorable disposition to Koreans in the first place. And having developed an intense affection for Lady Gi, he treated her as the preferred companion over his queen. When he tried to promote Lady Gi to official status as the secondary consort (second wife), it aroused staunch political opposition because it digressed from the standard practice of taking imperial queens only from a certain Mongol clan. In 1339, after she gave birth to a son, who would later become the Yuan monarch, the emperor's determination stiffened, and over weakening political opposition he had her crowned as the secondary imperial consort in 1340. In 1365, as the Yuan dynasty's grip over China was dissolving, Empress Gi ascended to the position of primary imperial consort.

In that intervening quarter-century, Empress Gi exercised great influence over the Yuan court and, by extension, Korea. In addition to her connection to the emperor, she controlled a special government organ, created specifically for her use, with wide-ranging tax collecting authority. Through this agency, she amassed tremendous power and initiated several grand projects. After a while she served in effect as the monarch, as her husband gradually lost interest in state affairs, and she even led a failed attempt to nudge her husband off the throne in favor of her son. The official Chinese history of the Yuan dynasty, written by the succeeding Ming dynasty, charged Empress Gi with corruption and extravagance, suggesting that her behavior contributed to the demise of Mongol rule. Empress Gi intervened in her home country of Goryeo as well, particularly through her family members, whose status and influence increased considerably. Empress Gi's father was formally invested as a "king" in the Yuan empire, and her mother in her old age received ritualized visits from the Goryeo monarch. Not surprisingly, according to official Korean accounts from the succeeding Joseon era, the Gi family is remembered almost exclusively for its lavish lifestyle and venality, on display both among the common people and within Goryeo elite circles. Outright theft of others' property, including slaves, for example, reached such severity among her siblings in Korea that Empress Gi herself had to warn them. One of her older brothers in particular, Gi Cheol, who once led the Eastern Expedition Field Headquarters and held greater authority than the Goryeo monarch, was especially singled out for his depravity. Indeed, his biographical entry in the *History of Goryeo* falls under the section on "Traitors" and recounts the sordid deeds of the entire Gi family. Little wonder, then, that when the last Goryeo monarch under Yuan domination, King Gongmin, unleashed an anti-Yuan offensive in 1356, he purged Gi Cheol and his family. For this, Goryeo suffered a reprisal invasion ordered by the empress, but this was successfully fended off, a reflection of the weakening Yuan as a whole. Little remains known of the fate of Empress Gi, who fled with her son, the next Yuan emperor, to the Mongol homelands ahead of Chinese rebels who would go on to establish the Ming dynasty.

Despite this inglorious end, Empress Gi's life and times present an intriguing picture of Goryeo's adaptation to the Mongol overlord period. She was likely most responsible, for example, for spreading Korean influence in China—through her political command, to be sure, but also through her incorporation of Korean females and eunuchs in the Yuan court. They in turn contributed to the flowering of a "Korean style" in the Chinese capital, from clothing and food to lifestyle. As a Korean observer at the time noted, it became fashionable for elite males in China to take Korean concubines, who exuded an aura of beauty and sophistication. Chinese sources, too—and often not in a flattering way—noted that Korean women, in particular, wielded strong influence over popular taste in China. Such a phenomenon may have represented a peak in the export of Korean culture in premodern times, and not until the early twenty-first century would Korean culture, popular or high, enjoy such widespread emulation and appeal outside the peninsula.

This presents, then, another reminder that the Mongol period, while certainly a time of humiliating subjugation to a foreign power, also left a more favorable imprint. We certainly cannot discount the horrific circumstances of the long Mongol siege of the mid-thirteenth century, or of the way Lady Gi and countless other captives wound up in China in the first place. But while Koreans' first experience of integration into a global order constituted a mixture of brutal conquest and cultural exchange, it also shared core features with the experience of other subject peoples in the Mongol empire who spanned all the way to Europe. And Lady Gi's rise to the heights of the Mongol court—and hence to a position as perhaps the most powerful person in the world at one time—demonstrates how Koreans throughout history adjusted to the realities of power among their neighbors. Indeed the long-term implications for Korean history are especially intriguing when compared to the subsequent experience of foreign domination in the twentieth century.

In the shorter term as well, there were major repercussions. The end of the Mongol period, for example, induced a concerted backlash among Korean elites, who, after two centuries of disruptions caused by both domestic and foreign usurpers, sought to restore a more stable and inward-looking form of monarchical rule. And in arousing the rebellions of the Red Turban bandits in the region, the Mongols were responsible also for the rise of Yi Seonggye, a Korean military leader who made his name in repelling these invaders on the peninsula. Together, these two outcomes of Mongol rule contributed directly to the death of the Goryeo dynasty itself, and to the birth of a new dynastic order in Korea under Yi's command.

7 Goryeo-Joseon Transition

CHRONOLOGY

1383	First meeting between General Yi Seonggye and Jeong Dojeon
1388	General Yi Seonggye's overthrow of the Goryeo ruling order
1392	Establishment of the Joseon dynasty
1398	Killing of Jeong Dojeon; abdication of the throne by Yi Seonggye
1400	Yi Bangwon's ascension as the third Joseon monarch, King Taejong
1418	Beginning of the reign of King Sejong the Great, son of King Taejong
1446	Promulgation of the Korean alphabet

YI BANGWON'S PURGE OF JEONG DOJEON, 1398

Six years after the founding of the new dynasty, for which he played the role of mastermind and lieutenant, Jeong Dojeon was killed by Yi Bangwon, the fifth son of the dynastic founder. The prince, furious over Jeong's betrayal in publicly backing Bangwon's half-brother for designation as the crown prince, now considered the scholar-official a major stumbling block to his own ambitions for the throne. Despite having worked in tandem to topple the Goryeo monarchy, the two had grown increasingly at odds over the issue of royal succession. Bangwon, uneasy at the prospect of not getting his just reward, purged his former partner, thereby eliminating from the scene the primary intellectual force in the expression of dynastic legitimacy. The inception of the Joseon era, then, established the basis of struggle between ambitious monarchs and pious officials that would feature prominently in the dynasty's politics thereafter.

Had it not been for this bloody moment, Yi Seonggye, the dynastic founder, would have enjoyed unquestioned primacy in the saga of the dynasty's birth. Like Gim Yusin and Wang Geon, the leading figures in the Silla unification and Goryeo founding, respectively, Yi was a military figure from the geographical fringes of the reigning kingdom. And it was Yi's audacity, foresight, and capacity to mobilize a wide range of followers— from military men to scholar-officials and even foreigners—that made possible the monumental change of a dynastic turnover. In contrast to Wang, however, Yi had to deal with potential trouble not from rival warlords but rather from rival sons. When he formally proclaimed his new kingdom in 1392, Yi could not have foreseen that the monarchy he labored to establish would almost immediately begin to fray from the ravages caused by his own progeny. From the historian's vantage point, this particular episode—indeed, the broader process of dynastic transition from Goryeo to Joseon—brings into relief major issues surrounding the Joseon dynasty as a whole and even premodern or "traditional" Korean civilization itself.

JEONG DOJEON: FROM MASTERMIND TO POLITICAL POWER

In 1383, after nine years of political exile, the up-and-coming Confucian scholar-official Jeong Dojeon visited the northeastern frontier of Goryeo. There, in General Yi Seonggye's home region, Jeong had a fateful encounter with this future founder of the next Korean ruling house. Whatever took place in their meeting, it was enough to forge a strong alliance, with Jeong hitching his ideals and destiny to the man who had amassed heroic feats in repelling marauding Japanese pirates and Red Turban raiders (Chapter 6). As it turned out, this bond could be characterized as an alliance of mutual convenience, with Yi using the scholar as much as Jeong used the general. When, as Goryeo's second-ranking military officer, Yi Seonggye was sent to lead a Korean expedition to invade Ming dynasty China during a border dispute in 1388, he recognized this as folly and instead turned his army toward the Goryeo capital. There he arrested his commander and effectively took control. Waiting for him was Jeong Dojeon, who directed changes that allowed Yi to take control, including the forced abdication of the sitting monarch in favor of Yi's hand-picked one. Jeong's increasing influence accompanied his accumulation of political offices, and he even went on a diplomatic mission to China to soothe the concerns of the Ming court. Jeong's rivals managed to send him to a brief exile in 1391, but to his rescue came Yi Bangwon, who killed many of these opponents, including the most prominent loyalists to the fading Goryeo monarchy. In 1392, freed from his imprisonment with the help of Bangwon, Jeong Dojeon joined dozens of other top scholar-officials in officially pleading for Yi Seonggye, the man who had effectively ruled the country since 1388, to establish a new dynastic order. For all of these efforts on Yi's behalf, Jeong Dojeon won designation as Dynastic Foundation Merit Subject, First Rank.

Jeong's role invites comparisons with other lieutenants of military leaders who established new political orders in Korea, such as Gim Chunchu, the mastermind behind General Gim Yusin's campaigns to unify the three kingdoms (Chapter 2), and later Kim Jong Pil, the dutiful assistant to General Park Chung Hee in the 1960s (Chapter 23). Unlike these two, however, Jeong Dojeon would not survive the turmoil of the takeover process, and so he resembled more the many scholar-officials in the Joseon era who became embroiled in political disputes concerning the monarchy and paid for this involvement with their lives. Like his successors, Jeong was driven by a fierce insistence on his own interpretation of Confucian ideology, and by the official's obligation to remonstrate the monarch when the latter strayed from the proper path. As part of the earliest cohort of Confucian officials in the Joseon, however, he helped draft the original blueprint of the dynastic order and thereby exerted a far greater influence than his peers would later. Jeong was by no means the only important figure in this regard, and to some historians his contributions did not necessarily exceed those of other "founding fathers" of this era. But clearly Jeong stood as the most versatile and influential in establishing the fundamental contours of early Joseon government and society.

Jeong, for example, authored many of Joseon's foundational documents. These included an early version of the dynastic legal code that, after decades of gestation, would be promulgated in final form some seventy years later. In this and other works, Jeong displayed a penchant for crafting a working compromise between Confucian ideals, on the one hand, and practical politics, on the other. His model for government organization harkened explicitly to the ancient *Rites of Zhou*, one of the core works of the Confucian canon, and his reverence for China's classical age affirmed a universal civilizational order centered on Korea's allegiance to the Ming dynasty. He did not view this arrangement in terms of China and Korea as separate countries as much as partners reviving the original glorious connections of the mythical era when a Chinese sage,

Gija, purportedly brought high civilization to Korea. Jeong also helped to further institutionalize Confucian meritocratic ideals through an emphasis on using examinations instead of connections to recruit government officials. This likely reflected his own relatively low birth status (he came from a lineage of local officials, it appears), a point exploited by his enemies throughout his career. Also arising from his own experience—namely, his near-decade spent in political exile—was his emphasis on the welfare of the peasantry, the meek majority whose struggles he witnessed directly in the remote corners of the country. And as if his political and philosophical works were not enough, Jeong helped to design the layout of the new capital city of Hanyang (Seoul), drafted an official history of the Goryeo dynasty—which served to legitimate the establishment of the Joseon—and even composed musical paeans to the new dynasty and its founder.

These accomplishments mattered little, however, in the face of naked monarchical ambition, and Jeong's death stood as one of many episodes of bloodshed that would surround Joseon royal succession. Jeong's downfall began with his public support of Yi Seonggye's decision to appoint Yi Bangseok, the founder's youngest son, as the crown prince. Yi Bangwon, who had long supported Jeong's preeminent standing in the circles of high ministers, considered this a betrayal and took action, just as he had done several years earlier when he did away with scholar-officials, like Jeong Mongju, who had opposed the toppling of the Goryeo monarchy. Now Bangwon set his sights on Jeong Dojeon, whom Bangwon tracked down and executed in early Autumn of 1398, just as he did also the crown prince. The dynastic founder, unable to bear any more of this mayhem among his children, abdicated in favor of another son and returned to his home town of Hamheung. Bangwon killed yet another fraternal rival in 1400, setting the stage for his ascension to the throne later that year as the third Joseon monarch, King Taejong. The tension would not end there, as Taejong's efforts to make amends to his father by sending royal emissaries to Hamheung appear to have been poorly received. In popular retellings of this period, the now "Senior King," still infuriated by his son's bloody actions, either incarcerated or outright killed a series of these "Hamheung messengers," or *Hamheung chasa*, a term that still today serves as shorthand for people, sent for errands, from whom nothing is ever heard. The father finally relented and returned to the capital, where, in a final fit of rage, he is supposed to have fired an arrow in Taejong's direction, narrowly missing him.

A RENAISSANCE, REVOLUTION, OR COUP?

These disturbing, in some ways horrific, circumstances during the opening decade of the Joseon era can elicit a wide range of perspectives on the significance of the dynastic turnover, and even cast doubt on its authenticity as a major historical event. Indeed, different schools of thought regarding the true meaning of this transition have arisen, with heightened historiographical stakes: an assessment of Confucianism's impact on Korean and Joseon history; the location of "legitimate" Korean tradition, especially the underlying tendencies in social and family customs; indeed the larger issues regarding the flow of premodern Korean history, such as stability versus change, external inducement versus internal propulsion, and so on. In fact, the prominence of both Yi Bangwon and Jeong Dojeon can illuminate and support each of the main perspectives on the historical significance of the dynastic transition.

Historians who view this process as a kind of Confucian renaissance emphasize the primacy of ideology in driving the events. Officially, at least, the scholars, officials, and even military men like Yi Seonggye drew explicitly from the teachings of what Western historians commonly call "Neo-Confucianism" in establishing the new dynastic order. Neo-Confucianism, a scholarly and ideological movement that, in Korea, began to brew in the late Goryeo era, had begun in Song dynasty China in the eleventh and twelfth centuries. It sought to resuscitate and refashion the classical texts of Confucianism into a moral philosophy that could be applied, expansively, toward addressing contemporary problems. The particular version of Neo-Confucianism that came to hold sway in the Joseon dynasty has often been called the "School of Nature and Principle," which more specifically referred to the firm link established between human nature and metaphysical doctrine. The proper understanding and practice of human connections lay at the heart of Confucian moral teachings, with filial piety—reverence for one's parents, explicitly invoked in the Confucian Five Relationships—serving as the core value that, when broadly applied, guided all human interaction. The "great chain" of Confucian cosmology began with the individual's self-cultivation of filial piety through ritual and learning, which in turn facilitated the achievement of familial and social harmony, a just political order, and peace under heaven.

One can see why, then, Jeong Dojeon, Yi Bangwon, and other Joseon founding fathers perceived in Neo-Confucianism not only an update to the millennium-long influence of Confucianism as a group of political doctrines, but a comprehensive approach to ethics, politics, social order, economy, and culture. The impressive range of Neo-Confucian legislation in the first few decades of the Joseon era reflected this ideology's systematic reach, and indeed the intricate attention given to even the realm of the family was among the most striking features (Chapter 8). Nevertheless, it bears noting that some Neo-Confucian practices, such as the state examination system, aristocratic domination based on a kinship system of common descent, and even male primacy in tracing family heritage, had long existed in Korea. Conversely, most of the new legislation inspired by Neo-Confucianism, especially in regard to instituting a patrilineal lineage system, took centuries to implement. In short, it can be said that ideology, however important, cannot account for all or even most of the thrust behind the dynastic turnover.

An alternative viewpoint claims that the founding of Joseon represented a revolutionary moment, but one driven by material changes and socioeconomic imperatives more than by ideas. The agitation of lower-level elites functioned as the indispensable source of support for Yi Seonggye's efforts to dismantle the late Goryeo order. To this vanguard, the significance of Neo-Confucian doctrine was utilitarian—in the service of class interests of the middle and small-scale landowners struggling against the capital elites and estate landlords. The rise to prominence of both Jeong Dojeon, from a lowly local official background, and Yi Seonggye, scion of a military family in the far northern fringe of the Goryeo realm, would seem to validate this perspective. Despite the attractiveness of this theory, however, in suggesting a deeper impulse for social change and hence a compelling story of historical progress, it appears somewhat overdrawn. Notwithstanding the dynastic founder's family history and Jeong Dojeon's own humble origins, extensive studies of the social background of the new capital elites have shown that, for the most part, they came from the Goryeo aristocracy.

A third view, in fact, considers the dynastic turnover as representing neither a social nor an ideological revolution, but rather a historical moment limited in significance, at least initially, to the realm of politics. It required a combination, in other words, of a military strongman's grab for power and a committed group of scholar-officials, like Jeong Dojeon, who had long attempted to implement major reforms, both in line with Neo-Confucian doctrine and in order to curb the abuses of the Buddhist establishment. The dynastic transition, then, represented the culmination of institutional reforms that had begun in the late Goryeo dynasty to address decays in the socioeconomic and political system.

It took simply the decisive contribution of military and political power (and ruthlessness) provided by Yi Seonggye and his son, Yi Bangwon, to bring this promise to fruition, which also enabled the aristocratic elites to maintain their social prerogatives. Critics of this stance, which appears to emphasize continuity over historical rupture, have objected to what appears an insufficient consideration of the wider circumstances of political change, especially one as momentous as the toppling of a five-century-old dynastic order. One could also level the charge that this interpretation suspiciously resembles the one put forth by Japanese colonialists to justify the takeover of Korea in the early twentieth century: What happened for a decade or so beginning in 1388 was merely a drawn-out palace coup. Few historians could seriously be expected to dismiss the dynastic turnover as just a coup, but the resistance to this theory reflects a wariness of undervaluing the effect of large historical forces in what appears, on the surface, a momentous turning point.

YI BANGWON'S IMPACT

Whatever the judgement on the historical meaning of the dynastic transition, one must account for the role of Yi Bangwon. Upon ascending the throne to become King Taejong (r. 1400–18), he placed the floundering new dynasty on firm footing as a Confucian polity. Under his direction, the Joseon state established the basic structure of government that would endure until the late nineteenth century, particularly in defining the state's deliberative and administrative authority. These duties were headed respectively by the High State Council and the Six Boards, a kind of cabinet-like division of managerial responsibility. For the provinces, the early Joseon reforms extended state jurisdiction to the farthest reaches of the realm and institutionalized the eight-province division of the country that, in modified form, still is in effect today (at least in South Korea). King Taejong also took decisive steps to further disenfranchise the Buddhist establishment, the only viable rival to the new dynasty in its claims to ideological supremacy. He did this by closing down many temple complexes and appropriating the Buddhist clergy's human and material resources. And further attesting to the state's ambitions for population control, he instituted the obligation to carry an "identity tag" for people traveling outside their home regions. Above all King Taejong strengthened the position of the monarchy in relation to the bureaucracy, presenting himself as the model of an authoritative and sagely Confucian monarch.

King Sejong the Great

It seems only one monarch in the long history of Korean royalty commands the unquestioned and universal appellation of "the Great" following his name: Sejong, the fourth king (r. 1418–50) of the Joseon dynasty. King Sejong enjoys a standing in Korean civilization that is akin to George Washington's in the United States, with his name attached to everything from universities and cultural institutions to civic organizations and state projects. That his portrait graces the most familiar South Korean bill, the 10,000 won bank note, is itself a reflection of his supreme stature in Korean civilization. Most Koreans attribute to him what is widely considered the nation's signature cultural accomplishment, the promulgation of the native Korean alphabet in 1446. They also know that he instituted innovative state policies and sponsored the invention of advanced scientific instruments such as the rain gauge, water clock, and sundial. He is seen, in short, as having come closest to the ideal of the sagacious monarch who promoted the welfare of the common people above all. But one can also summarize his accomplishments and historical significance with the reminder that, perhaps more than anything else, King Sejong fortified the Joseon state's great project of Confucianizing Korea.

Even the development of the Korean alphabet itself was part of Sejong's wide-ranging efforts to enhance the state's dissemination of Confucian teachings. Overlooked in the ceaseless and ubiquitous mythologizing of this feat (there is even a national holiday honoring the alphabet) is the fact that Sejong, in addition to standardizing the Korean—that is, "proper"—pronunciation of Chinese characters, found the alphabet a potentially breakthrough instrument for public education. In his famous preamble to the "Proper Sounds to Educate the People" (Hunmin jeongeum), the document introducing the new alphabet, Sejong emphasized not only that the Korean language is different from Chinese, but also that the common ("ignorant") people needed a simplified system of written communication. The Joseon government in fact soon began to publish numerous didactic works featuring glosses with the new alphabet, all preaching the core principles of Neo-Confucianism. And indeed, Neo-Confucian scholarship and education was the basic charge of the Hall of Worthies, a state research institute that Sejong established soon after ascending the throne. Today there remain questions about the precise balance of contributions from the Hall of Worthies and King Sejong to the alphabet project, but perhaps in accordance with the Confucian values that Sejong so eagerly sought to instill, there was no difference: He gets the credit.

As noted above, the Confucian transformation of Korea took a very long time to accomplish, but Taejong's actions helped to set the parameters of Confucianization, characterized by a comprehensiveness of ambition and scope, especially under the direction of the state. Some modern historians have criticized such steps taken by the Joseon founding fathers as having forced the Koreans to subsume their native ways, indeed their cultural autonomy, to the foreign ideology of Neo-Confucianism. The early Joseon's explicit reference to the Confucian canon as the basis for comprehensive changes appears indeed to have set the stage for an obsessive and at times stultifying preoccupation with asserting the country's Confucian credentials. But Confucianism, like Buddhism, also contained the potential to highlight and heighten native customs and identity. Taejong's son and successor, King Sejong, commonly considered the greatest of all Korean monarchs, served as convincing testimony to this potential (see text box).

8 Confucianism and the Family in the Early Joseon Era

CHRONOLOGY

THE DRAFTING OF LADY YI'S WILL, 1541

In 1541, a family inheritance document was drawn up to designate the division of an aristocratic female's possessions, mostly in the form of slaves. Though normally an unremarkable event, this particular occurrence was notable because some of the recipients of this estate, along with its attendant responsibilities, included a mother and son who later became the most celebrated such tandem in Korean history: Sin Inseon, better known as Sin Saimdang, the venerable poet, painter, and calligrapher; and her son, Yi I, better known by his pen name of Yulgok, recognized as one of the foremost Confucian scholar-officials and a towering genius. This will is valuable also because it represents one of the few surviving such documents from the early Joseon era, and because it distributes the estate of a female to her female offspring—something that would become increasingly rare.

In 2007, South Korean officials chose Sin Saimdang as the historical figure to grace the new 50,000 *won* bill, the fourth bank note in South

Image 8 *Lady Sin Saimdang (front) and one of her bamboo paintings (back) featured on the Bank of Korea's 50,000 won bill, issued June 2009. (Courtesy of Bank of Korea.)*

Korean money, and the first new one in several decades (see Image 8). Given that the hallowed figures on the other three bills were all men, including Lady Sin's son Yulgok, anticipation over the selection of the new personage had drawn great attention, with the tacit understanding that the figure would be a female. To the surprise of many, however, when the selection committee announced its choice, a strong reaction arose from women's organizations and feminist groups, who viewed Lady Sin as a representation of the harmful impact of Confucianism and of traditional customs in general. This opposition provided a reminder of, among other things, the ongoing significance of the early Joseon era, in particular of the Confucianization of society and family, in Korea's past and present.

EARLY JOSEON CONFUCIANISM

It is commonly accepted that the Joseon dynasty, which endured from the late fourteenth to the late nineteenth centuries, solidly Confucianized Korean civilization, effectively rendering Korea's premodern era inseparable from Confucianism itself. In modern times, this has provided the impetus for an ongoing reconsideration of Korean tradition by distinguishing the Joseon era from a "pre-Confucian," and presumably more genuine, Korea. In North Korea, the official historical view dismisses Confucianism as a reflection of backward feudalism and toadyism. In the South, the nationalistic thrust of such a critique has fused more recently with the continuing struggle over the proper place of Confucian teachings, especially regarding females and the family, in contemporary identity. While this division of Korean history tends to obscure the millennium of Confucian influence on the peninsula before the Joseon dynasty, the notion that the Joseon rulers and social elites instituted Confucianism as a totalizing, dominant thought system appears warranted.

The early Joseon state stood at the center of these efforts at Confucianization and, regardless of whether Confucianism drove the dynastic transition or simply acted as a convenient political tool (Chapter 7), the state was infused with this greater purpose. Due to the immediate demands of state strengthening and centralization, Confucian statecraft in the early Joseon appears to have had a major impact even in the economy. Officials pursued a grand effort to fortify state finances while attempting to abide by Confucian ideals of eliminating unjust tax burdens and of reinforcing the centrality of agriculture over other economic activities, such as commerce. This required, then, a land tax policy of shifting revenues toward the state and its local agencies at the expense of other social sectors that, in the Goryeo era, had grown wealthy and powerful, especially the landed aristocracy, local elites, and the Buddhist establishment. These measures did not go so far as to completely monetize the economy, however; land taxes were paid in kind through grains and cloth. A complex system of personal tribute taxes also constituted a large proportion of the state's revenues. The population was responsible for service duty, including military service and labor for state projects, as well as for providing material goods, ranging from luxury items to household goods, for government organs, the royal family, and even foreign dignitaries. The precise balance between land taxes, personal service, and tribute items is difficult to gauge, but all of these duties had the effect of reinforcing the centrality of agriculture in the country's economy. Commercial activity and foreign trade appear to have been relatively unchanged or even curtailed through the central state's increasing control over the circulation of material resources.

The Confucian ethos, and hence Confucian statecraft, expressed little interest in encouraging private accumulation.

Confucianism did, however, encourage the pursuit of intellectual wealth, and the first two centuries of the Joseon dynasty witnessed the peak of Confucian philosophy—if not the peak of philosophy as a whole in Korean history. Through a richly productive exchange of correspondence, memorials, and publications, Confucian intellectuals participated in a thriving republic of letters in sixteenth-century Korea that tackled fundamental problems in connecting the cosmos to human experience and morality. Among the most preeminent figures in these developments were Yulgok and Yi Hwang, better known as Toegye (who also is canonized through his appearance on a South Korean bill). Although they were not of the same generation and likely met only a couple of times, Toegye and Yulgok stood as dueling representatives of a great debate that consumed Korean philosophy in the sixteenth century and went on to exert a profound impact on politics and society the rest of the dynasty (Chapter 10). The foremost issue, known sometimes as the "Four-Seven Debate," revolved around how to reconcile basic psychological drives behind moral behavior (the "four basic feelings" and "seven emotions") with the Neo-Confucian metaphysics of reality and being. While he appears to have further refined and clarified the orthodoxy, Toegye gained acclaim for unveiling a convincing schematic for self-cultivation. Yulgok, meanwhile, won renown for tackling these questions through a novel, synthetic, and practical approach of addressing pressing political and economic concerns.

CONFUCIAN FAMILY LAW AND WOMEN'S STANDING

As suggested by such deep-seated connections between the philosophical and a wide range of political and social concerns, Confucian teachings had a comprehensive impact on Korean customs, ritual practices, and human interaction, even down to the level of the family itself. Indeed the signal Confucian transformation came in the realm of family law, with the most dramatic effects felt in the familial and social standing of women. The intimate setting of the family, though, is also where entrenched customs naturally take the longest to change—as witnessed in modern Korea, for example, with the century-long, grinding effort to *overturn* Confucian family practices.

The Joseon dynasty eventually did manage to install a new, Confucian family system. The legislative blueprint appeared in the opening decades of the Joseon era, at the turn of the fifteenth century, and was based largely on "Master Zhu's Family Rituals," written by the great twelfth-century systematizer of the Neo-Confucian renaissance in Song dynasty China, Zhu Xi. *Master Zhu's Family Rituals* designated four such ceremonies and contained detailed instructions on how to carry them out: capping (a coming-of-age ritual), wedding, funeral, and ancestor worship. With the exception of capping, these rituals had long been practiced by Koreans, but the Neo-Confucian instructions integrated them systematically into a cosmology that extended to dictums on politics, society, religion, and other realms. Because of their divergence from previous practices and their centrality to the overall Confucian program, the propagation of Confucian family teachings received a lot of attention from the state. Scholar-officials and even female royal family members glossed Zhu Xi's work, with a consideration of native Korean circumstances, in order to disseminate publications on core Confucian principles. This effort received a further boost by the promulgation of the Korean alphabet in the mid-fifteenth century.

The Confucian family laws also demanded a commanding patrilineal system, one that not only traced family identity and legitimacy through the males, but also required that all rituals conform to this orientation. This had a wide-ranging impact on women's social and familial standing, which, while not approaching equality with that of males, had hitherto been relatively high, as demonstrated by the personal possessions of Lady Yi. To be sure, in overriding the patrilineal thrust of Confucian teachings, Koreans were to maintain the powerful native practices that held the social status of the mother as equally important to that of the father in determining an individual's status. But in general the Confucian family rituals, especially the ancestor worship requirements, helped to downgrade the female's role and influence as independent actors in her family's ritual life and social identity. The lifelong responsibility of male descendants, primarily the first sons, to observe regular sacrificial rituals carried an acute economic burden, for example, and this demanded that inheritance practices, too, be gradually shifted toward that of males.

Historical events and documentary evidence from the early Joseon era bear witness to the fits and starts of this extensive effort to implement Confucian family law throughout the realm. Work on producing a final version of the dynastic code, or *Gyeongguk daejeon*, which would serve as a kind of constitution for the remainder of the Joseon, in fact took over seven decades following the establishment of the dynasty, with promulgation coming finally in the early 1470s. But the dynastic code represented just the first step, and the greater challenge of

Confucianization lay in getting the people, beginning with the aristocratic elite, to follow the code's instructions in their own family practices. This is why sources such as Lady Yi's will of 1541 are so illuminating, for they reflect the ongoing, though not always smooth, transition to a Confucian family system that would eventually transfer privileges—as well as responsibilities—exclusively to males.

Lady Yi's inheritance document in fact suggests the resilience of older practices mixed with the demands of the new, even as late as the mid-sixteenth century. Strikingly, it shows a female, albeit a female aristocrat, holding considerable economic resources in her name and, apparently, at her disposal. Lady Yi would go down in history as the maternal grandmother of the great philosopher Yulgok, whose deeply affectionate biography of his grandmother provide all we know about her, aside from the information presented in the will. As to be expected for a local aristocrat, Lady Yi had impeccable family credentials, with both of her parents coming from prestigious lineages. She had grown up in Gangneung, on the east-central coast, and had wed a young man from Seoul with the surname of Sin (pronounced "sheen"). Following long-established practices, after her wedding the couple lived initially in the wife's natal home before, in accordance with Confucian teachings, moving to Seoul to be with the husband's family. But she quickly returned to Gangneung, with blessings from her husband and in-laws, to care for her aging parents. She and her husband lived apart like this, interspersed with frequent visits, for over a dozen years. In Gangneung she raised their five children, all daughters, including the second daughter, who would become the mother of Yulgok.

The 1541 will, however—drafted nearly thirty years, as it turned out, before Lady Yi's death—provided no special consideration for that second daughter. In accordance with a long-held custom, Lady Yi's substantial estate of 173 slaves was divided more or less equally among her five daughters, with the inheritances ranging from twenty-nine to thirty-five slaves each. The will meticulously notes the name, age, sex, family relationship, and current residence of each of the slaves, who were scattered around the country. While this shows a continuation of long-held inheritance practices that divided estates equally among children regardless of gender or order, Confucian demands made their presence felt in the special designation of the "ritual heir," the descendant responsible for leading the ancestral rites. The extant inheritance documents from the early Joseon show a gradual increase of this provision until it became standard practice by the late sixteenth century. Here Lady Yi's will is especially instructive, for, in the absence of any sons, the person designated to lead the ancestral ceremonies was none other than a five-year-old grandson, Yi I (Yulgok), who was given land and five slaves to provide the financial wherewithal to sustain this task indefinitely. One presumes that, had Lady Yi died soon after this document was drafted, either this boy's father or an uncle would have temporarily taken responsibility, but this provision is still notable on two levels: first, that it was the third son of the second daughter who was chosen, suggesting that this boy—who later, as a thirteen-year-old, would pass the introductory level state civil service examination, in first place no less—was already demonstrating his precociousness; and second, that no daughter, despite receiving a substantial inheritance, could be deemed fit to lead the sacrificial rites, suggesting strongly that some legal and, by now, customary restrictions on females were taking hold.

In the late Joseon era, this practice would become even more restrictive, with far greater social consequences. By the eighteenth century, the increasing centrality of the ancestor rites in the Confucian lineage system standardized the practice of primogeniture, or preference for the oldest son, not only in selecting a ritual heir, but, due to the cost of such a responsibility, in inheritance practices as well. Daughters and even younger sons received far less, if anything, and when it came to the children of concubines, the exclusion was complete. Indeed, when families in the late Joseon era encountered a similar situation as that of Lady Yi in 1541—that is, lacking a (non-concubine's) son—the prevailing practice was to adopt a nephew, however distant, from the same lineage, to act as both the ritual and family heir. Customs like primogeniture that later developed out of the Confucian family system thus weakened the standing of women in many ways. They left women with few possessions and hence little economic independence, in stark contrast to Lady Yi. They diminished women's ritual and lineage roles. And they stigmatized the descendants of secondary wives, whose status as concubines reinforced the centrality of sexual exploitation in the social hierarchy.

It is no wonder, then, that contemporary women in South Korea look back on the early Joseon with deep regret about what might have been—that is, without the incorporation of Confucian family practices. In modern terms, as noted above, the Yi family inheritance document and other evidence suggest strongly that pre-Joseon Korea was relatively "advanced" when it came to the social and familial standing of females. Without Confucianization, so the thinking goes, the country might have taken a more enlightened historical path. The sixteenth century, more specifically, is fascinating in this regard, for it could have represented the last gasp of relatively high female standing before the momentum of state instructions and customary practices would overwhelm it. At the court, for example, for two decades in the early sixteenth century, practical power was wielded substantially by two women: The first was the mother of a young king who acted as his regent, and the second was her niece, who had begun her life as a slave and ascended to a position in the court that allowed her to push for greater social opportunity for the lower classes. And in the literary realm, two other women of the sixteenth century, Heo Naseorheon and Hwang Jini, who advanced the great forms of native poetry, *sijo* and *gasa*, appeared far more accomplished than Sin Saimdang.

Given this, one could suggest that Lady Sin might not have been the Bank of Korea's best choice even from her own historical period. In any case, one can understand the disappointment expressed by women's organizations over the selection of Lady Sin, long celebrated for her supposed dedication to Confucian family values in her role as a daughter, wife, and mother. Critics of this choice suggested that Lady Sin's claim to fame was based not on her artistic talents, however admirable they might have been, but rather on the fact that she raised a celebrated scholar and statesman who, along with his admirers, placed Lady Sin on an undeserved pedestal. Lady Sin, in other words, was seen as a paragon of traditional (male-centered) Confucian—not modern—virtue, and hence her selection was considered somewhat patronizing. Tellingly, before the selection South Korean women's organizations and feminist groups had put forward another female, Yu Gwansun, as their preferred candidate for the new bank note. As a cultivated teenage girl armed with modern schooling, Yu had been martyred while rallying her home town's residents to participate in the independence movement of 1919 against Japanese colonial rule. Within the overarching, persistent framework of nationalism and modernity, then, Sin Saimdang serves as another symbolic object of contestation over the place of tradition, especially the Confucian heritage, in contemporary Korean identity. And remarkably, all four historical figures, including Sin Saimdang, who are now celebrated on the South Korean bills hail from the first two centuries of the Joseon dynasty.

9 The Great Invasions, 1592–1636

CHRONOLOGY

THE RETURN TO DUTY OF ADMIRAL YI SUNSIN, 1597

Though little known outside of Asia, the East Asian war of 1592–8 stands as one of the major events in world history. For the first time since the aborted Mongol invasions of Japan in the thirteenth century, the major civilizations of East Asia became embroiled in a single conflict, with consequences that would far exceed any other in this region until the late nineteenth century, indeed perhaps until the Pacific War of 1937–45. Begun through the Japanese invasion of Korea in 1592 in a bid to conquer China itself, this war, fought exclusively in Korea, brought together all three countries in a conflict lasting nearly seven years. The destruction was enormous—to the Chinese who sent huge armies in Korea's defense, and even to the Japanese. In Korea, the scale of the devastation can scarcely be imagined: hundreds of thousands killed, millions injured or uprooted, and a poisoning of relations with Japan that would never disappear.

That Korea survived this onslaught is itself a miracle. The most common Korean view relates that the country was rescued by its greatest military hero, Admiral Yi Sunsin, who helped staunch the destruction in 1592 by leading the Korean naval forces to key victories. Not long after his heroics, however, Admiral Yi found himself in a Seoul jail, awaiting judgment on charges of insubordination and treason. When, after four years of stalemate, peace talks collapsed and the Japanese sent another invasion force in 1597, Admiral Yi was freed and ordered back to the Korean coast to coordinate his command with the Chinese allies. In a decisive naval battle against an enormous Japanese flotilla in the fall of 1597, Admiral Yi gained victory and prevented the Japanese from establishing supply lines along the west coast. This helped bring the conflict to an end in 1598. But the significance of this conflagration would extend both geographically and temporally thereafter. It may have even paved the way a few years later for the rise of the Manchus, who also launched destructive invasions of Korea. For the Koreans, these wars exposed grave problems in the Joseon polity, but they eventually also provided an opportunity for sharpening the Koreans' sense of national identity and civilizational standing.

PROBLEMS IN THE KOREAN RESPONSE

Although some Korean officials and commanders had suspected trouble brewing in Japan and even prepared for a conflict, the utter scale and catastrophic force of the Japanese assault in the spring of 1592 came as a shock: a landing force of hundreds of ships and tens of thousands of soldiers. The county officials of Dongnae, now part of the city of Busan in the southeastern corner of the peninsula, managed to send messengers on horseback to Seoul before the siege overwhelmed the Dongnae fortress. But the samurai soldiers, splitting their invasion routes northward, tore through the country so quickly that within two weeks they were at the gates of the capital. After much hand-wringing with every report of the collapse of the country's defenses, King Seonjo abandoned Seoul and fled northward, eventually all the way to the border town of Uiju. The capital, devoid of official authority, was ransacked by angry, hungry, and frightened refugees, who pillaged public granaries and burned down palaces and government buildings, including those that contained slave registers.

Amid the chaos, the Korean court had turned to its formidable navy, sending two naval commanders for the southernmost provinces, Won

Gyun and Yi Sunsin, to engage the Japanese within days of the invasion. Admiral Yi Sunsin, in particular, enjoyed tremendous successes in these battles, destroying much of the Japanese fleet and thereby managing successfully to cut off Japanese supply lines along the southern coast. He is credited in particular with skillful deployment of smaller, highly maneuverable attack ships, including the famed "turtle boats" that were protected by a spiked armored shell. These breakthroughs proved sufficient to hold off the invaders until Chinese forces, sent by the Ming emperor at the request of the Korean monarch, arrived in sufficient numbers to turn the tide of the war. In the opening weeks of 1593, the combined Korean–Chinese army laid siege on Pyongyang fortress, occupied by the Japanese since the previous summer, and then pushed the invaders southward. As the Japanese retreated to their encampments along the southern end of the peninsula, negotiations began for a peace settlement, and an extended stalemate ensued for the next four years.

Meanwhile, in spite of the recognition of his skills accorded him by the court, Admiral Yi found himself embroiled in the factional struggles among high officials over responsibility for the stunning failure to prepare for, then counter, the invasion. Factionalism, a form of party politics, had evolved from the early-Joseon conflicts among the throne and high officials (Chapter 7) into a system, exploited and institutionalized in King Seonjo's reign, of bitter, often inherited divisions among the literati as a whole. Thereafter, factional differences, the configuration of which developed through further divisions over the seventeenth and early eighteenth centuries, corresponded to struggles over royal succession and political appointments as well as to differences in policy and philosophy. Even marriage boundaries were set by factional identity, which was not limited to the upper echelons of powerful aristocrats in the capital but also drove social and political interaction among local elites as well. Perspectives on the larger significance of Joseon dynasty factionalism have varied widely among historians, but tellingly the Japanese who again invaded Korea in the early twentieth century cited factionalism as another example of the debilitating Korean political system.

Regardless of its ultimate significance in explaining Joseon dynasty politics as a whole, factionalism did play a major role in this period of great invasions from 1592 to 1636, as partisan disputes became entangled in formulating the government's responses. One key example of this phenomenon came in the two years preceding the Japanese attack, when the Korean monarch sent a diplomatic mission to Japan to gauge the intent of Toyotomi Hideyoshi, the Japanese leader. The embassy's report to King Seonjo showed a division among its top two officials, members of rival factions. In implementing a response, one official's warnings of an imminent Japanese invasion lost out to the reassurances of peace by the second official, whose party enjoyed the upper hand in court. The government's fateful decision not to mobilize the country in preparation for war proved disastrous. And, once again, factional politics affected the government's handling of the crisis amidst the war, as Admiral Won Gyun, who, in contrast to Yi Sunsin, had largely failed in his efforts to defeat the enemy at sea, blamed Yi for not carrying out orders to support him. Amid the stalemate during peace talks, Won's political ties to those in power in Seoul produced the astounding scene of Admiral Yi's becoming incarcerated, and indeed of even being sentenced to death. The scramble to save his life by a few top officials was enough to prolong the stay of execution until the second Japanese invasion of 1597, which highlighted the folly of locking up Admiral Yi in the first place.

Freed from prison and reinstated to his command, Yi turned his attention to the southwestern coast. There, in the famed Battle of Myeongnyang, his depleted fleet of twelve ships lured the vanguard of the hundreds-strong Japanese armada into the tricky, powerful currents of the straits off Jindo Island, which provided the advantage needed to destroy many Japanese ships and drive the rest away. This outcome proved crucial in cutting off Japanese supply routes to the west coast of the peninsula. Meanwhile, the allied forces, bolstered by waves of reinforcements sent by Ming Emperor Wanli, fought a series of gruesome battles with the Japanese, who again retreated to their fortresses along the south coast until receiving the order to withdraw from Korea in the summer of 1598. Hideyoshi's death in the fall further hastened this withdrawal, but as the Joseon navy chased the retreating enemy in a final major battle in late 1598, Admiral Yi was struck down by gunfire.

NARRATIVES OF HEROISM

Yi Sunsin's death in a blaze of glory has always served the great narrative of heroism centered on this figure, whose feats of bravery and skill in the face of impossible odds are commonly recounted by Korean schoolchildren. By all viable historical accounts, Yi Sunsin was indeed an accomplished soldier, gifted strategist, and charismatic commander. From a prominent aristocratic lineage that had produced mostly civilian officials, he chose another path in his youth and, after passing the military examination with honors, soon ascended the ranks of the military officialdom. As naval commander of Jeolla province, he stood as one of the few officials who foresaw the danger from Japan, and his preparations appear to have served him well once he engaged in battle, as chronicled in his diary-like official reports to the court. These documents, as well as other eyewitness accounts and government records, all point to Yi's great deeds. But perhaps the source that contributed most to the glorification of Yi Sunsin as Korea's greatest war hero was the *Book of Corrections* (*Jingbirok*), written by Yi's staunchest supporter in the upper echelons of government officialdom, Yu Seongnyong. Yu had acted as one of Yi's early patrons before the outbreak of war, and the *Book of Corrections*, in reference to the lessons that must be learned from the country's failures, likened Yi to a great spiritual force who almost single-handedly saved Korea. And Yi's stoic righteousness in the face of factional injustice only heightened the impression of his purity.

In the modern era, another example of valor has gained prominence in the conventional perspective on the Japanese war: the "righteous army" (*uibyeong*) guerrilla groups mobilized throughout the country to attack the invaders and obstruct the Japanese lines of communication and supplies. In the North Korean account of this war, for example, it is the righteous armies, representing the mass of the common, down-trodden people, who came to the rescue when the upper classes, including the monarchy, utterly failed to protect the nation. Such a populist perspective has become more accepted in South Korea as well, but, as scholars have pointed out, these militias were organized and led by local aristocrats or officials and thus replicated the hierarchies of society at large. The rise and effectiveness of these units may have been attributable not to their mass character, in other words, but rather to their aristocratic leadership, which served, in the long run, to strengthen local elites' standing in the process of helping to save the country. To what extent such mostly autonomous militias, which included bands of Buddhist monks as well, played a decisive role in the war's outcome remains a point of contention. It appears that indeed, the difficulties of obtaining provisions and of holding ground in the face of smaller-scale Korean attacks (and threats thereof) hindered the Japanese in achieving greater military successes in the interior of the country. But regardless of the precise impact of these guerrilla units, it seems fitting—considering who suffered the brunt of the Japanese invasions—that they would be featured prominently in the national memory of the war. Indeed, their deeds lingered in the popular imagination thereafter, as seen in the reprisal of the "righteous army" moniker for ragtag military groups that formed at the turn of the early twentieth century to resist, once again, the Japanese. In this sense, the prominence of the righteous armies in the narratives of national struggle reflects the intensification of anti-Japanese sentiment in the development of Korean identity.

There remains, however, one final major factor in the war's outcome that, in Korea at least, has not been readily highlighted: the Chinese. The precise balance of contributions between the Ming forces and the Korean defenses cannot be measured precisely when accounting for the allied military victories, but the Chinese role was likely far greater than what most Koreans have come to known. North Korean accounts understandably do not even mention the Ming dynasty's assistance, for this would run counter to their hyper-nationalist narrative of Korean history. Even in South Korea, conventional perspectives on the war give little credit to China, a sentiment shown as early as Yu's *Book of Corrections*, which mostly depicted the Chinese negatively, focusing on their abusive behavior, their commanders' neglect of Korean concerns in peace negotiations, and their battlefield failures. Other scholarship, however, has found clear evidence that the Chinese forces played not only a key role in the war's outcome, but an indispensable one.

THE REGIONAL ORDER REMADE

The significance of the Chinese contribution highlights the fact that, notwithstanding Korea's suffering, this war may have been the most widely encompassing event in East Asia until the modern era. Indeed the consequences extended even to an area originally untouched by the invasion, Manchuria. While there remains debate over the precise connections between the Japanese invasions and the Manchu conquest of Korea and China three decades later, the instability reverberating through the region likely had a staggering effect.

Often overlooked when considering the fallout from the Japanese invasions of Korea is the pronounced impact on Japan itself, much of which, ultimately, was in fact beneficial. The lessons learned from the failure of Hideyoshi's grandiose scheme, not to mention the expenditures of resources and lives, cast a long shadow over Japan's subsequent history. In addition to megalomaniacal delusions of ruling the entire region, along with perhaps some strategic commercial interests, Hideyoshi's primary reason for launching the campaigns appears to have been to provide an outlet for the energies of his retainers. They had helped him reunify Japan after centuries of fragmentation, and they dutifully executed his invasions of Korea. Thereafter, however, Japanese leaders would not again venture beyond their borders for over 200 years. In fact,

the man who emerged as Hideyoshi's successor, Tokugawa Ieyasu, instituted a peaceful, stable, and in many ways thriving dynastic rule, the
Tokugawa shogunate, based partly on a policy of "closure" to the outside
world until the middle of the nineteenth century. The grimly salutary
effects of Hideyoshi's misadventure would extend to unforeseen realms
as well: The tens of thousands of Korean war captives—mostly peasant
commoners, but also artists, potters, smiths, ship builders, even officials
and scholars—taken to Japan, where many were enslaved, appear to have
made a lasting contribution to the development of Japanese culture and
technology. Some prisoners of war were then sold to secondary slave
markets run by Asian and Western merchants, and indeed, a few Koreans
ended up traveling as far as Europe. Still other abductees escaped or
were repatriated in the years immediately after the war, as the Tokugawa
shogunate worked to reestablish diplomatic and commercial ties with
Joseon. Indeed, official relations were restored stunningly quickly, within
a decade of the war's end, and thereafter Joseon allowed a Japanese
trading post to operate in Busan in return for sending periodic, ornate
embassies to Edo (present-day Tokyo), the Tokugawa capital.

As for China, the dedication of massive resources to the war against
Japan—an act, admittedly, that was not devoid of self-interest, since
Korea served as a buffer against the irksome and unruly Japanese—could
not have helped the Ming dynasty's increasingly precarious grip on rule.
After more than two centuries, the Ming government, having concentrated its energies on internal stability through limited foreign adventures, found itself having to beat back not only a suddenly expansionist
Japan, but also Chinese rebels and ultimately yet another "barbarian"
group to its immediate northeast. The Manchus, descendants of Jurchen
tribesmen who periodically organized themselves into a formidable military force, had suddenly done so again while the rest of the region was
preoccupied with recovery from the Japanese invasions.

By the 1620s, the Manchus, following the familiar pattern of the
northmen of East Asia in previous eras, appeared on the verge of striking Korea on their way to the big prize of China itself. The specter of
this invasion instigated a major political struggle within Korea over
how to respond. Eventually the king, Gwanghaegun, who favored a policy of accommodation with this new power, the Qing, was overthrown
by his ministers, fiercely mindful of the great national debt owed to
China, in favor of a more explicitly pro-Ming monarch, Injo. This soon
brought forth the first Manchu invasion of Korea in 1627, to be followed by the finishing blow in 1636, which led to King Injo's surrender
in ritualized humiliation to the Qing ruler just outside of Seoul. This

cleared the way for the Manchus' march into Beijing in 1644 and their takeover of China.

Despite having succumbed to the irrepressible Manchu force themselves just a few years earlier, the Koreans were shocked by the Ming dynasty's fall, which constituted, from the their perspective, an event approaching the level of a cosmic shift. Despite Joseon's diplomatic subordination as a tributary state, the legitimacy of the Qing dynasty of the Manchus was never accepted by most Korean elites, who scorned these "barbarians" and even retained fantasies of pursuing a "northern campaign" to overthrow the Qing. Koreans, now stripped of their long-held assumptions about civilizational order, were compelled to reconsider their own existential standing. And here, a belief hardened among the Korean upper class that, with the fall of the mighty Ming, only Joseon remained as a bastion of (Confucian) civilization. This accompanied the equally fascinating emergence of a more widespread sense of collective consciousness among lower groups of people as well, as seen in the expressions of popular culture from the seventeenth century onwards (Chapter 12). Indeed, the rallying cry of Yi Sunsin, righteous armies, and others around the common cause of national survival might have fortified the idea of Koreanness itself.

10 Ideology, Family, and Nationhood in the Mid-Joseon Era

CHRONOLOGY

1644	Qing's conquest of Ming dynasty China
1674	Ascent to the throne of King Sukjong
1680	Marriage of King Sukjong to Queen Inhyeon
1688	Birth of crown prince to a royal concubine, Lady Jang
1689	King Sukjong's divorce from Queen Inhyeon, marriage to Lady Jang, purge of Westerners faction
1694	Remarriage to Queen Inhyeon, demotion of Lady Jang; restoration of Westerners to power
1701	Death of Queen Inhyeon; execution of Lady Jang

THE BIRTH OF A SON TO LADY JANG, 1688

In late 1688, news quickly spread that Lady Jang, the favored concubine of King Sukjong, had given birth to a son. Though certainly not an unusual event in the annals of the Korean monarchy, in the tense atmosphere of court politics at the time, it carried strong repercussions. For Lady Jang, known commonly as Jang Huibin, was not just a royal concubine. Through her actions and her unwitting status as a political symbol, she also embodied the tensions and conflicts involving fundamental issues of Korean identity and civilization that had roiled the capital for years. Lady Jang had so smitten the monarch that he promptly designated the newborn as the crown prince, divorced his own queen, who had yet to bear a son, and promoted Lady Jang as her replacement. The vehement objections to this move from many top advisors, including the most notable Confucian scholar of the era, unleashed a storm of political strife. Within fifteen years, this conflict would ultimately victimize dozens of high officials on all sides and end with Lady Jang's own execution ordered by the monarch himself.

A riveting story that has been replayed countless times on Korean television dramas and movies, this episode's historical significance extended far beyond the realm of the inner palace quarters. It underscored, for one, the conflicts surrounding ideological and factional struggles, family practices, social organization, and even civilizational identity that had been stirring for decades as the country recovered from the Japanese and Manchu invasions (Chapter 9). These broader implications in turn highlight the significance of this middle period of the Joseon dynasty, when some of the most familiar features of Korea's Confucian society matured into form.

KING SUKJONG'S TRIANGLES

The mid-Joseon era, in turn, can be further divided: the half-century of devastating invasions from 1592 to 1636, and the many decades thereafter of recovery, reckoning, and reconstruction. The political figure dominating the latter period was King Sukjong, who in his teens ascended the throne in 1674 and survived to reign for forty-five years. This longevity alone suggests a strong monarch ruling at a time of welcome stability, which indeed was the case for the country as a whole. Sukjong bolstered Korea's defenses and stabilized its northern frontier, implemented major tax reforms that contributed to the growth of agricultural production, and chipped away at the social discrimination against lower status groups in the government and military. All these deeds for the public good, however, are overshadowed in the prevailing historical perspective by his private failings—his quick-tempered, inconstant, and often scandalous behavior.

The consequences of these personal weaknesses might not have extended beyond his private quarters had he not ruled amidst the intensification of factionalism among officials and scholars, which he actually furthered. The bitter partisan wrangling of the late sixteenth century, which affected Korea's preparations for and response to the Japanese invasions, had again undermined Korea's preparations for and response to the Manchu threat beginning in the 1620s (Chapter 9). But it did not stop there; following the Manchu conquest of Ming China in 1644, factional divisions in Korea became tied to intricate debates about the country's place in the larger realm of civilization. Indeed, since the early Joseon era, philosophical differences had often spawned political rivalry and bloody conflict (Chapter 7). But beginning in the late sixteenth century and over the course of the seventeenth, this dynamic became solidified into permanent divisions corresponding to intellectual and political descent lines from the two great philosophers of the sixteenth century, Toegye and Yulgok (Chapter 8). The followers of Toegye, known as the "Easterners," then split further into the Northerners and the Southerners, and those who formed around the teachings of Yulgok, the "Westerners," eventually split into the Old and Young Doctrine factions. Over the second half of the Joseon dynasty, these affiliations would dominate the political sphere among those vying for power in the capital and even frame social and political associations in the provinces, home to local aristocrats whose access to bureaucratic posts became increasingly foreclosed. These rivalries also had a generally debilitating impact on monarchical authority, but Sukjong managed to use factional hostilities as a political tool to increase his leverage by triangulating between bitterly opposing sides.

Sukjong was also immersed in another, better-known triangle, however—the love triangle involving his wife and his concubine. The troubles arising from this particular dynamic were commonplace in upper-class Korean families throughout the Joseon era (and beyond), but, when these private travails racked the royal family, they often had a pronounced effect on politics. The two-decade spectacle involving these three figures resulted in major political upheavals leading to the deaths of dozens and, remarkably, determining the relative power of political groups and ideologies for the next two centuries. It also highlighted the tensions of the mid-Joseon era between the ongoing efforts at Confucianization and stout customs—socially, culturally, and in the realm of the family—continuing to resist a complete makeover.

According to both official and unofficial historical sources, Sukjong's second wife, Queen Inhyeon (his first wife had died at an early age), was widely revered for her grace and character. But as time passed these qualities were overshadowed by the lack of a male heir. In the meantime, the king grew strongly fond of one of his concubines, Lady Jang, who had developed a reputation for her spellbinding beauty and cunning. She even suffered expulsion from the palace for her potentially dangerous effect on the harmony of the royal family. Queen Inhyeon herself, credited with selflessly putting her husband's desires above her own, urged that Lady Jang be allowed to return. In early 1688, when news of Lady Jang's pregnancy spread, it seemed to validate Queen Inhyeon's noble move even as it threatened to unleash yet another struggle for royal succession. When, in answering the monarch's fervent wishes, Lady Jang bore a son, King Sukjong's affection for her grew immeasurably. Amid this euphoria, the monarch named the newborn the crown prince, a move quickly met by vehement political opposition.

The high officials belonging to the Westerners faction passionately protested this move, arguing that Queen Inhyeon was young and thus could still bear a "legitimate" crown prince. Not only did King Sukjong react angrily to this protest by purging some of these men, he immediately ratcheted up the confrontation to another level by divorcing Queen Inhyeon, stripping her of her title as queen. He accused her of insufficiently embracing, both figuratively and literally, the baby boy, and further rationalized this move as necessary for the crown prince when he eventually became king. The uproar that followed induced another purge of the Westerners, this time killing the faction's intellectual leader, Song Siyeol, who was made to drink poison. In 1694, however, King Sukjong, fickle as ever, changed his mind again and returned Queen Inhyeon to the palace, demoting Lady Jang back to her original status as a palace lady and assigning the Southerners permanently to the political wilderness. This would not be the end of the commotion, however, for Queen Inhyeon, still without having borne a son, died suddenly in 1701. When it was discovered that Lady Jang, in her attempt to regain the monarch's affections, had constructed a shamanistic altar where she put curses on Queen Inhyeon through the use of figurines, King Sukjong blamed her for his queen's death and had Lady Jang executed. But Lady Jang, as if remaining true to her reputation, would not go quietly and fiercely resisted any dignified death. The executioners had to force feed her the poison.

If we take a step back from the titillating combination of sex and politics that enveloped this long-running spectacle, we can properly place it in the larger currents of Korean history and even draw comparisons to similar situations in other parts of the world. To many readers, this episode will evoke thoughts of the notorious behavior of King Henry VIII of England, which took place a century-and-a-half earlier but established the basic divide that continued to spur bloody sectarian conflicts in the kingdom thereafter. Like King Sukjong, Henry desperately wished to divorce his queen for a favored concubine, and, like Lady Jang, Anne Boleyn in the end paid the ultimate price for the monarch's inconstancy in the face of pressing concerns over royal succession. In both settings, the political order was upended and led to the execution of a widely revered man of letters, whether Song Siyeol or Thomas More, who led the righteous opposition in defense, respectively, of Confucian or Catholic orthodoxy. And in the wider consequences as well, there were important similarities. While a new religious order like the Church of England did not materialize from these circumstances in Korea, in both countries the larger stakes concerned the country's place in the realm of the dominant religio-ethical civilization.

In this sense, Song Siyeol and Lady Jang stood as opposing symbols in King Sukjong's most important triangle. In determining the future direction of Korea's Confucian civilization, the monarch had to balance his personal desires against the two different priorities represented by Jang and Song. Song Siyeol, in fact, had served as the resilient ideological fount of classical East Asian and Neo-Confucian orthodoxy for much of the seventeenth century. Since the 1640s, he had engaged in prominent battles against scholar-officials arguing for Korean exceptionalism in the Confucian world order. The latter view, given the loss of Ming China to the barbarians in 1644, emphasized Korea's position as the lone standing source of civilization and called for modifications to the orthodoxy that would accommodate historical change and national interests. Song, on the other hand, in condemning such "heterodoxy," always maintained that Korea, precisely because of the demise of the Ming, must firmly adhere to traditional understandings. Little wonder, then, that Song is sometimes cited as "Korea's Zhu Xi," in reference to the great Chinese scholar credited with formulating the foundation of Neo-Confucian doctrine in the twelfth century. In stark contrast, Lady Jang can be seen as representing the nativist impulses of folk religion, the primacy of the crown, and the complications of hereditary social hierarchy. She also represented the heritage of strong Korean women whose public prominence reached a high point in the mid-Joseon era.

FAMOUS FEMALES

Neither Lady Jang nor Queen Inhyeon, who have always been joined at the hip in historical lore, wished to be swept up and exploited by the political combatants of the day. Likewise, neither likely could do anything to prevent their fates from being determined, in the end, by a mercurial monarch. But in other ways, these two opposing females served as models of strength in Joseon Korea, although in very different ways. Queen Inhyeon has always stood as the paragon of Confucian female virtue. Unable to gain the affection of her husband due to the lack of a son, she subsumed her personal feelings and interests by inviting Lady Jang back into the palace. And when Lady Jang gave birth to a boy, Queen Inhyeon again selflessly supported the monarch's designation of the baby as the crown prince. Lady Jang, on the other hand, has traditionally been portrayed as the evil opposite— the stubborn, licentious, and decadent *femme fatale*. But she could also be considered a model of the boisterous, passionate, clever Korean female who more recently has been celebrated, especially in mass culture, as a forerunner to the confident modern woman who takes control of her own destiny.

Unlike Lady Jang, most palace ladies, who were servants attending mostly to female members of the royal family, had little chance of becoming a royal concubine, much less of exerting great influence on political affairs. But, as with other fortunate females, they could express themselves through a discreet but historically significant medium of empowerment at the time, vernacular writing. The Korean alphabet had been devised and promulgated in the mid-fifteenth century (Chapter 7), but well into the nineteenth century Chinese remained the dominant form of writing in the circles of learned elites and government affairs. Girls and women, who could not expect to become literate in the high culture, took advantage of the alphabet's great functionality to leave behind a treasure trove of valuable writings, ranging from letters and diaries to public documents, poetry, novels, and chronicles. Among the most illuminating examples of the latter came from a palace lady who apparently had witnessed the Queen Inhyeon–Lady Jang spectacle. This author penned the "Biography of Queen Inhyeon," a sympathetic portrait of the queen that still stands as a precious unofficial source of information about these events.

The vernacular culture exerted perhaps the greatest influence in regard to females by spotlighting the social class of "gisaeng" courtesans. Like the Japanese *geisha*, the *gisaeng* carried out both sexual and artistic functions. And, like the palace ladies, many courtesans were attached to government service, usually provincial or county offices. This reflected also their "base" social status, which put them in the same larger category as slaves. Their sometimes scandalous love affairs and renowned talents in music, dance, and letters gave these women prominent standing in the folk culture as a whole, while the lives and accomplishments of certain *gisaeng* became legendary. In fact, a disproportionate number of famous females from the Joseon era were *gisaeng*. In addition to Hwang Jini, the early-sixteenth century figure celebrated both for her great beauty and extraordinary literary skills, many other *gisaeng* gained fame for their talents and romances. The sorrowful tales of their forced parting from their lovers became the basis for some of the great literary and musical expressions of premodern Korea (Chapter 12), which constitute a rich source of insight about Korean culture and society at the time.

The prominence of such low-status females in the historical memory of the Joseon dynasty, especially of the mid-Joseon era, also testifies to the profound decrease in the standing of females as a whole, especially of the aristocracy. It became rare, for example, for daughters to gain a comparable inheritance as their brothers, especially the oldest son, and movement and visibility for women were significantly curtailed. These developments also went hand-in-hand with the hardening of the hereditary social hierarchy beginning in the seventeenth century. Indeed the social and political discrimination against the offspring of concubines and remarried widows, a semi-Confucian legal measure from the early Joseon, now took firm root throughout society. These concubines' descendants, including those of *gisaeng* courtesans, became a distinctive hereditary status group that, by the nineteenth century, swelled in numbers to constitute a major social force.

LATENCY OF THE MID-JOSEON ORDER

As suggested by the formation of these conventionally "traditional" Korean social patterns, the mid-Joseon era stood as a time of reconstruction and systematization in the wake of the great invasions. The Japanese assault might have been more devastating in terms of human and material loss, but the Manchu invasions, particularly the Manchu conquest of China shortly thereafter, dealt a greater blow to Koreans' sense of self and propriety. At the heart of the political conflicts and social strife lay the task of formulating a national identity as the self-perceived sole remaining Confucian civilization. The bloody strife that embroiled Song Siyeol and others also demonstrated that a significant strain in Korea's sociopolitical leadership sought to assert national interests that transcended Confucian orthodoxy. And as the Lady Jang episode demonstrated, the self-styled rationality of Confucianism, now after nearly three centuries as the official social ideology, still had to contend with deeply-rooted, countervailing impulses and practices.

One possible consequence of the persistence of such tendencies was the rise of money as a social factor, particularly amid the economic expansion and advances in agricultural techniques and production of this era. Lady Jang, who is conventionally known as someone from low social origin befitting her position as palace lady, actually entered the royal compounds through the maneuvering of her wealthy family. Her social status, in fact, was that of a "jungin"—hereditary lineages of technical officials such as translators, physicians, and accountants. Her father was an interpreter who, like many others in his social class, grew rich through trading while accompanying embassies to China, handling transactions with Japanese merchants operating in Busan, or engaging in the intermediary commerce between the two neighboring countries. Like him, sub-aristocratic members of society who could not hope to enter high office or marriage relations with the ruling aristocracy (see text box) could turn to wealth to gain influence and privileges that otherwise were denied them. Their economic activities also lubricated the heightening pace and quantity of material exchanges, including in luxury items from abroad, in the second half of the Joseon era. The Lady Jang story thus unveils a significant undercurrent of economic growth and social fluidity in her time, which had the potential to facilitate major political changes as well.

That Lady Jang's ascent to the royal palace created such an uproar, however, testified also to the reverse: the firm limits to social mobility irrespective even of material wealth. The chaos of the invasions led to a determination on the part of the aristocracy, armed with its class cohesion and status consciousness, command over political institutions, and Confucian learning, to maintain its dominant social standing in the ensuing era. This system allowed room for sub-aristocratic groups, such as the technical official class, to gain a small measure of social mobility through economic accumulation, but the preeminence of birth, marriage, and lineage in determining sociopolitical power remained intact.

Secondary status groups

One of the enduringly fascinating features of Korean civilization since the beginning has been the commanding influence of hereditary status in determining both social interaction and structure. And perhaps the most compelling manifestation of this social hierarchy was the emergence, in the mid-Joseon era, of the secondary status groups. To a greater extent than the aristocracy or commoners, the secondary status groups embodied Joseon Korea's systematic integration of political power with the delineation of ascriptive social privilege.

Five secondary status groups came into distinctive form beginning in the post-invasions recovery period of the seventeenth

→

century: the lineages of technical officials, or *jungin*, such as the family of Lady Jang, specializing in foreign languages, medicine, law, astronomy, accounting, calligraphy, and painting; the hereditary clerks, or *hyangni*, carrying out the day-to-day administration of the provincial and county offices and who descended from local rulers of the Goryeo era; the ubiquitous concubine descendants, who constituted one of the largest social groups in the latter Joseon era and whose existence and welfare increasingly aroused fierce controversies and conflicts; the local elites of the northern provinces, victimized by a regional bias with origins deep in Korean history; and the military officials who, in an earlier era, stood as equals to their civilian counterparts. Though originating under different circumstances, these secondary status groups all suffered discrimination both socially and politically, and hence embodied the core principle linking hereditary social status to political power, or, to be more precise, to bureaucratic eligibility. Their existence as sub-aristocratic groups, in other words, both determined and was determined by their limitations in gaining government office.

The secondary status groups thus acted as a kind of buffer between the ruling aristocracy and the majority mass of commoners. Hence, they embodied the complicated mixture of the rock-solid principle of hereditary status and the sporadic possibilities for some social mobility. They had a foot in the realms of both the ruling class, with whom most of them had an ancestral connection before being sloughed off into secondary status, and the ruled, with whom they could commiserate about the injustices of the system. They represented, then, the Joseon social structure in its full range of characteristics, from the dominant Confucian ethos and socioeconomic system to popular culture and sentiment (Chapter 12). And therein lay the latency of their historical significance: while they absorbed social conventions and internalized the Confucian orthodoxy, as time passed they demonstrated an increasing desire for social recognition and privilege, which nevertheless remained largely thwarted until the modern era.

11 Intellectual Opening in the Late Eighteenth Century

CHRONOLOGY

1750	Birth of Bak Jega
1752	Birth of King Jeongjo
1562	Birth of Jeong Yagyong; execution of Crown Prince Sado, Jeongjo's father
1765	Hong Daeyong's trip to China
1776	Death of King Yeongjo; beginning of King Jeongjo's reign
1778	Bak Jega's visit to China; drafting of "Discourse on Northern Learning"
1779	Appointment of Bak Jega to a post in the Royal Library
1780	Bak Jiwon's trip to China
1790	Bak Jega's third trip to China
1800	Death of King Jeongjo
1801	First Catholic persecution; Jeong Yagyong sent into exile

THE RETURN OF BAK JEGA TO KOREA, 1778

In 1778, Bak Jega, a little-known intellectual, gained the privilege of accompanying a close friend on a tribute mission to China. So inspired was he by this trip that, upon his return later in the year, Bak wrote the *Discourse on Northern Learning*, at once a travelogue as well as a wide-ranging social commentary on the ills of his native country. Through this work, Bak Jega voiced the views of a scholarly movement that drew together some of the country's brightest minds, who together pushed for a thorough renovation of Joseon society, and particularly its economy, by looking to the example of contemporary China. While Koreans had a long history of adopting Chinese models, for over a century before Bak's trip most

Korean elites had dismissed Qing dynasty China, established by the Manchus in 1644, as a country ruled by barbarians.

From the vantage point of Bak Jega and those in his intellectual circle of "northern learning" advocates, the urgency of reform directly corresponded to the challenge of overcoming this long-held, ethnicized bias against the Manchu-run Qing dynasty—the "north." Nearly all of these scholars had visited Qing China and come back with an eye-opening impression of its socioeconomic advancement. These advocates of northern learning declared not only that Koreans must overcome their prejudices against the Manchus, but that this must in turn spur a comprehensive reconsideration of long-held Korean tenets and practices, including those of the Confucian orthodoxy. In this way the northern learning movement constituted, however briefly, an apt capstone to the Joseon dynasty's "golden era" of the late eighteenth century, marked by peace, relative political stability, and cultural flowering. Little wonder, then, that this period is also preferred by Koreans as a truer representation of the latter Joseon era, before the ravages of the nineteenth century led to the tragedies of the twentieth.

UTILITY FOR THE GREATER GOOD

The unofficial motto for the northern learning school, appearing repeatedly in the writings, was "iyong husaeng," a term that can be translated in many ways, including "utility for the greater good," and reflects an approach to solving problems practically and logically. Historians tend to identify the northern learning cohort as part of a wider scholarly movement in the late Joseon era called "practical learning" (*silhak*), but this was a coherence constructed mostly by modern historians. Furthermore, one could argue that all Confucian reform proposals that targeted policies affecting the lives of people, by their very nature, were a reflection of "practical learning." The northern learning movement, however, was real—nearly all of this cohort's figures had a singularly influential experience of visiting China, befriended each other and, in their writings and advocacy activities, supported common core principles. These ideals in pursuit of "utility for the greater good" included an embrace of foreign models, especially the scientific teachings of the West; an encouragement of manufacturing, trade, commerce, and even consumption, as well as the concomitant removal of the social stigma attached to profiteering and commercial activities; and the leveling of the social hierarchy. Together, these positions, in fact, went about as far as one could in questioning Neo-Confucianism itself—or at least its domination in Joseon Korea—without explicitly rejecting it.

The apex figure of this movement was Hong Daeyong, who visited China as part of a tribute mission to Beijing in 1765. There he became well acquainted with Chinese scholars, Catholic clergymen, and many accounts of the world beyond the peninsula. Hong's experience left him in stunned awe, and he meticulously recorded his observations in a travelogue he wrote following his return. In this and other works, Hong noted the extraordinary energies in the daily lives and economic activities of the Chinese, even beyond the capital of Beijing itself. He took this as an impetus to launch a general critique of Korean customs and Confucian orthodoxy, most clearly in evidence in his "Uisan Mountain Dialogue," which features a conversation about the world and nature between the imaginary characters "Empty" and "Substantive." Needless to say, Empty reveals himself as a thinly veiled caricature of the Korean scholar mired in the abstractions of Confucian philosophy. As seen in this work and others, however, the interaction with Chinese and Western scholars seems to have most affected Hong's view of the larger cosmos, and indeed it is Hong's scientific writings for which he became best known. In them he propounded and legitimated, mostly through deduction, the ideas of a round, rotating earth that encircled a stationary sun, and of humanity's commonalities with the rest of the natural world. Some historians consider Hong Daeyong the greatest scientific thinker of the Joseon era.

Hong's circle of like-minded colleagues included his protégé Bak Jiwon, who finally took his own trip to China in 1780 and returned to write the best-known travelogue of this period, the "Diary of the [Journey to the Chinese Emperor's] Summer Palace." Like Hong, Bak admiringly described the lives of the Manchu-ruled Chinese, whose use of advanced practical technologies seemed directly connected to their productivity and flourishing material culture. This work was far more than a travelogue, however; his experiences were often theatrically presented in the form of episodic commentaries, essays, interviews, and even "fictional" tales, to which he applied the extraordinary literary skill that placed him among the most innovative writers of the Joseon era. Indeed, some of Bak's best-known works have in common a satirical portrayal of late Joseon society and mindset (or their Chinese equivalents as stand-ins), often masked as detached observations. In his "Tale of the Yangban" or "Tale of Heo Saeng," for example, Bak takes aim, both directly and indirectly, at Korea's hereditary social hierarchy, in which one's social status corresponded little, if at all, to one's contributions to the greater good. These stories depict a parasitic aristocracy that relied upon empty learning and the privileges accorded by birth, while people of lower standing were engaged in socially productive, practical work and even growing rich.

Such themes were perhaps most systematically integrated into a prescriptive for national renovation by the work and writings of Bak Jiwon's close friend Bak Jega, whose renown extended to poetry, painting, and calligraphy despite the social stigma of his being the son of a concubine. Bak Jega's appointment in 1779 to a high position in the Royal Library by King Jeongjo, newly enthroned three years earlier, allowed him to further elaborate on the points made in the *Discourse on Northern Learning* and to influence the formulation of government policy. By the time the final version of the *Discourse* appeared in print more than two decades after its unveiling, it contained the most systematic expression of the northern learning program, garnished with the wisdom gained from Bak Jega's experience in government service.

Among the most striking ideas appearing in this work and in Bak Jega's policy proposals was the explicit endorsement of the pursuit of private wealth. According to Bak, the core problem facing Korea was widespread poverty, both in relation to China as well as in absolute terms. This condition stemmed in part from the ruling Confucian ethos of austerity that discouraged the consumption of high-quality goods, which in turn weakened the incentive to produce, improve, and circulate material items. One solution, then, was to encourage the *yangban* aristocracy to engage freely in commerce, trading, and artisanal production—all areas of activity that, in the Joseon era, had been scorned as unbecoming of the nobility. This would, Bak stated, discourage idleness and serve as a model for "pursuing profit," which in turn would enrich everyone.

Korea was also beset by decay in the infrastructures of commerce and manufacturing, according to Bak. Along these lines, he seemed almost obsessed with the simple wagon, which was the first of dozens of novelties—ranging from sericulture and paper currency to buildings and boats—that he described having seen and studied while in China. He noted that ancient Koreans effectively used wagons, and even in contemporary times one could find a few of them in scattered areas. So why were wagons not in greater use as a central mode of transportation and transport? Nothing so encapsulated his homeland's backwardness, Bak appeared to say: Widespread use of wagons internally, in conjunction with open trade externally, would boost the circulation of goods, promote the diversification and improvement of locally produced specialty items, and improve the economy as a whole.

Indeed the northern learning school's "utility for the greater good" motive constituted very much a materialist proposition: Only after the basic economic conditions are addressed can other concerns be tackled. In laying out the interconnectedness of the material with other realms of existence, these scholars in fact aped the great Confucian chain of being, as expressed famously by Confucius himself in *The Great Learning*, a core book of the classical canon. But instead of locating self-cultivation at the most fundamental level, the northern learning advocates designated material well-being. This in effect overturned the long-held spiritual and ritualistic basis of Joseon Neo-Confucianism, and it was even done with the rhetorical tool of appealing to the classics. In his introduction to the *Discourse on Northern Learning*, for example, Bak Jega quotes the ancient sages to emphasize the economic foundation of ritual and morality— that the people's material welfare must be secured before focusing on enlightening them on ritual propriety. In this sense the northern learning school presented one of the most compelling intellectual challenges to the Neo-Confucian orthodoxy.

THE SPROUTS OF MODERNITY?

Historians have thus suggested that the northern learning school, as part of the "practical learning" trend, demonstrated the stirrings of Korea's own drive toward modern ideas and institutions. The calls for a centrality of the people's welfare and the leveling of the hereditary social hierarchy seem to have represented such ideals. And the increasing pursuit of profit in economic activity, the formation of cottage industries in mining and manufacturing, as well as an uptick in regular markets and trading networks suggest indeed the growth of a commercial economy. Economic historians have dug up evidence of late Joseon increases in productivity, commerce, wage labor, population, urbanization and, in the agricultural sector, the adoption of new techniques and technologies such as double cropping and seedling transplantation. And even scholars of art and literary history have uncovered a growing culture of material exchange and consumerism in books, art works, and artisanal products that connected Korea to larger networks extending to China and beyond. Northern learning scholars certainly would have embraced such developments. But their systematic observations and analysis of the continuing *weakness* of such an economy in their home country suggests that late eighteenth-century Korea, despite such advances, fell far short of the critical mass necessary to overturn the basic production modes. Significantly, this was also the uniform observation of foreign visitors to Korea a century later.

This takes us to the historical significance of the northern learning school, given its seeming lack of a major, immediate impact. Was it simply an interesting but ultimately inconsequential intellectual movement? As suggested above, the "what if " questions surrounding these promising developments of the eighteenth century are particularly bitter-sweet due to the solipsistic decay, leading ultimately to calamity, that followed in the nineteenth century (or so it seems—see Chapter 13). The underlying historical issue, though somewhat crudely put, is whether the internal development of Joseon society had enough within itself to trigger the shift toward the modern. There appears to be a search for a reassurance, almost cathartic in tone, of the validity of Korean tradition and civilization before the nineteenth century as a way to accept the sacrifices and ultimate accomplishments of the modern experience. Over the past few decades in South Korea, as seen in scholarship as well as in various forms of public history, this search has been narrowed to several benchmarks for the advances of the late eighteenth century, such as capitalism, Catholicism, and royal absolutism. And in this regard, even more than the northern learning advocates, the historical figures who have drawn the most attention are two with direct personal connections to Bak Jega: the great philosopher Jeong Yagyong, better known as Dasan, and King Jeongjo.

Jeongjo in fact brought Bak and Jeong together to work in the Royal Library. The king was an accomplished scholar in his own right. And his charge to his officials in the Royal Library was to compile and organize a grand repository of works in order to advance scholarship and government policy, just as the Hall of Worthies had done for King Sejong. Like Sejong, Jeongjo has won great acclaim for personifying the ideals of the sagely Confucian monarch. He was the third in a triumvirate of long-reigning, powerful, reform-minded leaders: Sukjong (r. 1674–1720), Yeongjo (1724–76), and Jeongjo (1776–1800). King Yeongjo, the longest reigning monarch in Korean history, not only brought stability but introduced a series of state reforms, including a major update to the dynastic code, that spurred cultural and social advances. Many restrictions on hereditarily discriminated groups were eliminated under his leadership, and he is lauded for having striven, somewhat successfully, to control the factional strife among his officials through his policy of "grand harmony." Despite these accomplishments, however, Yeongjo also is remembered for a family tragedy that he facilitated: In 1762 he ordered that his violent, mentally disturbed crown prince wither away while locked in a rice chest on palace grounds. King Jeongjo, Yeongjo's grandson and the doomed prince's son, had witnessed this horror as a child and came of age, as the next crown prince, under the guidance of his grandfather, the same man who had ordered his father's death. It is a wonder that the psychological scarring did not overwhelm Jeongjo, but in fact, once he ascended the throne in 1776, he strengthened his grandfather's reformist policies while rehabilitating his father, known posthumously as Prince Sado. Indeed, to celebrate the sixtieth birthday of both of his parents in 1795, Jeongjo formally led a lavish royal outing to his father's new gravesite south of Seoul, in Suwon, where a grand fortress was constructed in Sado's memory.

Jeongjo's own accomplishments as monarch might have matched those of his predecessor in half the time, although it is widely lamented that he did not reign longer. While maintaining Yeongjo's efforts to overcome factionalism through appeals to unity, Jeongjo was keen to promote cultural advances through the circulation of new ideas. His interest in new models and publications from China and his desire to cultivate talented young officials appear to have brought Bak Jega to his attention. A year following the publication of Bak's *Discourse on Northern Learning*, King Jeongjo appointed him to a compiler's position in the Royal Library. Bak in fact was one of four new pathbreaking officials in this post, all of whom concubine's children, who embodied Jeongjo's policy of opening the path toward higher government office for these long-discriminated men. Indeed, Bak appears to have enjoyed the favoritism of King Jeongjo, who in 1790 sent him as a special ambassador to China.

By then Bak had served for a decade in the Royal Library, where he befriended and mentored other young officials, none more accomplished than Jeong Yagyong. Beginning with his entrance into government service in the 1780s, Jeong went on to become one of Korea's foremost intellectuals and is today commonly cited as the greatest thinker of the late Joseon era. He was certainly one of its most prolific authors and versatile minds, even designing the Hwaseong Fortress in Suwon mentioned above. He produced hundreds of masterful writings on topics ranging from the core Confucian pursuits of statecraft, philosophy, history, and social criticism to economy, science and engineering, architecture, and religion. In the realm of religion, in fact, Jeong may have been the first major scholar-official of his time to embrace not only the scientific but the religious and philosophical teachings of Catholicism. He may have even converted.

Korean visitors to China had begun to notice the Catholic presence in the form of Jesuit priests in Beijing in the sixteenth century, but it was not until the closing years of the eighteenth century that the potential challenges from Catholicism became a serious issue in Korea. The first Korean Catholic was in fact Jeong Yagyong's brother-in-law, Yi Seunghun, who was baptized in China in 1784. Soon, Korean and foreign missionaries secretly pursued their work in Korea itself, converting thousands by the turn of century, including many from the aristocracy and secondary status groups. Over protests urging a harsh crackdown on a set of teachings that appeared to promote an abandonment of one's social and ritual responsibilities, King Jeongjo cautioned patience and treated this religion as a superstitious curiosity that should be monitored. Following Jeongjo's death in 1800, however, the Joseon court pursued a mass persecution of Catholics. The witch-hunt ensnared Jeong Yagyong's immediate circle of friends and family members, many of whom were executed, and implicated him enough to send him into exile.

Jeong Yagyong would never recover his political or intellectual influence, even after his exile of eighteen years ended while he was in his mid-fifties (he would live into his seventies). But the second half of his life that he spent in exile and recovery proved extremely fruitful for him intellectually: It allowed him to reorganize his thoughts, synthesize the various strains of reformist policies that had circulated in the late eighteenth century, and witness directly the plight of the people in the countryside. As a result, he could provide an exhaustive diagnosis of Korea's systemic ills. His proposed solutions in many ways reflected the influence of the northern learning school, especially the embrace of new technologies, though with less enthusiasm for copying the Qing model. In contrast to his friend Bak Jega, Jeong directed more of his attention to fixing statecraft, with an emphasis on original Confucian doctrine and on the premise that good society began with good governance. This perspective was reflected in his most famous work, *Core Teachings for Shepherding the People*, which harkened back to the classical Confucian focus on self-cultivation and care for the people as the basis of proper governance. At one level, *Core Teachings* was a handbook on how to be an effective county magistrate, based on Jeong's own experiences as both a magistrate and exiled observer, and on his deep knowledge of both Chinese and Korean history. At another level, the reform measures advocated in this work extended to more general lessons on statecraft from the local government all the way to the central state. Jeong argued, for example, that Joseon statecraft relied too much on stilted formalities, like the examination system to recruit officials, that valued rote learning and empty philosophy over practical administration. Hence the county magistrate was improperly prepared for his job, becoming dependent on clerks, servants, and local elites and often falling victim to unscrupulous behavior by both them and, eventually, himself.

That Jeong Yagyong, like Bak Jega and Bak Jiwon, faded into the political or intellectual wilderness in the early nineteenth century sharpens the contrast with their prominence in the late eighteenth century, and in turn accentuates the sense of what might have been. Their fates, then, constituted a regrettable end to the intellectual and cultural flowering of Joseon's golden age: with a whimper instead of a bang. The bang, in another form, would have to await the tumult of the ensuing era.

12 Popular Culture in the Late Joseon Era

CHRONOLOGY

17th c.	Publication of the *Tale of Hong Gildong*
1844	Publication of the *Hosan Unofficial History* by Jo Huiryong
1850s	Standardization of *pansori* librettos by Sin Jaehyo
1858	Publication of the *History of Sunflowers*
1862	Publication of *Observations from the Countryside* by Yu Jaegeon

PUBLICATION OF *OBSERVATIONS FROM THE COUNTRYSIDE*, 1862

"Many upstanding people have lived in our country, which stretches for hundreds of miles in all directions. How can it be, then, that we know about only a few of these people whose stories deserve to be passed down through our words and literature?" So asks the scholar and renowned painter Jo Huiryong in the preface to the book *Observations from the Countryside*, on behalf of the book's author, Yu Jaegeon. Yu's work featured biographical portraits of almost 300 people whose lower social status had prevented their upstanding actions and lives from having become more widely known. Their backgrounds ranged from the well-educated but subordinated technical officials in the government—or *jungin*, like Yu himself—to local military officers, clerks, doctors, artists, peasants, and merchants, as well as slaves, monks, and other "mean" people. People of all such backgrounds lived as models of filiality, morality, self-cultivation, and sacrifice, Yu wanted to show.

Observations from the Countryside typified the small flurry of such publications in the mid-nineteenth century. Biographical compilations of lower-status groups, including a work, *Hosan Unofficial History*, that had appeared a decade earlier and was authored by Jo Huiryong himself ("Hosan" was one of his pen names), were published in tandem with a growing cultural movement headed by non-aristocratic literary figures like Yu and Jo. In turn, these activities partook in a prominent trend: a greater awareness of the plight of regular people through the increasing expression of their voices in popular cultural forms, from novels to music, dance, and painting. The most well-known folk stories today in Korea, in fact, originated in the latter part of the Joseon era, which compels nothing less than a reconsideration of traditional Korean culture itself. Indeed, literature and art reflected social reality in a way that both circumvented and challenged the existing hierarchies.

TALES OF THE PEOPLE

Little wonder, then, that the adventures of Robin Hood-like righteous bandits held a prominent place in this body of literature. Such tales provided a scenario that, on the one hand, espoused orthodox values of righteousness and benevolence, and, on the other, addressed the yearnings of lower status groups through escapist fantasy. One such story was *The Tale of Hong Gildong*, about a concubine's son abused by both his family and society at large due to his birth status. Unable to endure the rampant prejudice against him, he runs away and leads a group of bandits that attack corrupt officials and distribute the booty to those exploited by them. This tale ends with Hong and his followers settling into a kind of socialist utopia without hierarchies and discrimination. In written form, *The Tale of Hong Gildong*, which appeared in the early seventeenth century, might have represented the first Korean novel in the vernacular. Clearly, however, the story did not originate with its putative author, Heo Gyun, but rather had circulated since the times of a real historical figure named Hong Gildong in the fifteenth century. The legendary elaboration on his life probably drew also from a similar story involving another, better-documented bandit, Im Kkeokjeong, of the early sixteenth century. Im's adventures were similar, but his background was even lower than that of Hong Gildong: Im came from the social outcast group of butchers, tanners, and other "unclean" people.

Another marginalized group, namely women—or, more often, girls—also appeared prominently in the popular tales circulating in the late Joseon. Like those of the righteous bandits, these accounts of virtuous females from lower backgrounds showed that Confucian values had penetrated the masses. The most famous such fable is *The Tale of Chunhyang*. Chunhyang, the teenage daughter of a courtesan concubine, falls in love with and betroths the son of the local county magistrate. While her beloved returns to Seoul and becomes a successful young official, she endures a series of hardships stemming from the next magistrate's evil

cravings for her in expectation that she, like her mother, would s
"duties." Chunhyang, though, resists by insisting that she remain faithful
to her husband despite her social background, and in the end the young
man returns as a secret government inspector and rescues her just before
she is to be executed. The *Tale of Sim Cheong* was another popular narrative of a virtuous woman who demonstrated the core Confucian values
of filial piety, loyalty, and sacrifice. Sim Cheong, having acted on her
belief that she could cure her father's blindness by sacrificing her own
life, is instead rescued from the underworld and delivered intact to the
king, who falls in love with her and marries her. The story ends with a
joyous reunion with her father, whose sight is restored. Like Chunhyang,
the reward of reunion comes from Sim Cheong's faithfulness to her
Confucian duties. The larger message of cosmic justice arriving through
good acts also drew from Buddhist undercurrents as well as from the centrality of a common woman overcoming her tribulations despite the odds
arrayed against her. Indeed, these latter narrative elements are the most
compelling and likely accounted for the popularity of these stories.

It appears, in fact, that both the tales of Chunhyang and Sim Cheong
began as songs used in shamanistic ceremonies, a genre that ultimately
developed into what we now call *pansori* (see below). The elaboration and
transmission of these tales in written form were made possible by the
gradual spread of the vernacular as a means of communication among
those unable to acquire the high culture of literary Chinese. Despite the
great invention of the native alphabet back in the mid-fifteenth century,
for the most part the elites shunned the use of what they called this "vul-
gar script." Until the end of the nineteenth century, then, the alphabet's
usage and development remained consigned to the lower social orders
and, significantly, females. But these groups benefited from what is today
commonly touted as the greatest strength of this alphabet—namely,
its efficient simplicity and versatility—and likewise, beginning in the
seventeenth century, there appeared a surge in mostly informal works
employing the vernacular. Not surprisingly, the popularization of the
tales of common people accompanied their increasing use of the Korean
alphabet. That these tales also featured compelling plots and characters
(including historical figures), especially for the benefit of illuminating
social injustices, also contributed to their popularity, one believes.

OTHER CULTURAL FORMS

Pansori, a distinctive "opera" genre that emerged in the eighteenth and
nineteenth centuries, stands today as perhaps Korea's best-known

traditional musical form. The singer or singers, accompanied by a drummer who keeps the beat and occasionally shouts responses and encouragement, recount a sprawling tale full of characterization, plot twists, and long monologues. The great challenge to the singers comes from the demand to voice several different characters, as well as the narrator, and from the enormous stamina necessary to pull off a complete performance. The most popular works of the *pansori* repertoire, such as the "Song of Chunhyang" and "Song of Sim Cheong," invariably date from the late Joseon era, and the successful transmission of these works through the ages owed much to the efforts of systematizers, in particular Sin Jaehyo of the early nineteenth century, who standardized the librettos and performance styles.

Mask dances (*talchum*), a theatrical performance genre comprised of one to several characters dancing to accompanying instrumental music, also became standardized in the late Joseon into the form that we know today. As the name suggests, the performers wore masks of exaggerated expressions representing the status and emotion of the characters involved. Their "dances" combined choreographed displays and spontaneous movements that, when supplemented by spoken dialogue, furthered the story along its trajectory. The different elements of artistic expression that went into this Korean version of the *Gesamtkunstwerk*—theater, music, song, dance, colorful costumes—usually served a satirical purpose. The aristocratic and other characters with pretenses to authority, including even Buddhist monks, were usually depicted with ridicule, as if this comedic context presented the most effective means of expressing the grievances of regular people. Not coincidentally, like Sin Jaehyo, the great systematizer of *pansori*, the creative figures behind the promotion and development of mask dances came mostly from the ranks of the hereditary local clerks, the *hyangni*. Due to their administrative duties, these clerks were literate, organized, and able to measure the pulse of the local mood.

Examples of the final major art form of the late Joseon, genre painting, have come down as among the most cherished and representative expressions of traditional Korea. Unlike dramatic singing and satirical mask dances, which boasted a history of development before their respective standardized forms in the late Joseon, genre painting—the depiction of daily life—could not draw upon a definitive heritage before the eighteenth century. The extant Korean paintings preceding that period are mostly portraits, Buddhist works, landscapes, or drawings of plants and animals. In fact one has to turn all the way back in time to the Goguryeo tomb paintings (Chapter 1) to find a similarly lively attention to people in everyday settings. But unlike these Goguryeo paintings' preoccupation with the elite, the eighteenth-century genre paintings are concerned also with showing commoners and even low-born peoples, featuring subtle hints of the social critiques that were more openly expressed in the tales, songs, and mask dances. In style as well, due likely to the influence of Western painting techniques by way of China, one sees a turn in perspective and spacing that corresponded to the shift in subject matter to the commonplace and ordinary. So representative of "traditional" Korean life and culture have these paintings become that the two most prominent masters of genre painting are also the two best-known painters in Korean history, perhaps even the two best-known artists: Gim Hongdo, whose expertise extended to all other painting forms but is most beloved for his uncanny, sympathetic depictions of commoners and slaves (and the occasional aristocrat) going about their daily lives (Image 12); and Sin Yunbok, whose beautiful renderings of glamorous courtesans and aristocratic lovers evoke scenes in *The Tale of Chunhyang*.

Image 12 *"Wrestling," by Gim Hongdo, eighteenth century. (Courtesy of the National Museum of Korea.)*

POPULAR CULTURE AND SOCIAL CONSCIOUSNESS

A remarkable aspect of late Joseon popular culture is that the subject matter of these works seems to have reflected the lower social status of those responsible for their production, standardization, and dissemination. When we dig a little deeper, however, we find that actually the creative forces—whether court painters like Gim Hongdo and Sin Yunbok, clerks promoting the mask dances, or the *pansori* composer-authors like Sin Jaehyo—came not from commoner or low-born populations, but rather from secondary status backgrounds: families of technical officials in Seoul, hereditary clerks in the countryside, or the descendants of concubines. The artists and intellectuals of secondary status background, however, were neither revolutionaries nor even effective agitators. While they suffered from the restrictions of the aristocratically driven hereditary status system (Chapter 10), the secondary status groups also played an integral role in maintaining the Joseon structures of state and social authority. They were caught, in other words, between a fervent desire to emulate the rituals, behaviors, and education of the aristocracy and thereby be considered social elites themselves, and the frustrations at the fruitlessness of most such efforts to attain true recognition for their talents. This explains why, perhaps, their artistic works rarely featured themselves, but rather focused on mostly downtrodden commoners and the low-born.

Such ambivalence in the face of social restrictions appears, for example, in the spectacular stylistic flourishes in the works of Jo Huiryong, the artist and author of the *Hosan Unofficial History* noted above. But these experimental expressions were framed within traditional literati themes and genres such as paintings of plum blossoms and bamboo. And the greatest innovations from the likes of Gim Hongdo and Sin Yunbok, who like Jo belonged to the *jungin* secondary status group, appeared in the context of their government service, in subordinate standing, in the Office of Painting. Even Sin Jaehyo's *pansori* librettos, full of allusions to the Confucian canon, point to this absorption of the dominant culture and value system. The capital-based poetry societies of the late eighteenth and nineteenth centuries likewise reflected this reality. While talented authors of non-aristocratic background organized themselves into a separate literary movement, they did not produce vernacular verse on issues of social justice, but rather poetry in literary Chinese on conventional themes. Meanwhile, the subject matter of their contributions to the vernacular poetic form, *sijo*, remained mostly the yearning for love, nature, and contemplation.

In contrast to this more reflective tendency, however, there arose also an undisguised effort among the secondary status groups to proclaim a higher place for themselves in the social order. And here the genre of choice was not poetry but rather the prose of biography. Works of literary biography had long contributed to the emergence of a national literature—in the true sense of the term, given these works' frequent use of the vernacular. They included the court diaries written by palace ladies, biographical novels of historical figures, and heroic accounts of virtuous women, honorable men, and loyal commoners who resisted the Japanese and Manchu invasions of the sixteenth and seventeenth centuries (Chapter 9). Similarly, the biographical works produced by the secondary status groups, written mostly in literary Chinese, profiled eminent figures from their own ranks. Published genealogies, for example, mimicked aristocratic genealogies in highlighting accomplished family members while attaching the ancestral lines to those of the aristocracy in order to accentuate common descent. A similar appeal for greater social recognition could also be found in narrative histories honoring the lives of exemplary hereditary clerks. And by the mid-nineteenth century, the rising tide of concubine descendants and their grievances resulted in the *History of Sunflowers*, whose title referred to an allusion made by an earlier king attesting to the unswerving loyalty of these people, much as sunflowers always pointed to the sun. This work included biographical portraits of many such honorable Koreans from the past, historical accounts of the institutional and legal discrimination against them, and a documentation of appeals from famous nobles throughout the Joseon era to overturn this bias.

The most notable breakthrough, however, in expressing the consciousness of social rectification in the guise of popular culture came via the biographical compilations, such as *Observations from the Countryside*, of people from all non-aristocratic backgrounds. The profiles of "Interpreter Hong" or "Filial Lady Yi," for example—among close to 300 separate biographical portraits in *Observations*—provide examples of lives worth remembering as well as a clear sense of the common people's adherence to shared values, despite their obscurity. As the author of *Observations* notes in his preface, "Since long ago there have been wise and good people throughout the countryside who have gone unnoticed [because of social status]. How could the disappearance of their memories not be lamentable?"

Such a sentiment raises some intriguing questions about the way these cultural expressions later became venerated through the modern processes of constructing and defining national tradition. What does it

mean, for example, that Korea's representative folk tales and other artistic products, from *pansori* and mask dances to genre paintings, became
those that mostly reflected the views, plight, and grievances of people
who were often victimized by the socio-political order of the late Joseon
era? How does one square this phenomenon, in turn, with the undeniably strong impact of the aristocratic culture and mentalities, particularly
the power of social status and status consciousness, that have helped to
drive Korea's modern transformation, all the way to the present day?
Whatever the answers, the popular culture of the late Joseon era appears
to have left an indelible imprint on Koreans' sense of collective identity
and history.

13 Nineteenth-Century Unrest

CHRONOLOGY

THE APPEARANCE OF THE *GENERAL SHERMAN*, 1866

In the summer of 1866, residents of Pyongyang sighted something strange in the Daedong River: a black, iron-clad merchant steamship, with cannons, and carrying mostly Asian sailors but headed by a few pale-faced men. This American vessel, named the "General Sherman" after a union commander in the recent American civil war, had become stuck on a sandbar in the middle of the river. Impatient with the negotiations regarding their demands for trade, the General Sherman's officers began firing on the shore and even abducted a Korean negotiating official. Soon, the order came from royal authorities to attack the ship, and after a few days of fighting, Korean soldiers managed to set it afire. No crew members survived. The Pyongyang governor who directed the attack was Bak Gyusu, grandson of Bak Jiwon, the famed scholar-official of the late eighteenth century. As it turned out, the General Sherman was not simply a wandering intruder, but rather an ominous harbinger of imperialism, a force that had already engulfed China and Japan, and would soon push Korea into the currents of a new world order. Within a month, Korea would be attacked again, this time from French forces.

The arrival of imperialism, and all that it implied for Korea's exist-ence as a nation and state, dominates historical consideration of the latter half of the nineteenth century. It forced Korea into the cutthroat system of international competition and aggression that would eventu-ally strip the country of its autonomy. While imperialism ushered in the modern era, however, internal upheavals also played a major role. Both sets of developments prompted, in turn, a concerted reform movement that questioned almost every facet of Korean society and eventually facilitated Joseon's formal "opening" through the Treaty of Ganghwa in 1876. Bak Gyusu, the Pyongyang governor, actually helped negotiate this agreement, and indeed he found himself in the middle of several seminal events in this era. He symbolizes, in turn, the complexities of passing judgment on the nineteenth century, the memory of which has long been dominated by perceptions of decay and decline.

THE NINETEENTH CENTURY ISSUE AND INTERNAL PROBLEMS

The nineteenth century, marked by both internal uprisings and external threats, continues to stand as a troubling historical theme in Korea's modern transformation. In this regard, the era is taken simply as the prelude to "the end," that is, the loss of national sovereignty and other calamities of the early twentieth century. Indeed, this foreboding shadow cast by the nineteenth century has sparked countering suggestions that, given the flourishing of culture and statecraft in the eighteenth century (Chapter 11), the nineteenth was more of an anomaly. Thus both per-spectives situate this period in longer, and presumably more significant, historical developments—that of the late Joseon era that preceded it, and of the modern era that succeeded it. While such broader historical approaches are always edifying, it is also necessary to take the nineteenth century on its own terms.

Many factors contributed to the nineteenth century's special, distinc-tive character, but we must look first to politics. Here, a major moment took place at the very beginning: the death of King Jeongjo in 1800. As discussed in Chapter 11, King Jeongjo has come to embody all that was hopeful and healthy in the late Joseon era, and his sudden death while still in his forties appears to have cut short a comprehensive reform movement. He was followed on the throne, coincidentally, by a suc-cession of four kings too young to exert their own authority when they began their reigns. Not so coincidentally, throughout the nineteenth century the court was dominated by royal family members, especially those of the queen. The resulting network of corruption extended all the way to local administration, which constituted a fundamental cause behind the eruptions of rebellious violence—the largest in the Joseon dynasty until that time—in northern Korea in 1811 and southern Korea in 1862.

The Hong Gyeongnae Rebellion of 1811–12 is striking for its many similarities to the Myocheong Rebellion of 1135–36 (Chapter 5): a charismatic malcontent, convinced by divination of Pyongyang's centrality in Korean civilization and, seething at the discrimination suffered by the country's northwestern region, leads a devastating uprising to overthrow the reigning dynasty. On both occasions, the government forces eventually crushed the rebels after a long siege, but the negative reverberations in Pyeongan province, and indeed throughout the country, would last for decades. The lingering bitterness over the Hong Gyeongnae Rebellion, however, would prove especially consequential because, unlike with Myocheong, the uprising was instigated by rampant corruption on the part of local government authorities. Indeed, the venality came at a particularly acute time, amidst very difficult economic conditions in the area. And this largely explains how, under the banner of regional solidarity, the rebel leaders could mobilize so many people from different socioeconomic and status backgrounds to join the cause.

While the court conducted a thorough investigation of the uprising, it could do little to overturn the most entrenched cause, which was not the material privation nor even regional discrimination, but rather local corruption. For misconduct by local officials was rooted in the chain of graft emanating from the increasingly interventionist central government, chronically beset by both a weak king and political strife among powerful officials jockeying for the spoils. This in turn exacerbated longer-term developments in local society that had been threatening the domination of the nobility, including cultural challenges from long-suppressed local actors and the increasing influence of private wealth amidst beleaguered state finances. In any case, the victims of this toxic brew of political conflict, empty state coffers, and besieged localities were mostly the tax-paying commoners, squeezed increasingly by both the central and local elites. Hence, smaller-scale uprisings continued, and it was almost inevitable that another major peasants' revolt would erupt. Half a century following Hong Gyeongnae it did, striking this time the southern provinces. In early 1862 residents around the southern coastal city of Jinju, fed up with the extortionate military commander there, rose up to kill local officials and take control of government offices around the area. The state hurriedly sent troops and dispatched none other than Bak Gyusu to investigate the uprising and mollify the local populace. This did little to stop the spread of the revolts around the southern provinces—and indeed all the way to some counties in the north as well. Eventually Bak came to recommend several systemic reforms in the taxation system to address the people's grievances. His recommendations, however, were swallowed up by the festering dysfunction of the central government.

Indeed, the most consequential outcome of the 1862 rebellions might have been to alter the growth of a nascent religious movement. In the tense atmosphere of southern Korea following the uprisings, the authorities arrested a wandering preacher, Choe Jeu, for spreading heterodoxy and subversion. He was quickly tried and executed in 1864, and hence began Choe's status as that of a martyr. By then, his teachings, which he labeled "Donghak," or "Eastern Learning" (or simply, "Korean Learning"), claimed several thousand followers in over a dozen localities. Choe's story, and that of his movement in the early years, diverged little from the familiar path followed by the founders of other religions: an early life of doubt and restlessness leading to a journey of self-discovery, followed by a moment of revelation of universal truths so powerful that they compelled the receiver of this vision to initiate a religious and social movement. The Donghak theology blended elements of native Korean spirituality, Confucian ethics and cosmology, teachings of a single divinity borrowed perhaps from Catholicism, and a timely message of universal brotherhood and equality. Most striking, however, were the distinctively Korean prayers and incantations, methods of divination, and healing practices. Even the name of "Donghak" referred to Korea—traditionally, the "eastern country"—and contrasted consciously with "Western Learning," or Catholicism. Donghak's incorporation of a strong native, even nationalist, identity compels a comparison to other nation-centered religious movements that arose in the nineteenth century: the Taiping in China and the Mormon Church in the United States, both of which were founded by extraordinary men who blended nativist elements with established religious practices. Not surprisingly, Choe's execution in 1864 only hardened the resolve of his followers, who remained underground for the next three decades before erupting in an explicitly nationalistic revolt in 1894 (Chapter 14).

To the governing authorities, Choe—despite his movement's profession of a faith that deliberately contrasted with Catholicism—looked very much like someone trying to spread a dangerous tenet like Catholicism.

Like Donghak, Catholicism, with its call for an ontological equality under a personal deity, was considered gravely threatening to the carefully crafted social order. While King Jeongjo had found this religion a curious but potentially disruptive superstition that demanded surveillance, after his death in 1800, the overwhelmingly hostile sentiment from the central elites was unleashed on the small but growing Catholic community in the country. The first state persecution of Catholics in 1801 killed several hundred converts, and when this failed to exterminate the movement, further roundups and mass executions occurred periodically over the next several decades. The final anti-Catholic campaign took place in 1866, and by then, thousands of Korean followers had been martyred. Even today parts of the South Korean countryside are dotted by memorials to individuals captured in a particular spot and executed for their faith. To Korean Catholics, these persecutions represented the searing trial that ultimately strengthened their church.

THE ARRIVAL OF IMPERIALISM

The Catholic persecutions also accompanied the onset of imperialism, a force that had already struck Korea's East Asian neighbors. Qing dynasty China had suffered actual military confrontation with these "barbarians from the oceans" (the British) beginning in the 1830s, and this set the tone for China's tragic difficulties with both internal and external challenges through the rest of the century. While not lacking in institutional reforms, the Chinese response to the impending crisis, for complicated reasons, did not amount to a fundamental reorientation of the country's sociopolitical system. Japan, on the other hand, managed to escape foreign depredation. This was due mostly to its relatively mild initial encounter with Western imperialism, in the form of the United States, which nonetheless sparked fiery domestic struggles that overthrew the Tokugawa shogunate and fueled an intensive drive for institutional reform. By the 1870s Japanese leaders sensed that influence over, and even conquest of, Korea would logically extend this self-strengthening effort, and hence they applied the same kind of gunboat diplomacy practiced by the West to "open" Korea to unequal terms of trade and diplomacy. The resulting Treaty of Ganghwa in 1876, for good reason, is commonly seen as the beginning of Korea's modern era.

The opening shots of imperialism, however, had been fired a decade earlier along the banks of the Daedong River in Pyongyang. The American officers and owner of the General Sherman had loaded the ship with goods and set sail from China in the summer of 1866, determined to force open trade relations with the recalcitrant "hermit kingdom." When the ship first stopped near the mouth of the river, the local magistrate warned that the Korean government forbade such relations with foreigners and demanded that the visitors leave. Ignoring this, the Americans sailed further up the river and, buoyed by some heavy rains, made it past the shallows to Pyongyang itself, only to get stuck after the rains subsided. Negotiations between Governor Bak Gyusu and the General Sherman's officers reached an impasse, and when the Americans abducted a government representative and held him hostage, hostilities broke out. After a few days of cannon, rocket, and archery fire going back and forth, Koreans floated a burning raft to set the ship ablaze, forcing the crew members to swim to shore, where they were killed.

Within a month, however, it became clear that these incursions were not going away, as a French armada raided villages and fortresses on Ganghwa Island on the west-central coast, establishing a temporary base. Soon, the French made their way up the Han River leading to Seoul, proclaiming themselves a punitive expedition and demanding reparations for the nine French priests who had been killed in the Catholic persecution earlier in the year. The Korean defenses successfully beat back the ships after several days of fighting, but not without heavy casualties and the loss of something equally valuable: hundreds of books and cultural artifacts taken by the French forces from Ganghwa Island. The fear of the Korean leaders, especially the xenophobic Prince Regent (father of the boy king) who had ordered the persecutions, had been that Catholicism was simply an instrument of Western imperialism. The French invasion seemed to validate these fears.

Ganghwa Island and the lower reaches of the Han River again served as center stage for imperialism five years later in 1871, this time for a punitive expedition carried out by American marines in response to the destruction of the General Sherman. As the French had done, the American invasion force cut a path of destruction on the island and along the banks of the river, suffering only a handful of casualties while killing hundreds of Korean soldiers. But once again, the invaders ultimately beat a retreat without accomplishing their aims of battering the capital. And once again, this episode intensified the anti-foreign sentiment among Confucian scholars, high officials, and a court still dominated by the Prince Regent's policies of anti-foreign resistance. He responded by erecting stone tablets in front of government offices throughout the country inscribed with a stern warning: "Western barbarians are invading. Failure to fight amounts to appeasement. Appeasement is treason."

Image 13 *"The Martyrdom of Reverend Thomas," depicting the attack on the General Sherman in 1866. Painting by Gim Haksu. (Courtesy of the Council for the 100th Anniversary of the Korean Church.)*

A countering sentiment, however, was also forming among some influential officials, led by Bak Gyusu himself. Soon after the 1871 episode, Bak went on a diplomatic mission to Qing dynasty China, and he returned with a resolve to change the Korean court's policy of fierce resistance to engagement. Despite his efforts to repel the General Sherman, Bak was actually intrigued by the possibilities of learning from the outside world beyond China. He belonged to a small circle of such advocates for greater opening, which included also two gentlemen who, unlike the aristocratic Bak, came from the secondary status group of technical officials, or *jungin*: O Gyeongseok and Yu Honggi. O, an interpreter, had brought back books from his trips to China that aroused the interest of both Pak and Yu. Together, these three men stood as the founders of the Korean enlightenment movement, tutoring the first group of young activists who would gain prominence in the 1880s and 1890s and helping to change the court's diplomatic stance. Such a shift eventually materialized in 1875, when King Gojong, now with full monarchical authority, permitted the exploration of formal trade relations with Japan. As officials, both Bak and O played key roles in the negotiations that led to the Treaty of Ganghwa the next year.

The "Uphold Orthodoxy and Reject Heterodoxy" movement

The teleological tug of the nineteenth century can direct the observer's gaze toward the forces calling for "opening" among the Korean reactions to imperialism, but the more substantial and influential stance adamantly condemned the West. Advocates of this response formed a concerted movement beginning in the 1860s under the banner of "Uphold Orthodoxy and Reject Heterodoxy" (*Wijeong cheoksa*). This term starkly delineated the moral differences, and reiterated the urgency of acting on those differences, between the Confucian and Western civilizations. The practice of labeling opposing ideas as heterodoxy had a long history in the struggles over Confucian propriety in the Joseon era, but this time, as with the Manchus in the seventeenth century, the notion of heterodoxy carried an ethnicized contempt. In contrast to the Manchus who conquered Korea and China but sought to maintain Confucian civilization, however, the "barbarians from the oceans" challenged Confucianism's supremacy.

Though most readily associated in historical lore with the Prince Regent, or Daewongun, who ordered the Catholic persecution and feverishly beat back the American and French incursions in 1866, the intellectual leader of this anti-Western movement was Yi Hangno. Yi was actually one of the most accomplished philosophers of his time, but it was through his rationale for rejecting all intercourse with the West that his influence became paramount. Based on the premise of Confucian civilization's unalterability, Yi found the news of China's defeat at the hands of the British deeply disturbing and explained that such developments portended grave dangers for Korea as well. Even the slightest accommodation to such corrupting external influences, he noted, would place the Joseon state, populace, and civilization on a slippery slope toward disaster. Before Yi died in 1868, he served as mentor to the next generation of "Uphold Orthodoxy and Reject Heterodoxy" advocates, including those, like Choe Ikhyeon, who led armed guerrilla campaigns several decades later. For Yi, the events of 1866 only reinforced his original warnings, and although he eventually fell out of favor with the court, his calls for absolute resistance resonated with the Prince Regent, who made this stance the state policy.

→

The official North Korean historical view later claimed that leader Kim Il Sung's great grandfather led the people's charge against the *General Sherman* that year. In an odd way, this might as well have been true, for the "self-reliance" stance of the North Korean regime represented the logical extension of the isolationist Korean response to the nineteenth century. The makeup of the dangerous outside changed from Western imperialists to Western imperialists pushing capitalism, but the claims that contact with the external world endangered the survival of Korean civilization itself remained in force.

What followed was a series of study missions sent by the Korean government to Meiji Japan and Qing China to imbibe the basics of modern statecraft and technology. Participants in these trips, from high officials to young students, returned and helped implement major changes in government organization and direction in the early 1880s. The full-fledged "enlightenment" cause behind these developments challenges, in turn, the conventional view of the nineteenth century as one of decay and decline that led directly to the disasters of the twentieth century. Rather, the enlightenment movement, which drew considerably upon long-standing, internally-driven reform efforts—and, indeed, even upon the rise of the Donghak religion as well—showed that the nineteenth century also represented a logical culmination of the late Joseon era as a whole.

14 1894, A Fateful Year

CHRONOLOGY

1882	Soldier's uprising in Seoul; establishment of diplomatic relations with the United States
1884	Failed overthrow ("Gapsin Coup") of Korean government by radicals
1894 April	The Donghak Uprising
1894 July	Japanese occupation of royal palace
1894 July	Establishment of the Deliberative Assembly
1894 August	Start of Chinese–Japanese War
1895 April	End of Chinese–Japanese War
1895 October	Assassination of Queen Min
1896 January	Flight of Korean king to Russian legation

THE OCCUPATION OF THE ROYAL PALACE BY JAPANESE SOLDIERS, 1894

In July of 1894, Otori Keisuke, Japanese minister in Korea, presented to the Korean government a set of demands for domestic reforms that would protect Japan's security interests. Otori could act with such impudence because his soldiers were encamped in and around Seoul. They had been sent to the peninsula in the wake of the Chinese military's own entrance into the country, which had come, officially at the behest of the Korean court, to help pacify the Donghak Uprising. This rebellion had exploded in the southwest earlier in the spring and threatened to bring down the five-century-old Joseon dynasty. When the Korean government refused to respond directly to Otori's demands, Japanese troops stormed the royal palace and sent most of the government leaders scurrying. The Daewongun, father of the Korean king and former Prince Regent, returned to power with the support of the Japanese and formed a Deliberative Assembly, with sweeping governmental authority, to take charge of reform efforts. The Deliberative Assembly consisted of conservative opponents of the Korean government (like the Daewongun), as well as moderates and progressives who had long wanted to take control over a court dominated by the royal consort family, the Min.

This hodgepodge of elements in the Deliberative Assembly, however, soon developed into one of the influential actors in Korean history. What began, then, as an uprising against local corruption soon engulfed the country in a region-wide confrontation and helped to usher in a new age in Korea, a process driven by the elite admirers of foreign ways as much as by the peasant followers of the native Donghak religion. Over the long term, therefore, one could argue indeed that the Donghak rebellion led to the downfall of the Joseon dynasty, or at least of Korea's long-established sociopolitical system.

THE DONGHAK SPARK

In the summer of 1894, the ill will from the Donghak Uprising still festered in the countryside, for the end of the rebellion's fiercest battles earlier in the spring had not brought an end to the underlying troubles that had triggered the unrest in the first place. Venality by local officials had been a constant problem in the nineteenth century, but the exploitation practiced by the magistrate of Gobu county in Jeolla province, in the form of debilitating special taxes, appears to have come at a particularly sensitive moment. The local followers of the Donghak religion had been unhappy with deteriorating economic conditions, with the difficulties of rehabilitating the reputation of their martyred founder, Choe Jeu (Chapter 13), and with foreign, especially Japanese, commercial influence. When their grievances about excessive local duties went unheard, these Donghak villagers, led by their local religious leader Jeon Bongjun, swiftly ransacked the Gobu county office and redistributed the ill-gotten grain to the people. The rebellion thereafter spread like wildfire through the southwest, and within a few weeks, many county governments in this region had been seized. The battles against government troops, now supplemented by Chinese reinforcements, abated in the early summer of 1894 through a settlement, only to revive in the fall in protest against the Japanese occupation of Seoul. The bloody confrontations that ensued between the Donghak followers and the joint Japanese–Korean force ended the rebellion in the winter, but not before costing the lives of thousands of peasants.

Interpretations of the Donghak Uprising's historical significance have tended to focus either on the systemic ills of the late Joseon state, or on the suffering of the common people besieged by a stifling social hierarchy, government exploitation, and poor economic conditions. The former perspective tends to view the rebellion as the culmination of a gradual decay in the central government over the course of the nineteenth century. By contrast, the latter historical view, which accentuates the plight of the people, establishes the revolt as the basis and inspiration for the modern struggles against domestic oppression and foreign domination. The manifestos, declarations, and demands that the Donghak leaders issued in 1894 appear forward-looking: Calls for an end to social discrimination, for an expulsion of seedy foreign influences, and even for the redistribution of property seem, upon first glance, not merely progressive but revolutionary. And while the documentary evidence suggests that these historical assessments are somewhat problematic, especially regarding the claims for economic redistribution (likely an embellishment added later), on the whole both viewpoints appear warranted. The implications for Korean history, furthermore, were not limited to internal developments. The Donghak rebellion's most wide-ranging impact, in fact, might have come in helping to overturn the millennia-long regional order in East Asia.

A SHRIMP CAUGHT IN A WHALE FIGHT

The Japanese incursion in Korea following the Treaty of Ganghwa in 1876 would not go unmet by the Chinese, who understandably were not keen on allowing any challenge to their special position in Korea. This was, after all, a relationship that had endured, for the most part, since the Unified Silla period beginning in the seventh century. Thus in the 1880s Korea became entangled in the growing feud between China and Japan over dominance in northeast Asia, a situation that Koreans referred to proverbially as "the breaking of a shrimp's back when caught between fighting whales." This rivalry took many forms—in the availability of intellectual and institutional models, in diplomatic influence, and in commercial competition—and twice grew into military skirmishes in Seoul. In 1882, a group of common Korean soldiers, upset at their treatment compared to that of the new crack unit trained by Japanese advisors, rose up in revolt against the Korean government's growing ties to foreign influence. Taking the Daewongun as their inspiration and leader, the soldiers instigated attacks on Japanese compounds and threatened members of the royal family. But it was the Chinese military that put down the rebellion, and for good measure it also seized the Daewongun and took him to China. With that, the pro-reform elements in Korean elite circles, favorably disposed to following the Japanese model, felt emboldened. In 1884 a particularly brazen group of young radicals, impatient with the slow pace of change despite the signing of treaties with Western powers (beginning with the United States in 1882), killed conservative high ministers and took over key government buildings. Despite the tacit support of the Japanese officials, as in 1882, this putsch, known as the Gapsin Coup ("Coup of 1884"), ended through the intervention of Chinese soldiers. The coup plotters able to escape the backlash had to flee all the way to Japan.

Gaining the upper hand through this event, the Chinese established preeminent influence over the Korean government for the next decade through a "residency" headed by the powerful Chinese official Yuan Shikai. While scholars have termed this a "dark period," characterized by stifling Chinese intervention and commercial exploitation, the languid pace of Korean institutional reforms, and the house arrest of enlightenment activists such as Yu Giljun, the Chinese impact was not so clear-cut. Qing China in fact played a central role in the establishment of the first Korean telegraph lines, the Korean Customs Service, and even formal diplomatic relations with Western governments. Furthermore, Korea's state restructuring efforts continued, the enlightenment movement grew further through publication and educational activities, and moderate reformers remained in power, supported by a sympathetic monarch often hemmed in by his queen's ties to the Chinese. These tendencies might have produced an interesting result had the Donghak Uprising not triggered a clause in a treaty, signed in 1885 by the Chinese and Japanese, acknowledging each other's interests in Korea.

This treaty had called for the notification of the other side if ever there was a cause for dispatching troops to Korea. And this is exactly what happened in June of 1894, when the Korean government turned to China, almost reflexively, to help put down the Donghak. The influx of Chinese troops was met by a quick Japanese response, and before long this powder keg was lit. Under the pretext of protecting the Japanese consulate and other possessions, Japanese soldiers filled the Seoul streets. They provided support for the diplomatic pressure exerted by envoy Otori and others, who demanded fundamental government reforms that would ensure a Korean buffer against Chinese threats to Japan. When these troops chased away the conservative pro-Chinese government leaders, the Japanese orchestrated the creation of the Deliberative Assembly (*Gunguk gimucheo*), which would henceforth act as the highest governing body.

While the Deliberative Assembly went about its work, the Japanese forces prosecuted their confrontation with China, declaring war on

August 1, 1894 and swiftly gaining the upper hand. In a series of clashes, from Pyongyang, where the largest land battle of the war left much of the city in ruins, to Manchuria and the Shandong peninsula, to naval exchanges in the Yellow Sea, the Japanese won decisively. Just as they had attempted, but failed, to do in the 1590s, the Japanese sought supremacy in East Asia by provoking a direct confrontation with China in Korea, and this time the result was a shift in the East Asian regional balance of power that would endure for a century.

THE SPIRIT OF GABO

This momentous reversal of the East Asian order would present a psychological and cultural shock to the Koreans, akin to the effect of the fall of the Ming dynasty two centuries earlier (Chapter 10). But for many Koreans, China's downfall represented good riddance, a crucial external requirement for furthering the internal processes of enlightenment, reform, and self-strengthening. The Deliberative Assembly in fact could not have been clearer in its approval of this release from the centuries-long subordination to the Chinese: The first article of its reform program declared that Korea's official dating system would no longer be based on the Chinese imperial calendar but rather on the founding, in 1392, of the Joseon dynasty—1894, for example, was now designated "Year 503 After Foundation." The second article called for a new kind of diplomatic relationship between Korea and China. But the articles that followed definitively set the stage for the staggering changes in state and society that the Deliberative Assembly would initiate. In the rest of the first ten articles, in fact, the Deliberative Assembly declared an end to hereditary social status and slavery, a cessation of contract marriages of adolescents along with a lifting of the prohibition on widow remarriage, and the opening of the path to government service by commoners. By the time the Deliberative Assembly gave way to a cabinet-based government at the end of 1894, it had passed over 200 such bills, systematically overhauling patterns of Korean government, society, and economy that had been in place for centuries. With the exception of those concerning the governing structure, most of these resolutions were not immediately implemented into practice, but they provided a blueprint and impetus for reform that would continue for decades. The Deliberative Assembly, in short, kick-started the Gabo ("1894") Reforms of 1894–5, the significance of which would reverberate over the course of Korea's modern transformation.

The end of slavery in Korea

"Laws allowing public and private public slavery are completely abolished, and the sale of human beings is forbidden." One is tempted to take this resolution of July 1894, the ninth passed by the Deliberative Assembly, as the Korean equivalent to the American Emancipation Proclamation of three decades earlier. Indeed this comparison inspires thinking about the striking parallels as well as differences between the Korean and American forms of slavery. Korea's system was more ancient and endured in a population with no physical differences, while that of the United States was based on, and had a lot to do with furthering, the notion of race. But the two slave systems also shared fundamental features: hereditary slave status, the treatment of slaves as chattel property, and the dependence of the social structure and economy on their bondage. In both cases as well, the perpetuation of slavery and discrimination relied upon the insistence of the "one drop of blood" rule in the face of widespread sexual exploitation. The similarities extended, in fact, to the gradual and pained process of social emancipation following legal abolition.

The end of slavery in Korea, however, had actually begun long before the Gabo Reforms, both legally and customarily. After reaching a peak, according to estimates from household registration records, of approximately 30 percent of the population in the late seventeenth century, economic changes prompting the use of more wage labor made slavery gradually less efficient. And growing calls from scholar-officials condemning the practice as a violation of Confucian morality contributed to the government's decision to eliminate the holding of "public," or government, slaves (*gong nobi*) in the early nineteenth century. By the time the Gabo Reforms extended this ban to private slaves, slavery had already been significantly diminished. The official emancipation of 1894, then, was largely a symbolic gesture; indeed, some forms of servitude did not end, and even the first major revision of the household registration system in 1896 still made room for bound servants. It was not until the 1920s that household registers eliminated any possibility of accounting for them. Even these steps, however, did not totally destroy the reality of bondage, especially in the countryside, where servile laborers (*meoseum*) continued to tend to their masters until the Korean War (1950–53) period.

These legal steps of the late nineteenth and early twentieth centuries, however, were still significant, for once slavery, bondage, and the formal distinction of "mean" or "low-born" people were eliminated, their descendants truly enjoyed social liberation. This perhaps stems from the fact that hereditary slavery in Korea, though meticulously maintained through record-keeping and other factors, had not been based on physical differences like "race." In other words, in the modern era, with increasing urbanization and mobility, no one could really know who was a slave descendant. The contrast with America could not be starker. The flip side to this, however, is the contemporary Korean tendency, bordering on national amnesia, regarding this discomfiting component of the past: The casual claim that Korea's form of slavery was somehow less inhumane finds easy support in the quirky belief among almost all (South) Koreans that they are descendants of the Joseon aristocracy.

The makeup of the Deliberative Assembly and of the Gabo Reform governments was equally revolutionary. Of the twenty or so members of the Deliberative Assembly, half came from the non-aristocratic secondary status groups. And while the Gabo cabinets were formally led by men with traditional aristocratic ancestry, the ranks immediately below, from vice minister to administrators and their assistants, were filled with those from non-aristocratic backgrounds. This bespoke the prominence of secondary status groups, especially northerners and the *jungin* technical specialists, in the Korean enlightenment movement from the 1860s onward. Their ascendance to the higher ranks of the new officialdom, in breaking through the centuries-old barriers of hereditary status, had much to do with the particularities of their long-standing roles, but also with their readiness to discard traditional ideas and ways. This inclination, shared by the enlightenment activists as a whole—both aristocratic and not—also drew them to Japan as a model of reform and self-strengthening. Such ties were reinforced in the fall of 1895 by the assassination, at the hands of Japanese soldiers and Korean accomplices, of Queen Min, who from the beginning had been a thorn on the side of Japanese interests.

The uproar over this craven act eventually engulfed the political scene, and within a few weeks, anti-Japanese elements close to the monarch spirited away the Korean king to the safe haven of the Russian consulate, beyond the reach of Gabo leaders and Japanese soldiers. This provided the impetus for the widespread distaste for the Gabo government to erupt into a mob that helped to kill several top officials while chasing the rest to Japan. Thus ended the Gabo Reforms, the same way as they had begun back in the summer of 1894, with Korean progressives under the protection of the Japanese.

The forces unleashed by the events of 1894, however, would pave multiple paths of historical development determining the country's modern fate: China would weaken further and not regain its dominant standing in northeast Asia for another century; the Donghak Uprising would inspire countless other eruptions of armed anti-foreign resistance movements well into the period of Japanese colonialism (1910–45); and the Gabo Reforms would stand as a microcosm of Korea's uneasy transitions at the turn of the twentieth century—at once embracing the models of the outside world, but ultimately becoming swamped by forces beyond Koreans' control.

15 The Great Korean Empire

CHRONOLOGY

1896 April	Founding of the Independence Club and *The Independent* newspaper
1896	Revision of the household registration system
1897	Proclamation of the Great Korean Empire
1898	Start of the nationwide land survey
1898–99	Government shutdown of the Independence Club and *The Independent* newspaper
1899 May	Operation of the first streetcars in Seoul
1899 Sept.	Opening of the Seoul–Incheon Rail Line
1904	Opening of the Seoul–Busan Rail Line
1904	Outbreak of the Russo-Japanese War

OPENING OF THE SEOUL–INCHEON RAIL LINE, 1899

"The noise from the rolling fire-wheeled chariot was like that of thunder, as the earth and heavens shook and the smoke from the chimney of the engine erupted into the air," wrote a newspaper reporter who rode the inaugural train trip in Korea in September of 1899. "As I sat in the car and looked out the window, the whole world seemed to be racing past us, and even flying birds could not catch up." Such awestruck accounts accompanied the introduction of railroads throughout the world in the nineteenth century, as the enormous bellowing machines heralded the onset of a new era. In Korea, the opening of the first rail line between Seoul and Incheon, a distance of approximately twenty kilometers, took on a similarly epochal significance. This event furthermore came to reflect the mixture of confidence, potentiality, and uncertainty that came to mark the "Great Korean Empire," the brief period, from 1897 to 1910, when the Joseon kingdom formally became an "empire" like the foreign powers that surrounded the country. As with the railroad, this period witnessed the birth of many fundamental features of the modern era, not only in communications and transportation infrastructure, but in the wider realms of technology and commerce, and as well as in culture and institutions.

However profound its altering of life and perception, the railroad in Korea also cannot escape the uneasy connections to the history of national misfortune, for these early rail lines eventually facilitated the Japanese takeover of Korea. The initiation into the modern world, like the railroad, thus carried dangers as well, as the promises of "enlightenment" and progress were offset by threatening forces beyond the Korean people's control. It is this duality that renders judgment on the Great Korean Empire contentious. Once largely derided for its failures, this period is now mined for signs that Koreans sought to follow an autonomous, albeit precarious, path toward modern change.

KOREA AND THE NEW EMPIRES

At the turn of the twentieth century, Korea was immersed in the age of high imperialism. The social Darwinian ethos of the "strong eating the weak" played itself out in the global arena, and northeast Asia became one of the fiercest zones of competition. Once again, Korea, at the center and crossroads of this region, unwittingly stood as a target for territorial gain or commercial exploitation. The imperialist rivalry penetrated and, in turn, was appropriated by competing political groups at court. During the closing years of the nineteenth century a new imperial power, Russia, eyed the peninsula as a key component in its geopolitical strategy, and likewise the pro-Russian sentiment among higher officials, who looked upon Russia as a protector, gained the upper hand. But the Russian empire's ambitions clashed with those of another rising power, Japan. The Japanese empire had defeated Qing dynasty China in the 1894–95 war on Korean soil and gained Taiwan and parts of Manchuria as its war booty. At the turn of the twentieth century, however, Japan chafed against the constraints on its regional ambitions imposed by the European powers, especially Russia. And finally, China, too, lurched toward refashioning itself as a modern imperial power even while trying to fend off the Western forces.

Korea, traditionally China's most reliable tributary state, now sought to escape this subordinate relationship altogether. "Independence" from China had been a central motive behind the Gabo Reforms of 1894–95 (Chapter 14). And even after the fall of the Gabo government in early 1896, the Korean monarch and government advisors pursued autonomy not only from China but from all the ravenous powers that surrounded the country. After months of entreaties, from both within and beyond the court, to take a bold step in this direction, in 1897 the Joseon state officially joined the ranks of empires. On the surface, this seemed delusional, for Korea, a small country with no command over different ethnic or civilizational groups, did not look anything like an empire. But the distinction between empire and kingdom was also one of diplomatic recognition following self-declaration, and when the Chinese "son of heaven" no longer appeared as the pinnacle Under Heaven, Korean officials felt ready to take such a step. Hence the birth of the "Great Korean Empire," or "Daehan jeguk"—shortened to "Hanguk" then as now (at least in South Korea, or *Daehan minguk*)—and, with it, the coronation of the Korean monarch in 1897 as emperor. One of the best-known images from this period shows the monarch, Gojong, posing resplendently while dressed in a faux Kaiser uniform. Little wonder, then, that his reign was called officially that of the "Glorious Military" (*Gwangmu*).

The construction of the Korean state's new status and legitimacy went far beyond the emperor himself, however. It encompassed a range of changes, both symbolic and organizational. The ceremonial declaration of the "Great Korean Empire" borrowed from a mixture of old and recent traditions, surrounding the monarch in ancient customs and symbols while emphasizing that his ascent represented "the foundation of independence" in the new era. The standardization of other symbols accepted globally as emblems of state sovereignty soon followed, including a flag and national anthem, and even national holidays. The strengthening of the monarchical state progressed on the level of institutional changes as well. The formal description and proclamation of the "Imperial System," which appeared two years later in 1899, employed concepts and terminology establishing legitimacy in the vocabulary of late nineteenth-century international law. But most of the content in this proclamation reinforced the ties to the Joseon dynasty and proclaimed royal absolutism, with each article explicitly covering a different realm of governance over which the emperor had total control.

Even the economic activities directed by the royal house contributed to this emperor-centered state legitimacy, for they enveloped the monarchy in the aura of modern advances. The Office of Crown Properties and a host of other organs subordinated under the Royal Household Ministry took the lead in sponsoring major infrastructural projects in electricity, streetcars, waterworks, telegraph and telephone, printing, and minting. The Crown even rescinded the concessions already granted to foreign railroad and mining operations and took control over the further development of these industries. The Korean government that coexisted with the Royal Household Ministry as a junior partner of sorts did its part, too, particularly by revamping the household registration system and undertaking a nationwide land survey. Both efforts sought to increase the central administration's capacities for mobilization and extraction, and to a certain extent they achieved these goals.

TRADE AND INDUSTRY

It was the Royal Household Ministry, however, that was responsible for most of the many developments in commerce, industry, and infrastructure during the Korean Empire, which laid the foundation for the material transformation of modern Korea. In some areas, such as electricity generation, Korea benefited from a late developer status, gaining immediate access to recent technological breakthroughs through borrowing or copying. The first and most advanced electrical generation system in East Asia had been installed in the royal palace in Seoul in the mid-1880s and built by none other than the Edison Company. Within a decade, Korea's capital city boasted of hundreds of electric streetlights. By May of 1899, four months before the opening of the Seoul–Incheon railway, the Seoul Electrical Company unveiled, to great fanfare, the first streetcar line. The Seoul streetcars, appearing frequently in photographs that suggested a range of accompanying social and economic developments, would remain the most visible symbol of the rapidly changing capital in this era.

As an emblem of modern technology and progress, however, the railroad came to dominate the popular and historical consciousness in Korea during the opening decades of the twentieth century. The fanfare that greeted the opening of the Seoul–Incheon line on September 18, 1899, reflected the momentousness of the event, as dignitaries from the political, diplomatic, and business worlds gathered in a station on the south bank of the Han River, just outside Seoul, for the inaugural ride. News reports and official pronouncements heralded this event as the momentous opening of a new era. "On the inside, the rail cars were divided into three classes—high, medium, and low," noted one newspaper account, "while the outside of the cars was decorated in such a [lavish] way as to be indescribable." The train departed with the first group of passengers at 9am, and "within a short time" found its way to Incheon, where a magisterial welcoming ceremony awaited them at the station. At the festivities, according to another newspaper report, the head of the Japanese company that operated the rail line concluded his congratulatory address with three cheers of "Long Live the Korean Emperor" and "Long Live the Japanese Emperor." He was followed by Korea's Foreign Minister, who also ended his remarks by leading three shouts of "Long

Live the Korean Emperor." The reporter observed that the throng of people at the Incheon station looked "like a cloud," and pondered, along with a bystander, whether this signaled Koreans' overdue achievement of enlightenment. They also noted somberly, however, that this wondrous technology had been built by foreigners.

An American company had won the concession from the Korean government to construct the Seoul–Incheon rail line, which broke ground in 1896, but a few months before completion had sold these rights to a partially government-owned Japanese company. In hindsight it was clear that the Japanese had eyed this short stretch as a prelude to the larger prize of two "trunk lines" that would extend from the capital to the port city of Busan in the southeast and to Uiju in the northwest. These two lines, with the former completed in time to facilitate the Japanese effort against Russia in the 1904–5 war, would greatly aid Japanese expansionism. But the Korean imperial government had sold concessions for transportation and communication networks, mines, and industries to representatives of many countries. From the Korean government's (or monarchy's) vantage point, this constituted not a giveaway, but rather an opportunity to import commercial and industrial technologies while expanding the coffers of the state. The Korean rulers could hardly have envisioned that some of these ventures, especially the trains, would also serve literally as a vehicle for imperialist aggression.

The rise of Korean port cities

An unlikely symbol of the ambiguous position of the Great Korean Empire in modern Korean history is the city, or more precisely, the rapid growth of urban centers from the late nineteenth to early twentieth centuries. As with so much else associated with this period, the emergence of modern cities is entangled with the unsettling impact of external forces, in particular the transformation of the country into first a target of imperialism, then into a Japanese colony. Imperialist and colonialist interests, especially regarding trade and transportation, launched the rise of many of the familiar Korean cities today. These places include Sinuiju, Gaeseong, and Heungnam in the North, and in the South, Gunsan, Mokpo, and especially Daejeon, now South Korea's fifth largest metropolis, which went from small town to provincial capital in the early twentieth century. Outside the traditional centers of Pyongyang and Seoul, however, the two largest cities by the middle of the twentieth century were Busan and Incheon, which grew through the regional trading system.

Busan and Incheon had long served as ports in the Joseon era, but their significance increased dramatically after the 1876 Treaty of Ganghwa with Japan. Afterwards they functioned as two out of the three official "treaty ports," along with Wonsan (now in North Korea), where officially sanctioned foreign trade could occur. Through the accelerated influx of foreign merchants, interests, and conflicts at the turn of the twentieth century, the stage was set for these two ports to grow rapidly as Korea's meeting points with the larger world. Incheon, the gateway to the capital, grew into a hotspot teeming with Korean, Chinese, Japanese, and other foreign merchants, who set up their own communities and worked with the native population to gain favorable terms for extending their commercial ventures into the interior. Though the port became a battleground for the imperialist rivalry between China and Japan, by the end of the Russo-Japanese War in 1905 Japanese interests had gained the upper hand and soon began to construct not only railroads but also electricity, gas, and telegraph lines. Presently South Korea's third largest city and home to the country's gleaming flagship airport as well as other enormous developments, Incheon now touts its long ties to China and its status as Korea's most visible global hub.

Busan, by contrast, was always a creature of Korea's relations with Japan. A port that had long facilitated the limited official trade between the two kingdoms during the Joseon era, in the late nineteenth century Busan quickly developed into something akin to an extra-territorial base for Japanese commercial, agricultural, and military ambitions. By the turn of the twentieth century the harbor area had a large Japanese settlement and served as the primary entrance point for Japanese merchants wanting access to Korea's internal trading networks, and for Japanese companies supplying the amenities of the modern commercial world. Rail and electricity lines that began as short networks within Busan during the Korean Empire, for example, soon extended to neighboring areas in the southeastern region of the peninsula. And, not surprisingly, this Japanese largesse continued into the colonial period, when Busan's expansion swallowed up adjacent towns and eventually turned the city into an official provincial capital. The rapid development of Busan served the country well when, during the opening months of the Korean War in 1950, it functioned as South Korea's interim capital that held at bay the North Korean siege until American reinforcements, through an invasion of Incheon, provided relief. Today Busan, as South Korea's second city, ranks as one of the largest ports and most dynamic metropolises in the world.

Furthermore, as Korean governments discovered later in the twentieth century, it was difficult to isolate the country's general well-being from the influx of foreign capital, technologies, and industries. The economic gains simply would not have materialized otherwise, such as the blossoming of native enterprise and the training of countless workers in the skills of a diversifying economy. From the laborers who laid the tracks, mined the mines, and toiled in the nascent textile sector, to the operators of the streetcars and telegraph lines, Koreans began to forge a modern commercial realm. They were joined by the founders of the first Korean banks, some of which would survive for decades to come, and even of joint stock companies. Whether as transporters or handicraft manufacturers peddling their goods in the ports, or as traders taking advantage of their links to the heartland, or even as officials using their political connections to gain access to capital and materials, this first group of modern entrepreneurs made an indelible impact.

One of the best-known representatives of this early business class was Yi Seunghun. Yi hailed from Jeongju, lying north of Pyongyang and famed for its late-Joseon commercial development as well as for producing many prominent cultural figures in the early twentieth century. Yi traversed a variegated life course, but he initially made a name for himself as a manufacturer-merchant. He got his start as an apprentice in a local enterprise that produced brass wares, and by the late 1880s he established his own brass factory. During the Korean Empire Yi expanded his business activities through a trading company based in Pyongyang. This enterprise eventually gained a prominent position in the rapidly developing commercial sector, especially along the trading networks on the west coast between Pyongyang, Incheon, and Seoul. In addition to brass and other handicraft goods, his company traded in petroleum, medicinal products, and paper items. He also accumulated a small fortune as an investor in new enterprises. He was a founder in 1908, for example, of one of the earliest joint stock companies in Korea, the Pyongyang Porcelain Company. He was, in some ways, the first modern Korean tycoon.

THE SPIRIT OF ENLIGHTENMENT

For all of his success as an entrepreneur, however, Yi Seunghun is better known for his activities, made possible by his wealth, in education and publishing. He stood at the forefront of the cresting enlightenment movement through his sponsorship of educational ventures, most notably the Osan School in Jeongju, founded in 1907, which would go on to produce some of the best-known literary and intellectual figures of modern Korea. Such schools around the country would educate the first generation of Korean school children in the "new learning," the popular term for Western knowledge and enlightenment in general. Yi's interest in social edification also led him to support the activities of acclaimed nationalists, including An Changho. Yi's most celebrated accomplishment, in fact, came in 1919, when he stood as one of thirty-three signers of the March First Declaration of Independence from Japanese colonial rule (Chapter 17).

Yi Seunghun also engaged in newspaper publishing, a realm that began to wield social influence during the Korean Empire through the activities of the Independence Club, a civic group founded in 1896 by Seo Jaepil. Seo (anglicized as "Philip Jaisohn") had been a plotter of the Gapsin Coup of 1884 (Chapter 13), and then had fled to the United States and lived there for a decade before returning, with an American education and an American wife, to his homeland in 1895. The Club's program, which centered on "independence" from traditional ways as well as from China, was articulated in the *Dongnip sinmun*, the country's first modern newspaper. In its inaugural issue in April 1896, this organ served immediate notice of its radical agenda by its choice of the written language: the Korean vernacular, with even a page in English (*The Independent*). When Seo opted to return to the United States in early 1898, another enlightenment activist schooled in America, Yun Chiho, stepped in as the Club's next leader. Under Yun's guidance the Independence Club and its newspaper maintained the spirit of the Gabo

Reforms, constantly prodding the Korean government, monarch, and people toward modern change. The Club also erected the Independence Gate, still extant, at the same place where the Joseon dynasty monarch had ritually greeted the Chinese envoy, and it even organized a series of mass, open-air debates that promoted the participation of people regardless of social status.

In late 1898 the Independence Club was shut down by the monarchical government, which suspected the Club of republican leanings. *The Independent* newspaper had to follow suit a year later, but not before spawning a revolution in mass culture. People associated with the Club started other newspapers, which all sustained the general approach of using this medium to disseminate the information and knowledge that would help build a strong, independent nation and state. Of particular note was the establishment of the *Jeguk sinmun* ("Imperial Post") and *Hwangseong sinmun* ("Capital Gazette") in 1898, the former written in native script and targeted at the masses, the latter written in mixed Sino-Korean script and aimed at a more educated population. Both newspapers survived largely intact until 1910, serving as the twin pillars of the growing world of publishing during the Great Korean Empire. This sphere of public discourse received its next major boost after 1905, as the forced implementation of the Japanese protectorate in Korea provoked an urgent outpouring of publishing.

As with the trains and other technologies, however, the "new learning" embraced by the enlightenment movement also constituted a double-edged sword that marked the Korean Empire as a whole. As noted above, the railroad, for all its benefits, ultimately served in 1904–5 to facilitate Japan's prosecution of its war with Russia over supremacy in northeast Asia. And likewise, the discourse of "civilization and enlightenment" that dominated the public debate during this period proved just as useful to the imperialist forces wanting to conquer Korea as to those who touted this creed in defense of autonomy. To the Japanese (and many Koreans), Korea fell far short in its degree of civilizational advancement, and this justified a foreign power's efforts to take control of the country. For centuries dating back to the Spanish conquest of the Americas, after all, Europeans had deployed the same rationale to colonize much of the known world. Not surprisingly, Japanese and even many Korean elites argued that Japan had not only an interest but a duty in shaping Korea's future—out of security concerns, if nothing else, for Korea was too weak to withstand the pressures of Western imperialism. As it turned out, the promotion, importation, and implementation of railroads, streetcars, telegraph and electricity lines, mines, and other hallmarks of the modern world ultimately proved incapable of overcoming these geopolitical tides.

Thus we return to the problematic place of the Great Korean Empire in Korea's modern transition. Long stained historically by a perception of failure on the part of the state, elites, and even the masses to withstand imperialist pressures, the Korean Empire has recently enjoyed a revival in popular and scholarly interest. At one level, the responsibility for the country's loss of autonomy has shifted more to imperialism as a whole—and not just that of Japan—which escalated the complex political rivalries among Korean elites, including the monarch himself. Korea, then, could not have escaped unscathed in this era. At another level, historians and commentators have accentuated the need to appreciate the range of major advances that marked this period, whether in culture, economy, or politics. But such a view has served only to sharpen the condemnation of Japanese actions, for the Korean Empire showed that Korea was heading toward an autonomous modernity had the Japanese not intervened. The Japanese takeover and colonial rule from 1910 to 1945 represented, then, a dreadful "distortion" of national history that robbed the Koreans of the capacity to forge their own modern existence. This appears to go too far—one cannot write off thirty-five years of history, after all—but one can understand how the Korean Empire can be considered a crucial, if perhaps regrettable, component of Korea's modern transformation.

16 The Japanese Takeover, 1904–18

CHRONOLOGY

1904 February	Outbreak of the Russo-Japanese War; signing of the Korea–Japan agreement
1904 August	Signing of treaty allowing Japanese intervention in Korean government affairs
1905 September	Treaty of Portsmouth ending the Russo-Japanese War, recognizing Japanese supremacy in Korea
1905 November	Protectorate treaty establishing Japanese Residency General in Korea
1907 June	Arrival of secret Korean emissaries in The Hague for the World Peace Conference
1907 July	Forced abdication of Emperor Gojong; signing of a treaty giving Japan veto and appointment power in the Korean government
1907 August	Disbandment of Korean army; swelling of ranks of righteous armies
1909 October	Assassination of first Resident General Ito Hirobumi
1910 August	Signing of the annexation treaty; commencement of Government-General of Korea
1910–1918	Colonial land survey

THE SECRET MISSION TO THE HAGUE, 1907

On June 25, 1907, three Asian men bearing a Korean flag and a fierce determination appeared on the grounds of the Second World Peace Conference in The Hague, Netherlands. They had been sent clandestinely by the Korean monarch, Emperor Gojong, to plead their case for Korea's independence from the encroaching Japanese empire. This trio, however, was denied a platform before the gathered diplomats. From their perspective, they could not grant the Koreans formal recognition because Korea itself had no diplomatic presence on the world stage, having fallen into status as a Japanese protectorate in late 1905. The Koreans, however, sought to demonstrate that the 1905 protectorate "treaty" had been garnered fraudulently.

Declaring the protectorate invalid and illegal was not a simple matter, however, and neither was the Japanese takeover of Korea that began in 1904. How one views this process and the decades of Japanese rule that followed invariably dictates one's perspective on Korea's modern experience as a whole, particularly on the immense influence exerted by the external world. Seen in this way, the Hague incident showed Koreans taking matters into their own hands despite becoming swamped by powerful historical forces, including those that would rob them of their political independence.

AUTONOMY AND MODERN HISTORY

The Japanese conquest of Korea, which led to an experience of colonial rule that lasted until 1945, constituted the first time since Mongol suzerainty in the fourteenth century that Korea was directly controlled by a foreign power. Understandably, most historical perspectives have tended to focus on the political rupture and to treat the loss of Korean autonomy primarily as a matter of domination, victimization, collaboration, and resistance. They also extend this inquiry to raise questions about the nature and even historical validity of the period under foreign rule, so large was the imprint of Japan's conquest on the rest of Korea's twentieth century. In addition to imperialism, historians have cited numerous internal factors behind Korea's loss of independence, including a series of missed opportunities by the state and elites to avert the oncoming disaster: the reactionary responses to Western contact in the 1860s; the tepid changes of the 1870s and 1880s; the Chinese domination of the 1880s and 1890s; the incomplete reform movements of the 1890s; and the unsuccessful efforts, hampered by corruption and carelessness, to improve Korea's diplomatic, military, and economic conditions in the opening years of the twentieth century. Social and cultural factors cited include the stifling social hierarchy, the weakness of Koreans' sense of national collectivity, even the Korean customs regarding family, hygiene, and work. Undeniably, many if not all, of these factors did indeed ultimately contribute to the end result, but it is difficult to determine their relative significance, especially regarding events that took place as far back as the mid-nineteenth century.

On the other hand, one must also not overestimate the significance of the immediate circumstances, namely the 1905–10 Japanese protectorate period leading to outright annexation in 1910. First, such an approach would inflate the impact of two accords—the 1905 treaty installing the protectorate and the 1910 annexation treaty—as the boundaries for the takeover process. In fact, one could even argue that these did not even constitute the most important *treaties*, as those in 1904 and 1907 can be considered more consequential (see below). Such a fixation also leads to a preoccupation with the "legality" of the Japanese conquest, which, while not unimportant, is mostly moot given the larger historical forces at work. The takeover did not rely on a treaty, and it could not have been legal in any sense but the most absurdly legalistic. Finally, one must not exaggerate the rupture of 1910 by letting the annexation act as a conceptual black hole that sucks in all historical perspective. Indeed, it took another decade for the colonial regime to implant foreign rule securely. The colonial period itself subsequently developed in different ways at different times, and we must situate the colonial experience, as well as the takeover process itself, within the longer processes of modern change.

In the end, the most decisive factor was Japanese imperialism, and the series of events that led to Korea's loss of political autonomy began with the Russo-Japanese War. The rivalry between these two powers for dominance in northeast Asia had been brewing for some time, and the eruption of hostilities in early 1904 off the west coast of Korea provided the Japanese the justification for taking control of the peninsula. Without the Japanese ambition to first coerce Korea and then to control it directly, Koreans would not have lost their sovereignty—at least not to the Japanese and not at that time, and possibly not at all.

Having said this, it is imperative to maintain the centrality of Koreans in Korean history, an obvious point that often gets lost when revealing the multiple means by which a foreign power imposed its rule. Koreans not only challenged and resisted this effort, but in many ways also aided it, both willingly and not. The path leading to the loss of Korean autonomy, then, was paved by the interaction of imperialism and Korean consent. And one can further divide these factors into the "soft" and the "hard," with the latter in reference to the mechanisms of suppression that also engendered various means of resistance.

FORCE AND PUSHBACK

Until recently a historical narrative of domination and resistance prevailed in the common understanding of this period. Even with the emergence of a refreshingly more complex historical picture over the past two decades, it still bears reiterating that the loss of Korean sovereignty depended ultimately on force. The thousands of Japanese soldiers and policemen who entered the peninsula beginning with the Russo-Japanese War established the coercive framework for foreign domination, including the intimidation of Korean officials into signing cooperative treaties. The first such pact in February 1904, immediately after the outbreak of the war, allowed Japanese soldiers to be stationed on Korean soil. Later, in August, another treaty stipulated a strong role for Japanese advisors in the financial, military, and diplomatic sectors of the Korean government. This served as prelude to the protectorate treaty of November 1905, which followed a peace agreement between the warring sides, brokered by the United States, that recognized Japan's preeminent interests on the peninsula (in return, apparently, for Japanese recognition of American imperial interests in the Philippines). This notorious "1905 Treaty," signed by Korean ministers under coercion, established the Japanese protectorate government, the Residency-General. The Residency-General controlled the Korean government's foreign and financial affairs and implanted regional consulates around the country overseeing the Japanese migrant population and military presence. Ito Hirobumi, the venerable "senior official" at the center of Meiji Japan's modern transformation since the 1860s, arrived in Korea in early 1906 to serve as the first Resident-General.

At first, Ito appears not to have envisioned a complete takeover of Korea, but rather a civilizing mission that would curb Korea's potentially dangerous decay. This outlook took a dramatic turn in the summer of 1907, however, with news of the secret mission to The Hague. As a result, Emperor Gojong, who had been a thorn in the Japanese side, was forced to abdicate the throne over to his meek son, who became crowned as Korea's new emperor. A treaty to accompany this move put in place the framework for total Japanese control over the Korean government by allowing the foreigners to veto major policies and determine appointments to the highest posts. The disbandment of the Korean army quickly followed, along with the swelling of the combined Japanese–Korean military police force under Japanese control. The assassination of Ito on October 26, 1909, a few months after he stepped down as the Resident-General, appears to have accelerated the move toward outright annexation, which took place within a year thereafter. But, for all intents and purposes, the 1910 annexation merely formalized the Japanese political control over Korea that had been implemented in 1907.

An Junggeun, Ito's assassin, has long stood in Korea as the heroic representative of the combative resistance to the Japanese takeover.

An gunned down Ito in plain sight at a train station in Harbin, Manchuria, and, following a legendary interrogation in which he laid out the principles behind his actions, he was executed. Prior to this An had led some of the "righteous armies" operating throughout Korea and beyond, targeting Japanese soldiers as well as Korean collaborators—from officials and policemen down to villagers. These guerrilla groups, led by prominent elites such as the Confucian scholar Choe Ikhyeon, whose anti-foreign activism dated back to the 1860s (Chapter 13), had taken action sporadically since 1894. The disbandment of the Korean army in the summer of 1907, however, triggered an explosion in righteous army activities, as disaffected former soldiers entered the ranks. Battles raged throughout the peninsula, with one dramatic showdown taking place on the outskirts of Seoul in late 1907 involving upwards of 10,000 Korean resistors. Though they would never again be so well organized, they quickly formed the most serious obstacle to the Japanese takeover, and the full thrust of Japan's imperial might was directed at suppressing them. Pacification would not come until well after the 1910 annexation, and the bitter memories of the brutality deployed to hunt down the guerrillas would continue to fuel anti-Japanese activities indefinitely.

Notwithstanding his military deeds, An Junggeun also belonged to the wave of resistance leaders who, after 1904, had pursued their activities through education and publishing. The onset of the Russo-Japanese War and the growing awareness of Japanese designs instilled a sense of crisis that the nation's autonomy and even its future as a civilization were at stake. Sin Chaeho, who like An Junggeun would later engage in militant activities, was representative of those sounding the alarm. As a writer for a stubbornly critical newspaper during the protectorate period, the *Korea Daily News*, Sin, like many others, connected the country's imminent danger to the people's lack of nationalistic consciousness. His solution was to raise awareness of the nation's plight through the publication of works on the glories of ancient history, on the often tragic trajectory of national historical development thereafter, and on the pressing need to apply these historical lessons to asserting independence. Other historian-activists included Bak Eunsik and Hyeon Chae, who wrote long treatises on both recent and distant Korean history that sought to instill a sense of urgency. Still other educators, scholars, and journalists appealed for direct action. The most notable example was Jang Jiyeon, who penned a resounding "Lament of Wailing" in the *Hwangseong sinmun* newspaper immediately following the signing of the 1905 protectorate treaty. The newspapers and journals of the protectorate period stood often as the desperately final means, short of violence, to arouse Koreans and to appeal for international attention.

Little wonder, then, that one of the first steps taken by the new colonial government in 1910 was to shut down all unofficial newspapers and publication activities. The first decade of the colonial era, in fact, was marked by a general suppression of unauthorized activity, including in business, and became known as the period of "military rule" in reference to the heavy hand of colonial control and oppression. In addition to institutionalizing a new bureaucratic order and legitimizing the Japanese takeover, the primary aims of the colonial state were to ferret out and pacify the remaining sources of armed resistance, and to stifle any plots seeking restoration of Korean autonomy. For the latter concern, the Japanese authorities directed much of their attention and resources to mollifying the Yi royal house, for, as the secret mission to The Hague had proven in 1907, the long-standing monarch, Gojong, would not go quietly.

In the spring of that year, Gojong, unable to break out of the confines in which the Protectorate had placed him, dispatched three advisors to the Second World Peace Conference in The Hague. They met first in Saint Petersburg, where they joined up with a former Korean ambassador to the Russian Empire to plead their case for assistance to the Tsar himself. The Russian government, now more interested in allying with Japan, rebuffed them, and they proceeded to the Netherlands on their own. While they were denied a formal audience there, the three emissaries did manage to create a scene of protest, which caught the attention of the press. Indeed, according to the official proceedings of the Conference, one of the Korean delegates, Yi Wijong, pleaded simply for "a judgement on the legitimacy of the 1905 treaty." Later, at a speech he gave at the foreign press club in The Hague, he was more explicit: The Japanese have unjustly forced their way onto Korea against the wishes of the Korean people and their monarch; the 1905 treaty was signed at the point of a gun and sword, and hence is illegal according to the standards of international law; and the Korean people are determined to resist this injustice. Much of the press coverage of the Koreans came to sympathize with them, and this only furthered the resolve of the Japanese officials to take more decisive action.

THE DEFT HAND OF CONQUEST

The summer of 1907, including the forced abdication of Emperor Gojong, represented the culmination of incremental changes in the Korean government that the Japanese had promoted since 1904, the year the

Japanese military entered the peninsula to stay for good. Thereafter, the military and police, though not deployed specifically for struggles over control of government, stood as the undeniably powerful presence looming over the developments that led to the Japanese takeover. Under the cause of "reform" the Japanese Residency-General, which formally held responsibility only for Korea's diplomatic and financial affairs, pushed many of the most consequential changes. This process witnessed major amendments to the organization and manner by which the Korean government operated, all geared toward a more efficient means of mobilizing human and material resources as well as greater state control and surveillance. Notable targets of this project included the household registration, public health, penal, and legal systems, all of which included an explicitly expanded role for, and the implicit threat of, the police. The reorganization of the cabinet and, more importantly, the shift in appointment power to the Residency-General took place immediately after Gojong's abdication in 1907. Thereafter the highest posts in the central state, along with the provincial governorships and most of the county magistracies, were filled by Koreans with reliable ties to Japan.

The formal annexation of the summer of 1910, then, required few major changes to government structure or personnel. The first Governor-General, or head of the colonial Government-General of Korea, had been in fact the Protectorate's final Resident-General, Terauchi Masatake. He presided over an ambitious colonial state that more or less combined the pre-annexation Korean government and Residency-General while gradually expanding the state's regulatory and mobilizational capacities, including in the economy, education, and even religious affairs. The most consequential change to state organization might have been the creation of an agency to carry out the comprehensive colonial land survey, beginning in 1910. By the time of its conclusion in 1918, this enormous project would standardize the ownership of all plots of land and real estate, consolidate the large holdings of both public (the state) and private owners, and employ a legion of new officials, including thousands of Koreans.

The cultivation of Korean officials became perhaps the most overlooked major ingredient in the Japanese takeover. Upon annexation, the royal family and prominent elites were eased into submission through lavish monetary sums, nobility titles, and sinecures. More reliable and capable Koreans, meanwhile, were appointed to the colonial government, continuing a pattern that had begun in 1907, as noted above. The top Korean appointees after 1907, especially those to the provincial governor positions, had in fact spent most of the previous decade in Japan, having fled Korea following the collapse of the Gabo Reform government in early 1896. Their time in exile had hardened their belief that the only hope for their country lay in accepting Japanese direction, and upon their return to Korea they facilitated this effort. One did not need this formative experience in Japan to concur, however, as demonstrated repeatedly by the top Korean cabinet officials in the 1904–10 period: those who had signed the 1904 and 1905 treaties, colluded in transferring veto and appointment power to the Residency-General in 1907, and formally handed over the government and sovereignty in 1910. The central Korean figure in the latter two steps was Prime Minister Yi Wanyong, still reviled today as Korea's Benedict Arnold.

Yi Wanyong, however, represented only the tip of the collaborationist iceberg, for thousands of Koreans in all spheres of life acceded to the takeover process. Yi was actually related to Korea's royal family; he could count Emperor Gojong as a brother-in-law. While a tragic irony at one level, this was emblematic of the messy ties and blurry line between resistance and acceptance, and of the less-than-clear choices that many Koreans faced. While many prominent public figures, such as the historians and educators noted above, dedicated themselves to enlightening the people in the ways of the modern world for the cause of preserving national autonomy, others believed that saving the nation required the relinquishment of political independence. In addition to the maneuverings of Yi and other elites, there were also popular movements promoting the idea of joining the Japanese empire during this period. The most conspicuous of these groups was the *Iljinhoe*, or "Advance in Unity Society," which counted tens of thousands of members from a wide range of backgrounds, with many formerly belonging to the Donghak religion and social movement. Originally stirred into organizational activity amidst the Japanese entrance into Korea for the 1904–5 war, the Advance in Unity Society's primary goal was to agitate for a greater popular voice in government affairs, especially regarding taxation. To accomplish this, the leadership, led by a colorful figure named Song Byeongjun, embraced the annexationist cause in very public campaigns. It hence benefited from and contributed to the ongoing flowering of publishing for educational and political purposes. Although Song himself gained high office, the Advance in Unity Society ultimately failed to exert any lasting influence, even after annexation, for the very state power that it tried to curtail became the necessary instrument for implanting foreign rule.

The growth of the state facilitated the Japanese takeover, not only in enforcing a militarily supported conquest, but in penetrating Korean society sufficiently to render overwhelming force largely unnecessary. The "soft" features of the takeover, in fact, might have had a greater and more lasting impact in naturalizing foreign rule: changes to the financial and banking sectors, government investments in communications and transportation infrastructure, the construction of schools and technical training centers, and the establishment of hospitals and other mechanisms to improve health care and sanitation. To be sure, all of these measures were aimed first and foremost at easing the implementation of Japanese rule, catering to the Japanese migrants flooding the peninsula, and eventually enhancing colonial exploitation. But these steps improved the welfare of many Koreans as well, especially the already privileged. The majority of Koreans—those in the countryside—of course felt little to no change in their daily lives, and they likely sensed few compelling effects from the change in sovereignty. Many Koreans simply had little incentive to resist.

Did Koreans, then, "sell out" their country? For two large groups, this might have been the case: the thousands of elites and officials, like Yi Wanyong and Song Byeongjun, as well as other direct beneficiaries who provided legal and institutional assistance; and many, mostly lesser-known Koreans whose actions hinged not on payments but rather on implicit promises and hopes for material improvements and "enlightenment." But one could argue that many societies had to make such a Faustian bargain, often absent of considerations of national political autonomy, in coming to grips with the economic and political dislocations of the modern era. Whether in accommodation, resistance, or someplace in between, Koreans claimed a role in determining their own fate amid the maelstrom of external forces pushing upon them. They would undergo another such trial of autonomy and modernity following their liberation from Japanese rule in 1945.

17 The Long 1920s

CHRONOLOGY

1919 March	The March First independence uprisings
1919 April	Convening of the Korean Provisional Government in Shanghai
1919 Sept	Commencement of the "Cultural Rule" policy by colonial government
1920	Inaugural publication of the first two Korean newspapers of the colonial era
1921	Special exhibition of Na Hyeseok's paintings in Seoul
1925	First issue of the journal, *New Woman*
1927	Beginning of Na Hyeseok's extended visit to Europe
1929	Return of Na Hyeseok to Korea, divorce from husband

OPENING OF A SPECIAL EXHIBITION OF NA HYESEOK'S PAINTINGS, 1921

On March 18, 1921, a special exhibition of Western-style oil paintings opened in downtown Gyeongseong (Keijo), the official name of Seoul, the Korean capital, in the colonial era. It represented the first such show dedicated to the works of a single painter, but notably, the artist was a young woman in her mid-twenties, Na Hyeseok. Perhaps more remarkably, just two years earlier Na had been imprisoned for having participated in the March First Independence Movement, a mass uprising against colonial rule that brought forth bloody reprisals. Na's quick social rehabilitation and ascent to artistic distinction owed much to the rapid changes affecting Koreans at this time. Her new husband, for one, was a rising young Korean lawyer with connections to the upper echelons of colonial politics, business, and publishing. Indeed the sponsors of her exhibit were the two government newspapers of the time, one published in Japanese and the other in Korean. This exhibition thus demonstrated how the socio-economic transformation of colonial Korea facilitated the rise of groups and individuals who relied upon new opportunities and collectivities.

Na Hyeseok, in fact, proved a pioneering figure in more ways than one. She contributed vigorously to the flourishing public discourse of her times, in which she argued for greater recognition of both of her primary identities, as an artist and as a woman. Her life and work constituted a microcosm of the maturation period of colonial rule, the 1920s, that established significant societal patterns that would endure well past this decade. One could argue that the 1920s actually began in the opening months of 1919, when the independence uprisings led to the closure of the blunt 1910s and the commencement of what officially was proclaimed "Cultural Rule." Henceforth appeared a blossoming of cultural expression, associational activity, and articulations of nationhood through the reinvigorated realms of publishing and education. As the rise and equally dramatic fall of Na Hyeseok's public profile demonstrated, the transformation of Korea in the long 1920s was centered on social and economic developments that affected nearly everyone, but perhaps none more than Korean females.

THE MARCH FIRST MOVEMENT AND CULTURAL RULE

The loosening of social and political restrictions that marked the 1920s might have eventually happened regardless of the March First Movement of 1919, but certainly the uprisings spurred the colonial authorities to deploy substantial and immediate remedies. The first decade of the colonial period, that of so-called "military rule" characterized by the stifling of social activity, had suppressed the outward expression of people's discontent, but this served only to intensify the ensuing explosion. The trigger came from a confluence of three major events, one in Korea, another in Japan, and a third in Europe. In the West, 1918 was the year of reckoning of the Great War (World War I), and among the resolutions that the victorious powers advanced was to encourage self-determination among fledgling nations. The Euro-American victors meeting in Versailles had in mind, however, the peoples of Europe and did not envision the independence of overseas colonies, but this was exactly how their utterances were taken by liberation movements around the world.

Indeed, Korean students who had flocked to the Japanese metropole, especially Tokyo, in the 1910s found there not only greater educational opportunities but, ironically, also a much freer atmosphere of political expression and activity. They eventually published a Korean independence manifesto in February 1919, and soon they joined forces with like-minded students in their homeland to recruit social and cultural leaders for a mass demonstration for independence. The timing, however, would be determined by news in late February of the death of Gojong, the last autonomous monarch of pre-annexation Korea, and by the likelihood that people from throughout the colony would gather in the capital for his funeral. The drafting of the Declaration of Independence by a renowned writer, the assembling of eminent religious and social figures to serve as official representatives, and other secret planning for the demonstrations targeted March 1, two days before the funeral, as the date. On that morning, the thirty-three signers of the Declaration convened in Seoul to read aloud the document in Pagoda Park, and soon throngs of people marched down the streets shouting "Long Live Korean Independence!" This scene was soon repeated throughout Korea, and the scale and ferocity of the demonstrations stunned the authorities.

This undoubtedly accounted for the senselessly ruthless countermeasures by the colonial police and military police forces, with the cycle of suppression and resistance escalating into atrocities that included random shootings, massacres, and burnings of churches and entire villages. Perhaps the best-known victim of these reprisals, and hence also the most renowned female of this era in the nationalist annals, was Yu Gwansun. Yu was attending the famed Methodist girls' school in Seoul, Ewha, when March First broke out, but quickly went down to her home town in Chungcheong province to rally the locals for the cause. She was captured, brutalized, and eventually killed in prison, one of countless activists who became martyred. Even the colonial government's tallies totaled more than five hundred deaths and thousands of injuries over the course of the spring, with unofficial counts claiming exponentially larger numbers. Pacification would eventually come in the summer, but by then, much had changed.

One thing that did not change was Korea's colonial status, for the March First Independence Movement ultimately failed to achieve its primary goal of attaining liberation from Japanese rule. But the significance of March First, judged by its effects both internally and externally, was still enormous. Outside the country, representatives of disparate independence movements, military and otherwise, gathered in Shanghai in April that year to organize a government in exile. This effort soon faltered due to ideological and other divisions among the activists, but the liberation movements continued throughout the colonial period, if along divergent tracks. Within the peninsula, meanwhile, the March First Movement elicited a sweeping reevaluation of colonial rule on the part of the Japanese rulers. They were not ready to grant Koreans autonomy, of course, but they realized that harsh enforcement was counterproductive.

Hence, the new Governor-General, Saito Makoto, instituted a comprehensive reform program combining a discreet strengthening of bureaucratic and police forces with an outwardly more benign governing approach that allowed Koreans to pursue social, economic, and cultural activities more freely. This so-called "Cultural Rule," then, constituted a policy of co-opting Koreans into the colonial system by allowing them a greater stake in its development.

The scale and scope of the changes that followed were extensive. Press restrictions were lifted, and the two oldest Korean newspapers still circulating today, the *Donga Ilbo* and *Joseon Ilbo*, began publishing in 1920. In the economy, the state's growing exploitation of the colony's natural resources, particularly through an increase in agricultural output, consigned more Koreans to life as struggling tenant farmers, but it also provided greater commercial opportunities. Furthermore, the Government-General's easing of restrictions on native enterprise stimulated the formation of many more Korean companies, including those businesses that would later turn into the giant conglomerates dominating the South Korean economy, such as Samsung and LG. The most formidable and conspicuous of such family-owned enterprises, the Gyeongseong Textile Company, eventually expanded into various industries and even different regions, as it built factories and branches in Manchuria and elsewhere. The colonial state's extension of communication and transportation networks, meanwhile, spurred further urbanization and the concentration of wealth, development, and influence in these growing population centers. The accelerating migration out of the rural areas and the ensuing dissolution of traditional ties, both familial and otherwise, would have far-reaching social ramifications. Most striking of all, perhaps, the loosening of government restrictions led to a boom in organizational activity among Koreans, who joined thousands of clubs, associations, and other groups catering to countless interests and social identities.

These developments, together with the incorporation of legions of Koreans into the colonial state, also engendered a dramatic rise in social mobility. A fundamental transformation and even overturning of Korean social hierarchy had begun in the late nineteenth century, but the colonial circumstances intensified these trends, particularly in urban centers. In these areas, the Korean social structure looked very different from that of a few decades earlier, as the diversification of the economy and occupations, together with legal reforms, further minimized the impact of hereditary status. Descendants of previously despised groups such as butchers and shamans organized campaigns to gain greater acceptance, and many from secondary status backgrounds of the Joseon era ascended to the highest levels of the new social elite.

KOREAN FEMALES IN THE NEW AGE

The most dramatic impact of urbanization, early industrialization, associational activity, and greater educational opportunities in the 1920s might have been experienced by women. From *gisaeng* courtesans and peasants in the countryside to the housewives, wage workers, and "New Women" in the cities, females began to reshape the social landscape in unprecedented ways. In both environments, they found room to explore careers and claim a greater role in determining their own lives. This marked the beginnings of a female subjectivity that, through its growth in fits and starts the rest of the twentieth century, would leave a major imprint on the development of modern gender roles.

The most distinctive type of woman in the 1920s went by the terms "New Woman" or "Modern Girl," a phenomenon visible in contemporary China and Japan as well. Concentrated in Seoul, these females shared a background of having been educated in the major cities (though often they had moved from the countryside), a strong consumerist orientation, and family connections to the new social elite, often through marriage to urban professionals. The New Woman appeared frequently in the contemporary literature, often portrayed—and not always flatteringly—in clear contrast to the more traditional women still constituting the overwhelming majority, which symbolized the choices and dilemmas of the modern world. They also appeared in articles, notices, and advertisements in the burgeoning publishing sector targeting their bourgeois lifestyles, with publications like women's magazines dishing out knowledge and advice on everything from fashion to hygiene. Most of the readers were either students or graduates of the growing number of girls' secondary schools in the urban centers, and some could point to an experience of schooling abroad, especially in Japan, as the source of their worldly perspectives and tastes.

Urban, educated women appeared not only as emblems and consumers of the publishing world, but also as producers. Female authors, translators, essayists, and critics contributed to the construction of a distinctively modern Korean literary culture, the most formative period for which was the 1920s. New magazines and literary journals, such as *New Woman* (*Sin Yeoseong*), catered to women's interests and provided a forum for female writers. Na Hyeseok, though known better for her paintings and essays, also expressed her ideals of female emancipation through poetry and short stories, the earliest of which was published in 1918. Renowned female contemporaries included Gim Iryeop, who founded in 1920 Korea's first women's journal; Gim Myeongsun, whose novels explored the depths of female subjectivity; and later in the 1930s, Gang Gyeongae, a realist author whose works depicted the plight of Korea's underclass.

Korean women made their mark in other cultural realms as well. City dwellers eventually came to know of Yun Simdeok, for example, the great singer whose concerts became lavish spectacles, and of Choe Seunghui, the dancer who mesmerized audiences throughout the world before working as a propagandist for Japan's war effort in the 1940s. Na Hyeseok was the third figure in this famed Korean triumvirate of female artists of the colonial period. Having demonstrated her precociousness as a schoolgirl from a progressive family near Seoul, she went to Japan in her late teens to enroll in a girls' art school. She returned to her homeland just in time to get caught up in the 1919 March First Movement, which derailed her goals, however briefly. After getting married under the condition—unheard of at the time—that she be allowed to pursue her profession as an artist, Na further developed her career by displaying her works in public arenas, including the solo exhibition of her works in 1921. Motherhood and a brief move to Manchuria to follow her husband, who had become a diplomat in the Japanese empire, curbed her artistic ambitions somewhat. By the late 1920s, however, Na was on the move again, this time with her husband on a whirlwind tour through Europe, where in Paris she trained further in oil painting. She also became involved in a scandalous affair with a well-known and much older Korean nationalist figure, and within a year after her return to Korea in 1929, her husband divorced her, and she lost custody of her children. Although she experienced a few successes as a professional painter thereafter, her artistic career eventually suffered from her very public divorce and a lack of popular interest in her work. Thereafter she lived in obscurity, much of it at a Buddhist temple, until her death in 1946.

The relatively small number of Na Hyeseok's paintings that can be considered reliably authentic show indeed an accomplished craftsman deserving of status as one of the major Korean painters of her era, regardless of gender. But Na Hyeseok's historical significance stems more from her opinions as a social commentator and chronicler, and from her actions. Even in her student days in Japan she had expressed reservations about the prevailing "wise mother, good wife" ideal and insisted that females shape their lives in accordance with reason and self-confidence. In a 1921 newspaper editorial entitled "Painting and Korean Women," which provided a prelude to the opening of her solo exhibition, she deplored the social biases that prevented Korean women from developing an interest and talent in painting. This stood in contrast to the visibility of female poets and writers, she noted.

In her later writings, she expressed views that would have been considered radical even a half-century later. In a long magazine essay entitled "Thoughts on Becoming a Mother," published in 1923, Na shredded the niceties of the maternal ideal and asserted that her experiences contradicted everything she had been taught. She wrote of the difficulties of pregnancy, childbirth, and child rearing, and of the resentments she built up against society, her husband, and even her baby for impinging on her personal ambitions and freedoms. There must be a conspiratorial character to the social conventions that divided men and women into their respective roles, she wondered. Upon her return from Europe, she openly praised the model of gender relations that she had observed in the West and even speculated that cohabitation before marriage, or a "test marriage," could allow women to become better informed before taking the plunge. After the failure of her own marriage, in writings such as "A Divorce Confession," she called for the liberation of women's sexuality, lamented the social and familial conventions that constrained females, and condemned the hypocrisy of typical Korean males regarding chastity. She even put into practice her calls for female empowerment by suing Choe Rin, the nationalist activist with whom she had become involved in Paris, for "infringement on a woman's honor." She accused Choe, in other words, of abandoning her despite his role in the events that led to Na's public disgrace and divorce, and she demanded restitution. These actions failed to rehabilitate her artistic career or social standing, but Na Hyeseok demonstrated that Korean women could aspire to new levels of assertiveness, even if society as a whole remained mostly unaccommodating.

A group of women who embodied these continuing social constraints were the thousands of young factory workers who "manned" much of the burgeoning manufacturing sector, in industries ranging from textiles to food processing. From having been nearly absent in modern enterprises at the turn of the century, women accounted for a fifth of the factory work force in the early 1920s and a third by the mid-1930s. Both the pull factors of regular wages and city life as well as the push factor of rural immiseration brought these girls, caught between puberty and marriage, into the factories. Their lives, however, were in many ways Dickensian, as they were herded into tight and strenuous working conditions and paid paltry wages. And despite the allure of the big city, they could enjoy at most one day a week off, and usually they spent this day in their cramped dormitories recuperating from their 12-hour shifts. Furthermore, these jobs presented only meager opportunities for schooling, given the incessant work demands, and even for consumption, since whatever they earned in wages was usually sent directly to their families back home. The lives of these factory girls, then, fell far short of the glamorous existence of the "Modern Girl" lore. But their experiences offered them at least the foundation, however limited, of self-determination through work and training.

This phenomenon also affected the agricultural sector, though of course with differences in the scope and character of the changes. While most young women engaged in household or field work, new social forces, including private organizations and the colonial state itself, gradually made possible other opportunities—including, for a fortunate few, schooling. And here, too, women often stood at the forefront of generating the very changes affecting them as a group. An example comes from Choe Yongsin, an educator whose life and activities were dramatized in a famous novel of the 1930s. After having attended a girls' high school in the 1920s, Choe entered a women's seminary and thereafter used her newfound connections, in particular to the Korean YMCA, to engage in work to eradicate illiteracy and provide basic schooling to children in the countryside. Her close connection to church-sponsored activities hence exemplified the major role of religion, particularly Protestantism, in bestowing opportunity for rural women. Choe was one of numerous Christian women who served as translators for foreign missionaries, as liaisons for religious educators, and as pastoral deputies dealing with people, especially females, who could not be easily approached by ministers or doctors. In turn, these women used such experiences as stepping stones to higher callings, whether in religious or other kinds of work, and regardless of their social background.

RELIGION AND SOCIAL CHANGE

The connection between Protestant activities and new opportunities for Korean females bespeaks the larger issue of the relationship between religion and social change in the early twentieth century. This in turn compels us to consider one of the great historical questions about modern Korea, namely, how Christianity found such uncommon success compared to its fate in other non-Western countries. And while Catholicism, as well as Buddhism, also witnessed dramatic growth, the development of Protestantism is most notable. Foreign Protestant missionaries began their activities in the 1880s, having entered the country as attachments to the increasing diplomatic, educational, medical, and commercial presence of mainly North Americans. Through their resourcefulness in employing the Korean alphabet, provision of biomedical procedures and technologies, implicit promises of social liberation, explicit promises of salvation in the afterlife, and generally an unshakable aura of advancement, the missionaries found great success. They counted among their converts many of the most prominent Koreans in the early twentieth century, whose work soon overtook that of missionaries in expanding the religion's larger profile and in domesticating the church into something distinctively Korean. But the original North American connection proved just as important, both in broadening the religion's social impact and in shaping its core, conservative theological orientation. How colonial rule contributed to these developments, and how they in turn connected to the emergence of modern nationalism, as well as to modern ideological and geographical divisions, remain fruitful topics of historical inquiry and historical contention.

An early peak in Protestant growth had been reached in 1907 through the Great Pyongyang Revival, a gathering of thousands in what quickly became the center of Korean Christianity, the northwestern region surrounding the city of Pyongyang. In the colonial period Pyongyang came to be known as the "Jerusalem of the East," a designation pointing to its centrality in Korean Protestantism, but also to the incorporation of this faith in the city's self-identity as a beacon of freedom amid the darkness of foreign rule. Due to efforts by the colonial state to curb Westerners' influence in education, religion, and medicine, Protestantism as a whole became identified with resistance to Japanese domination. Indeed many prominent nationalists and independence activists, including sixteen out of the thirty-three signers of the March First Declaration of Independence, pointed to their Protestant faith as inspiring their work. Perhaps most noteworthy in this regard was An Changho, from Pyongyang, who began as a Christian educator and activist in the first decade of the twentieth century, and soon became one of the first Korean immigrants to the United States. Traveling to and from his home in southern California, which served as a base for the early Korean American community, An organized and inspired efforts to achieve Korean independence throughout this period. His life and thought exemplified the role of both religion and nationalism as havens of collective identity away from the colonial system, and in turn as further examples of the forces of social change that marked the long 1920s.

18 Nation, Culture, and Everyday Life in the Late Colonial Period

CHRONOLOGY

1925	Founding of the Korean Communist Party and KAPF
1931	Literacy campaigns for the countryside led by Korean newspapers
1931 Sept.	Manchurian Incident and invasion of Manchuria by imperial Japan
1932	Establishment of the Japanese puppet state of Manchukuo
1936 August	Olympic marathon victory by Son Gijeong; defacement of Japanese flag on newspaper picture of Son

THE DOCTORING OF A NEWSPAPER PHOTO OF THE OLYMPIC MARATHON CHAMPION, 1936

The first evening edition of the August 25, 1936 issue of the Korean language newspaper, *Donga Ilbo*, had cleared the colonial censors. But just as the authorities had feared, a second evening edition quickly published thereafter caused a stir. On its front page was emblazoned the picture of national hero Son Gijeong, who two weeks earlier had captured the gold medal in the marathon in the 1936 Berlin Olympics. The cause for alarm was not that Son himself, pictured solemnly on the medal stand, was prominently featured, but rather that the Japanese flag on Son's uniform had been rubbed out, leaving a black smudge in its place (see Image 18). Unbeknownst to their own editors and managers, a group of journalists had pulled off the stunt in a fit of emotion comprised of both pride and shame—pride that a Korean had reached a pinnacle of world sport, and shame that he had been forced to don a foreign conqueror's flag. Not surprisingly, the ringleaders were fired, blacklisted, even jailed, and the newspaper was shut down for almost a year.

Image 18 *Son Gijeong's photo,* Donga Ilbo *newspaper, Tuesday, August 25, 1936*

This episode surrounding the picture of Son Gijeong—or "Son Kitei," the Japanese pronunciation of his name by which he was officially known outside the peninsula—is commonly viewed as an act of nationalist defiance. This is undoubtedly true, but the event also presents a window into the overarching patterns of daily life in the late colonial period, in which recurring exposure to each other's lives through mass culture strengthened a sense of commonality. The newspaper, in fact, played the central role in circulating these observations, impressions, and ideas. This prodded Koreans to contemplate and reconsider their collective identity, through both an active engagement with pressing issues of nationhood and the more pedestrian pursuit of their lives.

EXPRESSION, WITHIN LIMITS

The brazen effacement of the Japanese flag on the picture of Son Gijeong, in fact, epitomized the cat-and-mouse game Korean publications played with state censors. The colonial regime itself had unleashed the expressive energies of the Korean people through the "Cultural Rule" policy launched with great fanfare in the 1920s (Chapter 17). By the 1930s, the Korean language print media fully functioned as the authoritative forum for discussing a range of issues concerning life in colonial Korea. The often heated opinions at times went so far as to condemn government policies and behaviors, wonder about the validity of foreign rule, and even promote specific steps toward independence. A full spectrum of ideologies found voice in these pages, although many offending passages were excised by the authorities before reaching the reader. The consequences for crossing the line—explicit calls for immediate liberation, for example, or criticisms of the Japanese monarchy—often were severe, including incarceration, but this was not a totalitarian system, at least not until the wartime mobilization of the 1940s (Chapter 19); Koreans, including those in the publishing world, were not brutalized for thought crimes.

After having nipped in the bud potentially disruptive social movements throughout the 1920s, in the 1930s the colonial state dealt with a more fully developed realm of public discourse and interaction. As for Korean publishers, the challenges of straddling the fine line between the overlooked and the forbidden reached another level following the Manchurian Incident of September 1931 and the establishment of the puppet state of Manchukuo a year later. Ironically, Korean newspapers served unwittingly as propagandistic conduits for the Japanese invasion of the Asian mainland, as reports on the Manchurian Incident, the imperial army's exploits, and Korean settler communities in Manchuria fed a growing competition for readership. But Korean newspapers in the late colonial period could also fuel anti-Japanese sentiment by covering, for example, the exploits of the Korean guerrilla groups operating in Manchuria.

Korean newspapers, though sometimes criticized by contemporaries as well as by later historians for a preoccupation with commercial gain, also displayed a Confucian sense of paternalism. They led public campaigns on behalf of Korean commercial products, for example, and pursued efforts to curb illiteracy and expand educational opportunities among the overwhelming majority of Koreans still living in the countryside. They sent educated youth to the provinces to operate and teach in village schools on subjects ranging from hygiene to history, and of course to propagate the use of the Korean alphabet. One could suggest that this, too, was more commercially driven—that the newspapers were simply looking to expand their readerships—than by any sense of social responsibility. Indeed press reports and editorials often did the bidding of the government through their coverage of state projects in schooling or public health, or of the Government-General's own efforts at rural welfare, such as agricultural cooperatives for water, fertilizer, and credit. But just as often, the authorities harassed these publications for publicly criticizing, through editorials or investigations, discriminatory government policies or practices and for thereby inciting nationalism.

More importantly, the Korean-language print media promoted both themselves and national interests by serving as the expressive outlets for the most important intellectuals and writers of the time, who established in these pages the foundation for modern Korean literature and thought. Rarely did a full-length novel, for example, become released outside the well-established mode of serialization in newspapers or magazines. The publications, in particular the monthly journals whose circulation sometimes outpaced that of the newspapers, also printed the reflections of philosophers and social commentators, the latest findings of scholars, and the work of budding poets. In turn, consumers of the popular press in the late colonial period formed the first mass reading public in Korean history, and publishers grew influential as purveyors of information, insight, and opinion.

THE QUOTIDIAN BLOSSOMING OF MODERN CULTURE

In reality, the novels and short stories found in the print media represented only a fraction of the totality of cultural production in the late colonial period that amounted to the formation of modern Korean culture itself. Indeed, the very notion of a Korean culture to be explored and appreciated as a distinctive, self-enclosed civilizational entity reached full bloom in this era. That this feat was achieved when Koreans did not possess political autonomy constitutes a great irony, but this was not unusual. Colonized or subject peoples throughout world history, if they could evade extinction itself, often forged a keener, sharper group identity. In the early modern era, this dynamic resulted in the creation of wholly new nationalities or, as in the case of India (and Korea), a rejuvenated sense of collectivity replenished by cultural enterprises now definitively identified with the nation.

In Korea, this project of constructing modern culture, through the combination of cultural production and systematic reevaluation of older cultural products, had begun at the turn of the century, but it was not until the late colonial period that a critical mass of achievements appeared. The colonial regime, while remaining on the lookout for explicit calls for independence, not only allowed these activities but actually promoted them, at least until the wartime period. Japanese officials believed, perhaps naively, that such efforts would act as safe outlets for frustrations on the political front and even result in a reinforcement of the civilizational bonds between Japan and Korea. Regardless, Korean intellectuals began to engage intensively in research that they labeled "Korean studies" (*Joseonhak*). Korean historical scholarship, helped in part by large-scale projects sponsored by the government, reached new levels of depth and sophistication, at times even challenging official views. Some scholars, such as Choe Namseon and Yi Neunghwa, incorporated their study of Korea's religious history into grand theories of their country's place in Asian civilization. Still others took on the task of systematizing and standardizing the Korean written vernacular, which had enjoyed increasingly widespread use since the turn of the century but still lacked usage standards. The Korean Language Society, composed of linguists and other leading researchers, took to fixing this problem by promulgating grammar and spelling rules and compiling an authoritative dictionary.

Also helping to spread the vernacular was the lyric poetry of this era, which expanded the expressive potential of the Korean language. This was shown by the three most renowned poets of the first half of the twentieth century: Gim Soweol, Han Yongun, and Jeong Jiyong. Gim's best-known poem, "Azaleas"—indeed the most famous poem of the modern era—taps into the powerfully recurring theme in Korean folklore of sorrowful parting and unrequited love. This theme appeared in everything from the "Tale of Chunhyang" to the semi-official national folk song of "Arirang," as well as in hit songs of the colonial period such as "Duman River, Full of Tears." It is also central to the title poem of Han Yongun's great collection of lyrics, *Silence of the Beloved*. While a passionate nationalist and Buddhist reformer in his activities as educator and essayist, in his verse Han couched his concerns about the contemporary condition in allegories of love, lament, and reconciliation. Jeong Jiyong, a Catholic and perhaps the most noteworthy stylist, painted serenely evocative images of nature and rustic life with breathtaking fluency. That Jeong, who worked as a secondary school English teacher, could consistently unveil his work in published journals, including those he helped to edit, testified to the flourishing literary realm of the late colonial period.

Other forms of popular culture, meanwhile, were also facilitated by advances in transportation and communication technologies, which shortened geographical and temporal distances, and by commercial developments that drove consumerism, especially in the cities. There, theatrical performances featured both foreign and native works, as well as creative stagings of traditional folk tales. And not surprisingly, retellings of famous Korean stories became embraced by the early Korean cinema as well, the first "talkie" of which appeared in 1935. And in music a star system of singers emerged in the 1930s, with their biggest hits becoming iconic works that remain cherished today, thanks in part to the proliferation of phonographs among the upper and middle classes. But it was the advent of the radio that was most responsible for the widespread dissemination of popular music and storytelling in the late colonial period. Radio supplied people with news and education as well as art and entertainment, infusing the growing listening public with a new sense of connection to each other and to the world at large.

Indeed the radio, specifically the regular live reports from Berlin, helped spur Koreans' interest in Son Gijeong's great Olympic quest. When the day of the marathon came, Koreans huddled around their radios in the late hours of Sunday, August 9, 1936. Immediately following an update around midnight that Son had joined the lead pack about a third of the way into the race, however, the broadcast, in accordance with its regular schedule, cut off the coverage from Berlin. While the rest of the country had to wait until the next morning for the results, a group of people gathering just outside the *Donga Ilbo* headquarters received updates from a newspaper employee who had managed to establish telephone contact with Tokyo and Berlin. They were the first to know when, around 2am, came finally the joyous announcement that, indeed, Son Gijeong had won the Olympic marathon, and moreover, that another Korean, Nam Seungnyong, had taken the bronze medal. The following day the country erupted in celebration, and the *Donga Ilbo* newspaper's front page struck an unabashedly nationalist tone, blaring over-the-top headlines of "Hail the Global Triumph!" and "The Greatest Victory in All of Humanity!" The giddiness over this happy occasion would linger, even inspiring, two weeks later, the reporters at the *Donga Ilbo* to alter Son's photo.

The journalists behind this act presented an extreme example of the double duty that Korean reporters often pursued in the colonial period—as eyewitnesses and chroniclers on the one hand, and as activists, opinion makers, and authors on the other. In fact, a great number of colonial period fiction writers also had worked at one time as newspaper reporters. The line between observer and storyteller tended to blur, along with that between popular and high culture, through this connection and the serialization of novels in periodicals. Furthermore, the themes explored by these literary works mostly focused on the here and now, and on daily events—as if, indeed, they were elaborations of newspaper reports. The first great concentration of canonical works in modern Korean literature emerged in the late colonial period and was suffused with the details of the everyday, from the tedious to the tragic.

Many of the most notable authors of novels and short stories, in fact, won their renown through portrayals of daily, often mundane life in late colonial Korea. Chae Mansik, known primarily for his masterpiece, the novel *Peace Under Heaven*, used his stories to satirize, critique, and observe bemusedly the often dumbfounding dynamics of modern existence. His short story, "A Ready Made Life," for example, depicts the legions of "petit bourgeois intellectuals" who, armed with an education and high tastes but no practical skills, drift about contemporary Seoul in search of jobs and a greater purpose in their lives. The lead character, one such "ready made life," rescues himself from his absurd destitution and desperation by returning to simple, indeed traditional, priorities. Another important chronicler of life in Seoul was Bak Taewon, author of innovative narratives that at times dispensed with literary conventions, such as plot, for the sake of chronicling the pedestrian. "A Day in the Life of the Novelist Gubo" (serialized in 1934), for example, is an autobiographical stroll ("Gubo" was Bak's pen name) through Seoul relayed through streams of consciousness and snippets of observations, in a narrative style that often changes tenses and narrator in the same paragraph. Scenes of the rapidly modernizing capital city attract the attention of Gubo, who notes the goings on in theaters, restaurants, coffee houses, and that great symbol of high-class urban leisure at the time, the department store. What he finds in the teeming metropolis, however, often leads to alienation and disenchantment. In the splendid Seoul train station, for example, he senses only a throng of lonely individuals: "Although the place is so packed with people that Gubo can't even find a seat to squeeze into, there's no human warmth. Without exchanging a word with those sitting next to them, these people are preoccupied with their own business, and should they happen to say anything to each other, it's only to check the train schedule or something along those lines." While the quick pace and social impact of changes in the urban landscape are enough to devote an entire novella to the impressions of a curious observer, the novelties of modern life are not necessarily celebrated. Indeed, the effects are often lamented and feared.

Realist depictions of the underbelly of modern life and of the sad, sometimes harsh struggles of common people had appeared earlier, most notably in the works of Hyeon Jingeon in the early 1920s. But the late colonial period witnessed an intensified politicization of literature through an explicit engagement with pressing sociopolitical issues. This trend was exemplified by KAPF, the Korean Artists Proletarian Federation, an organization founded in 1925 to rally authors toward the theme of class consciousness and the finer points of Marxism and historical materialism. KAPF also reflected larger social trends toward leftist activism, as seen in anti-Japanese anarchist activity beginning in the 1920s, the founding of the Korean Communist Party in 1925, the attempt to unify nationalist movements under socialist leadership in the late 1920s, and the agitation of factory labor movements and peasant unions well into the 1930s. Revolutionary leftist influence extended to the realms of social criticism, theater, cinema, music, and the fine arts, but had perhaps the most palpable impact on literature. The representative KAPF writer was Yi Giyeong. After publishing several harrowing depictions of struggling peasants in his short stories, Yi unveiled his great novel, *Hometown*, through serialization in the *Joseon Ilbo* newspaper from 1933 to 1934. *Hometown* chronicles the attempts by a colorful cast of villagers—in effect, Korea's proletariat, given the relatively underdeveloped factory labor force—to adjust to the exploitative forces of early capitalism. It employs the ready tropes of proletarian literature, such as the heroic socialist intellectual in the role of the vanguard, but the success of this novel owed much to the compellingly lifelike characters and a grippingly melodramatic story that transcended conventions. Indeed, the work of KAPF writers moved even Korean authors who were not members, or even leftist in inclination, to infuse their works with a greater social consciousness and attention to the people's daily travails.

Whether through such literary works or via the new media of radio, phonographs, or cinema, culture in the late colonial period revealed to Koreans the countlessly variegated manifestations of each other's lives. Cultural production gave meaning, then, to the dizzying onset of industrial change—the explosive proliferation of occupations and economic activities; the appearance of big machines, vehicles, buildings, and cities; and advances in transportation and communications, including especially the newspaper—that rendered contact with a greater world a recurring reality. By instilling a sense of collective plight and subjectivity, both as Koreans and as modern people, the revelation of larger society and the experience of daily life aroused a sense of transformation, modernity, and nationhood much more solidly than could calls to political action.

Even the occasional bursts of nationalist ardor served more as exceptions that reinforced the more powerful effects of the churning quotidian.

Contrary to the standard historical emphasis on nationalist resistance, then, the greater significance of the Son Gijeong photo incident lies in its illuminating the centrality of newspapers and other media in the regular unfolding of a new era. By providing a lens into the everyday, popular culture, mass entertainment and publishing both transmitted and reflected the modern experience. To be sure, debates about the propriety of colonial rule, ardent calls for independence, and enticing visions of a better, autonomous future continued to spark passions. To the large majority of Koreans, however, life in the late colonial period remained firmly wedded to the here and now. Even to those who could afford to dwell on the grander issues, it was an open-ended time, and anything seemed possible. That soothing ambiguity would come to a screeching halt, however, once the colony became mobilized for war.

19 Wartime Mobilization, 1938–45

CHRONOLOGY

1935	Official order for school children and public employees to bow to the Japanese emperor
1937	Eruption of the (Second) Sino-Japanese War
1938	Proclamation of wartime mobilization measures
1940	Shutdown of major Korean language newspapers
1940	Order to register Japanese surnames; organization of neighborhood patriotic associations
1942	Expulsion of Western missionaries
1945	Defeat of the Japanese empire in the Pacific War

THE VISIT BY AUTHORS YI GWANGSU AND CHOE NAMSEON TO JAPAN, 1943

Two of the foremost Korean intellectuals of the colonial period, Choe Namseon and Yi Gwangsu, made a discreet visit to Meiji University in Tokyo on November 24, 1943. At the height of the "Greater East Asia Holy War," the pair had come to assist the mobilization of manpower by urging Koreans studying in Japan to enlist as student soldiers. Afterward, the two writers gathered in a roundtable discussion to assess the motives, meaning, and reception of their message. They also recounted their own experiences as students in Japan forty years earlier. Their lives thereafter had traversed the entirety of the period under Japanese domination, during which they won recognition as among the most pioneering and influential figures in Korean letters. That they found themselves in old age promoting the dissolution of Korean identity itself constitutes a profound if not tragic irony, as well as a microcosm of the final years of colonial rule as Koreans became swept up by war.

Wartime mobilization exposed Koreans to the most devastating conflict in human history, brutalized them through sexual slavery and forced labor, and stripped them of basic features of their ethnic identity, including even their names and language. Just as significantly, these concluding years of Japanese rule came to dominate the perception of the colonial period as a whole, producing a bitterness and distrust among Koreans that would haunt their subsequent history. For despite the hardships and excesses of the war years, there remained a substantial minority of Koreans who took up the Japanese cause. Their numbers, in fact, likely were far larger than those of the celebrated independence fighters, working mostly from outside the peninsula, whose impact proved greater in shaping Korea *after* the liberation of 1945 than in bringing it about. As with Yi Gwangsu and Choe Namseon, the actions of these "collaborators" during wartime mobilization have continually challenged attempts to arrive at a reckoning of Korea's colonial experience.

INDUSTRIALIZATION AND STATE DOMINATION

Every society immersed in a modern war has faced the ferocity of mass mobilization. But while the litany of abuses can readily be dramatized as unrelenting horror, for Koreans the impact was uneven in its severity, depending on class, geography, and, terribly for many women, gender. And while the difficulties came in many forms and touched every facet of Koreans' lives, they mostly resulted from the intensification of two phenomena that had been growing for a few decades.

Manchuria as a cauldron of modern Korea

The formative years of the two dominant Korean political figures of the second half of the twentieth century, Kim Il Sung (Gim Ilseong) and Park Chung Hee (Bak Jeonghui), took place in Manchuria during the last decade of the colonial period. Kim Il Sung (b. 1912), who went on to rule North Korea for half a century, grew up mostly in Manchuria and eventually led the most successful of several anti-Japanese communist guerrilla groups operating under the command of their Chinese counterparts. On the opposing side, Park Chung Hee (b. 1917), long-time president of South Korea, came of age as one of a select number of young Koreans who gained training at a Japanese military academy in Manchuria. Though they both later exploited nationalist sentiment to bolster their respective rules, which in turn relied heavily on human networks forged in Manchuria, this strong contrast in their experiences as young men in Manchuria decisively shaped their respective destinies, and in turn those of their states. In fact, throughout the first half of the twentieth century, Manchuria, both before and after the establishment of the Japanese puppet state of Manchukuo in the early 1930s, served as Korea's great frontier, the place to which Koreans could escape to forge a new life. In turn the forms of communal existence established there appear to have influenced significantly the social and political patterns back home.

Manchuria's pivotal role in Korean history was not a modern novelty, however. Since the ancient beginnings of state formation in northeast Asia, the peoples of Manchuria had supplied an impression of the (uncivilized) "other" against whom Koreans conceived their own ethnic or national identity. As late as the seventeenth century, after the Manchus had subdued the Joseon dynasty on their way to conquering China itself, Manchuria continued to compel Koreans to sharpen their sense of self. The name for certain Manchurian tribesmen, *Orangkae*, in fact became synonymous with a common derogatory reference to the people to the north—whether Malgal, Khitan, Jurchen, Mongol, or Manchu—and turned into the default Korean term for "barbarian." This tendency also reflected the consciousness of a mythical era when Koreans were said to have ruled this territory, and in turn the likelihood that Koreans, deep in their collective psyche, understood that they and these "barbarians" might have common origins. Japanese colonial rulers also promoted this idea by integrating their two conquered territories of Korea and Manchuria into a single extension of the Japanese homeland, claiming that this reconstructed an ancient civilizational bond. Whether in spurring resistance to (Kim) or embrace of (Park) this process during the late colonial period, Manchuria's function as the cultivator of Korean leaders, and as an experimental cauldron of Korea's modern existence more generally, continued its long historical role of shaping Korean identity.

First was industrialization, which began sporadically in the early years of the twentieth century, received a kick-start in the 1920s, and revved up considerably in the 1930s following Korea's transformation into a base for Japanese expansion into the Asian mainland. The ensuing industrial and infrastructural development stimulated a cycle of commercial growth, occupational diversification, and urbanization. The mass movement of people extended beyond the peninsula as well, as peasants escaping rural poverty followed work opportunities to Japan and Manchuria, a semi-colony of Japan since the installment of the puppet state of Manchukuo in 1932. Such trends accelerated greatly following Japan's invasion of China in 1937 and the formal proclamations of wartime mobilization measures in 1938. The established sectors of early industrialization, such as textiles and food processing, were joined by the rapid growth of heavy industries catering to war: armaments, chemicals, machinery, and minerals such as oil and gas. Factories churning out these products were concentrated in special corridors along the west-central and northeastern coasts, and the numbers of Korean factory workers and managers increased exponentially in line with the equally enormous rise in industrial production. By the closing year of the war in 1945, industry accounted for nearly 40 percent of the total economic output in Korea, which a decade earlier had still been overwhelmingly agrarian.

This remarkable expansion was not designed to improve the lot of the Korean people themselves, of course. The deprivations of war mobilization were made worse by the colonial state's overbearing efforts to intensify not only the economic but also the "spiritual" fortitude of its subject people. The colonial state, in short, instituted a relentless drive toward *total war*. This in turn reflected the state's development into an entity that actually surpassed industrial growth as a structural force in the wartime years. In channeling the entire socio-political order toward supporting the war, for example, the colonial state forcefully blunted organized worker actions, even in the rural areas, where strikes by peasant unions had become increasingly vociferous. The searing trials of both urban and rural laborers in their struggles against landlords, factory owners, and the state would contribute greatly to the creation of a proletariat in the concluding years of colonial rule.

People felt the state's reach also in the radical assimilation policies of the wartime years. Colonial authorities had always mouthed assimilation as an overarching ideal and indeed had explicitly stated this as a goal for annexation in the first place. But the irreconcilable reality of ongoing legal discrimination in the colonial system—from bureaucratic recruitment and compensation to segregation in educational and business opportunities—had marginalized this objective. Beginning in the latter 1930s, however, as war loomed in the air, the colonial state began to institute measures to coerce an identification with the Japanese nation and polity—to turn Koreans into "imperial subjects"—that veered toward totalitarianism. In 1935 came a government order for Korean schoolchildren and public employees to begin their day with a ritual bow toward the east in honor of the Japanese emperor, soon followed by orders for everyone to make visits to Japanese religious shrines. These steps invited fervent resistance especially from certain Korean Christian groups, sparking a struggle that would end with the expulsion of all Western missionaries from the peninsula in 1942. The authorities also began to prohibit children from speaking Korean in school. The two major Korean language newspapers were shut down in 1940, a year before Japan escalated its conflict against China into a Pacific War that embroiled the United States. And as if to put a final stamp on the drive to suppress a separate Korean identity, in late 1940 came the ordinance requiring all Koreans to register Japanese-style surnames. The authorities instituted this measure, which was part of a revamping of the household registration system, mostly to streamline surveillance and mobilization. Many Koreans, furthermore, fiercely opposed or simply disregarded this directive. But soon it became clear that, for those whose livelihoods depended on the colonial system—professionals, for example—taking a Japanese name was unavoidable. The harrowing tales of honorable Koreans forced to dishonor their ancestry by registering new names tend to exaggerate the ultimate impact of this measure, but undoubtedly it symbolized well the broader forced assimilation campaign, which spread through slogans such as "Japan and Korea as One Body."

Also in 1940 came the organization of all Koreans into multi-family groups of Neighborhood Patriotic Associations, which furthered the colonial state's quest to achieve complete command over human and material resources through penetrating surveillance and control. These neighborhood groupings facilitated the implementation of public rituals, rationing, and a comprehensive system of extracting "common good donations" of both food and materials that forced people, especially in the last few years of the war, into desperate measures to feed themselves. Everything eventually became appropriated for war; indeed, the state even arrogated the choice of shoes and clothing that people wore. And the term "total mobilization" became pervasive, attached to a torrent of new regulations as well as to all kinds of groups organized according to occupation, region, and even religion.

For Koreans, it would be difficult to recall anything worse than the severe deprivations of wartime mobilization, especially in the countryside. However, two other phenomena would eventually approach this both in terms of severity and in their impact on Koreans' memories of this period. The first was the degeneration of workforce mobilization into forced labor. Eventually thousands of Koreans, whether they were initially drawn by real jobs, deceptive promises of employment, or simply abducted, filled the labor shortages in Manchuria, Japan, and newly conquered Japanese territories such as Sakhalin Island. In munitions factories, shipyards, mines, farms, and sweatshops, these Koreans led lives of unremitting toil amidst often dangerous conditions, with little food, no pay, few chances to escape, and diminishing chances of survival. Thousands of these Koreans in Hiroshima and Nagasaki were killed by the American atomic bombs dropped in August of 1945. The other, and by now the most publicized, wartime atrocity was the roundup of tens of thousands of young women into the "Comfort Corps" prostitution rings servicing imperial soldiers on the battle fronts throughout the expanding Japanese empire. As with the Korean laborers, most of these females were lured with promises of economic opportunity, while others were kidnapped or otherwise coerced, and still others, with a background in the licensed prostitution system of colonial Korea, "voluntarily" joined this wretched exercise. The horrors of this experience can hardly be imagined, which explains the social shame that kept these women silent for most of their lives. But beginning in the 1990s, as they neared their deaths, survivors gradually came forward with wrenching accounts of their ordeals. These stories incriminated the collusion of colonial authoritarianism with the long-standing nexus of sexual vulnerability and social status, a practice that readily fell prey to the depredations of wartime mobilization.

RESIGNATION, COLLABORATION, AND MODERN IDENTITY

Given such harm, how, one might ask, could there have been so many Koreans who collaborated with Japanese colonialism during wartime, and indeed actively promoted its excessive efforts at mobilization? At one level, this is not difficult to answer: Many Koreans earned their livelihoods or otherwise benefited from the colonial system. And many of them, as well as others, sincerely believed that the best outcome for the Korean people—not necessarily for Korea's status as a politically autonomous nation-state, which might have been considered less important—was incorporation into and support for the Japanese empire's pursuit of war. This would explain the numerous civil servants, businessmen, intellectuals, artists, educators, and other professionals who publicly encouraged fellow Koreans to contribute to the war effort and renounce their Korean loyalties. More confounding, however, was that key contributors to the formation of modern Korean identity later came to advocate its obliteration, as was the case with Yi Gwangsu and Choe Namseon.

It would be no exaggeration to call Yi Gwangsu and Choe Namseon the two most influential intellectuals of the early twentieth century, and indeed perhaps the two seminal figures in the formative period of modern Korean culture itself. Yi, author of what is considered the first modern novel (and possibly still the most famous one), *Heartless* (1917), became the standard-bearer for Korean fiction writing in the colonial period. And Choe, a pioneering poet and publisher whose innovations, beginning with his poems "Song of the Seoul–Busan Railroad" and "From the Sea to the Boys," along with his literary journal, *Boys*—all unveiled in 1908—established the stylistic foundation for modern Korean poetry. But these two figures' influence extended beyond literature, as both played active roles in educational campaigns, Korean studies scholarship, and, most intriguingly, causes for Korean independence. Choe, in fact, authored the stirring March First Declaration of Independence of 1919. His turn into a vocal supporter of the Japanese war effort, then, would be as if Thomas Jefferson had joined the British forces in the War of 1812. Granted, Choe shunned political activism and even demurred from actually signing the Declaration of Independence, but he also produced foundational works of scholarship on Korean history, religion, and language. Yi Gwangsu, for his part, helped write the independence declaration by Korean students in Japan in 1919, wrote stories that celebrated nationalist sacrifice and condemned colonialist discrimination, and published essays calling for reforming Korean customs and character to prepare for eventual autonomy. He also assisted and venerated the celebrated independence activist An Changho, who died in 1937 while recovering from a prolonged bout in a Seoul prison.

In the roundtable discussion following their November 1943 speeches to Korean students studying in Japan (see Image 19), Choe and Yi rehashed the by-then familiar arguments calling for Koreans' support for the war: that Korea had a great deal to gain from Japanese tutelage; that the real enemy was the Anglo-Saxon civilization that threatened to destroy the East Asian one; that it would be an honor for the individual, family, and the Korean people to sacrifice one's life for this great cause. Interestingly, Choe Namseon also alluded to the findings of his historical research, noting that in ancient times—before Korean civilization had become "soft" through a preoccupation with literary pursuits under Chinese influence—Korea was, like Japan, militarily oriented. Indeed, Choe notes, ancient Koreans who had migrated to Japan were likely the ancestors of the samurai themselves.

For his part, Yi, who appears in the transcript through his Japanese name, betrays an anxiety that his message should have been better received by the Korean students, who still seemed overly attached to their Korean identity. As if to accentuate what they see as such a naive innocence of youth, Choe and Yi spend the rest of the discussion recounting their own formative years, starting four decades earlier, as students in Japan. This experience, they note while praising each other, had provided the springboard for their major accomplishments in developing Korea's modern literary culture.

It is somehow fitting that these two literary giants took an intellectual stroll through the entire colonial experience. Much more had emerged than modern Korean literature and culture; the colonial period in many ways had stood as the intensive cauldron of modern Korea as a whole. Within a relatively short span of three decades, Korea had experienced nearly the full spectrum of changes that took one-and-a-half centuries

Image 19 *Choe Namseon, Yi Gwangsu, and children's author Ma Haesong at a roundtable discussion in Tokyo, November 1943. (Courtesy of* Seojeong sihak.*)*

to take hold in, say, colonial India: urbanization, industrialization, state domination, nationalism, communism, social restructuring, and so on. By the early 1940s much of the peninsula, especially the urban areas, looked fundamentally different than in 1910, and throughout the country a pervasive feeling of permanence arose regarding Japanese colonial rule. Even the dislocations of wartime mobilization reinforced the sense that Koreans were simply cogs in the wheels of the Japanese empire. For many Koreans, then, resignation, not "collaboration," was almost unavoidable and equated simply to accommodation with the inexorable changes of the modern era.

What complicates matters is that the wartime mobilization included the crimes of forced labor and sexual slavery, as well as the horrors of combat itself for those dragged or caught outside the peninsula. In other words, the ultimate judgment on the so-called collaborators cannot escape consideration of the colonial period as a whole, which in turn cannot disregard the excesses of the wartime years. Given what happened in the subsequent Korean War, it is not difficult to believe that, had Koreans retained autonomy, the wrenching trials of modern change would have resulted in savagery of one kind or another, either among Koreans or committed by Koreans on other people. The terrible events, however, cannot be detached from the reality that Korea was ruled by a foreign power, and this makes fingering and condemning Korean collaborators almost inevitable, however simplistic. The suffering of Koreans was one thing, but for Koreans to assist the Japanese colonial system in committing such abuses invites outrage. As in France's periodic soul searching regarding its Vichy past, the complicity to atrocities (in the French case, the Holocaust) is almost overshadowed by the more facile condemnation of national betrayal: collaboration with a longtime foreign rival turned hated overlord. In this sense, to most Koreans today, the wartime mobilization represented a fittingly ignoble end to the despicable enterprise of colonial rule as a whole. To forgive the Korean collaborators during the war would be as unfathomable as acknowledging any positive results from the colonial experience.

THE GRAND NARRATIVE: INDEPENDENCE MOVEMENTS

The most ready alternative to a more forthright engagement with the issue of collaboration during the war, and indeed during the entire colonial period, has been to celebrate the efforts by Koreans to fight for their independence. These are well known on the peninsula, hailed as evidence of a resilient national spirit. Among the renowned figures was Syngman Rhee, who spent most of his lifetime in the United States trying to use his patchy connections to the Washington elite in order to influence American foreign policy. Frequented touted also were Gim Gu and Kim Il Sung, who fought alongside, and under the banner of, the Chinese nationalists and Chinese communists, respectively, in their common struggle against Japanese imperialism. By the 1940s, in fact, Gim Gu acted as the *de facto* leader of the Korean government in exile that had originated in the spring of 1919. He even formed a Korean Restoration Army from his base in China, with hundreds of soldiers ready to charge into the peninsula. There are several problems with the conventional, almost obsessive focus on these movements, however: First, these organizations were all operating outside the peninsula; second, they were splintered and commanded little cooperation from each other; finally, and not unrelated to the first two issues, these movements had little to no effect on actually bringing about liberation from Japanese colonial rule.

The heroizing of these freedom fighters is understandable, given that they at least made great sacrifices for the cause of national autonomy, and given the demands of constructing the modern narratives of nationhood; indeed, North Korea as both a country and ruling system has always been utterly dependent on this story (Chapter 22). But as with North Korea, the independence movements' historical significance lies more in illuminating the history that followed than in understanding the history for which they are honored. That their role in achieving Korean liberation was far greater in legend than in actuality also speaks to the complexities of the colonial experience as a whole, which reached a disturbing climax under the circumstances of war.

20 The Liberation Period, 1945–50

CHRONOLOGY

1945 August	Liberation from Japanese colonial rule
1945 September	Formation of the Korean People's Republic
1945 September	Start of the Soviet occupation of the north and American occupation of the south
1945 October	Return of Syngman Rhee and Kim Il Sung to Korea
1945 December	First Soviet–American Joint Commission, announcement of trusteeship
1946 October	Mass general strike in the south
1947 April	Dissolution of the Joint Commission
1947 July	Assassination of Yeo Unhyeong
1948 April	The Jeju Island Uprisings
1948 May	Elections for members of the National Assembly in southern Korea
1948 June	Syngman Rhee elected president of southern state by National Assembly
1948 August	Proclamation of the Republic of Korea (South Korea)
1948 September	Proclamation of the Democratic People's Republic of Korea (North Korea)
1948 October	Yeosu-Suncheon Rebellion
1948 December	Passage of the National Security Law
1949 June	Promulgation of the South Korean land reform
1949 September	Dissolution of the Committee for Investigating Anti-National Behavior

THE MAY ELECTIONS IN SOUTHERN KOREA, 1948

On May 10, 1948, people formed long lines to do something they had previously only heard about: choosing government officials in a national election. These voters were electing legislators for the National Assembly, which would be charged with devising a constitution and a new government for southern Korea. That this new state would materialize three years after the end of Japanese colonial rule, and that its jurisdiction would cover only one half of the peninsula, encapsulated the uneasy circumstances leading to this momentous event. The jubilation that had greeted liberation in the summer of 1945 had quickly faded into a somber realization that freedom from Japan did not mean freedom from foreign rule. Indeed the division of the peninsula into separate northern and southern occupation zones headed by the Soviet Union and the United States, respectively, turned the peninsula into the opening Asian theater of the emerging rivalry between these World War II allies: the Cold War.

For Koreans in the southern zone, the American occupation would bring forth greater political and economic freedoms compared to the Japanese colonial period, but an almost equal stifling of their aspirations for national autonomy. The clashes between American priorities and Korean goals, the American disregard for Korea's internal dynamics that matched Koreans' ignorance of geopolitics, and bitter divisions among Koreans came to dominate the tense five-year period between liberation in 1945 and the Korean War in 1950. This so-called "liberation space" brims over with historical significance, primarily because it must be viewed in relative terms: as foreshadowing and leading to the Korean War, but also bound inescapably to the colonial experience. One can consider the liberation space foremost as a transitional period from colonial subjugation to national division, a short interregnum between two devastating wars, or a wasted opportunity to reset the country's modern historical trajectory. In any case, what took place at this time would cast long, dark shadows over the rest of the twentieth century, and indeed help frame the perspective on the entirety of the modern era.

THE PRIMACY OF POLITICS: A MULTI-LATERAL DYNAMIC

Korea's modern history appears dominated by politics, so intense and rapid have been the political changes and their repercussions. The intrusion of politics into other spheres of existence was never more acute than in the post-liberation period. Political interests and conflicts, from village disputes over property, family, religion, and ideology, to the geopolitical rivalry between the Allied victors-turned-occupiers, seem to have overwhelmed everything else. And further complicating the situation were the constant shifts in the political forces arrayed against and alongside each other: the two occupation armies and military governments, the various Korean organizations of all ideological stripes, the emigrant workers and independence activists returning to their homeland, those who benefited from as well as those victimized by the colonial wartime mobilization, and so on. There simply was little room in the liberation space for much else beyond politics.

This reality seemed far-fetched during the enormous celebrations that spilled into the streets beginning on August 16, 1945, the day following the Japanese emperor's proclamation of unconditional surrender that had been heard by some on the radio. The joyous, stunning news spread like wildfire, and for several days Koreans marched up and down urban boulevards shouting and waving placards and makeshift symbols like the Korean flag. For some, however, this was not a surprise. A few days before liberation, the Japanese colonial authorities had asked the man they considered the *de facto* Korean leader left in the country, Yeo Unhyeong, to form a provisional governing organization. Yeo, a moderate leftist, consented to this request and quickly formed the Committee for the Preparation for Korean Independence (CPKI). Scarcely could he have known that, upon the signal for Koreans to exercise their new freedoms, a host of other political groups would emerge to push a variety of interests and ideologies. This was a portent of things to come.

By early September the CPKI gave way to the Korean People's Republic (KPR)—like the CPKI a coalition of ideological and political interests—which served as the central governing institution connecting over a hundred local "people's committees" that sprang up around the country. The people's committees lie at the heart of a great historical debate concerning this period, namely, whether Korean politics, aroused by the destabilizing demobilization of wartime society—including the return of those Koreans who had been abroad—was leaning toward a leftist social revolution. Despite their name, however, the people's committees and even the KPR appear to have represented diverse concerns of disparate localities. Indeed the most pressing, common items on their agenda were to secure local order and begin rectifying the injustices of the wartime period, the first steps in the great challenge of decolonization. To be sure, many of the people's committees embraced the promises and prowess of Korean communists emerging from their underground existence, but clearly most of the participants had little inkling of the larger communist program. Indeed the KPR's original platform called for nothing more radical than standard labor laws and the redistribution of ill-gotten gains. There was hardly a set ideological agenda in this preparatory period of flux.

The KPR leaders, in fact, chose as their chairman a right-wing nationalist, Syngman Rhee (Yi Seungman)—the best-known independence activist—who still was making his way back home after a decades-long exile in the United States. With the American government's help Rhee arrived in Seoul in mid-October, ready to pursue his long-held dream of leading Korea's first independent government. His homecoming, however, came a few days after that of Kim Il Sung, the former leader of a communist guerrilla band in Manchuria, who accompanied the Soviet army into the northern zone and was introduced by the Soviet authorities to cheering crowds in Pyongyang. In late November, the final major independence fighter from abroad, Gim Gu, who had led the Korean Restoration Army and Provisional Government in China, made his triumphant return. All three figures returning to the peninsula would ultimately exert far greater power than their domestic counterparts.

That foreign-based Koreans came to wield such overriding influence in the post-liberation political space, a somewhat discomfiting reality in hindsight, had much to do with the fact that the Allied forces, and not Koreans themselves, liberated Korea. And, as the primary agents of liberation, the Allied powers determined the ultimate fate of the country, which meant that they were also the immediate agents of national partition. Well before the end of the Pacific War, the Soviets and Americans had agreed on an allocation of wartime responsibilities that would place the Soviets in a prime position in the northeast Asian mainland, while the Americans would be busy with Japan in the Pacific theater. When the Americans suddenly realized in August of 1945 that this would likely result in the Soviet Union's commandeering of the entire Korean peninsula, they proposed a split occupation. Surprisingly, the Soviets accepted, even though the Red Army could have easily driven down the entire length of the peninsula, and even though the thirty-eighth parallel dividing line placed Seoul in the American zone.

Thereafter the two military occupation governments determined what was politically acceptable in their respective zones. The Soviets, as unaware and unprepared for their occupation as the Americans were, had to deal with a strong right-nationalist and Christian tendency in the populace, particularly in the northwest. It recognized the Korean People's Republic and the people's committees while ensuring that Kim Il Sung and other Korean communists would gain the upper hand politically in the northern zone (see Chapter 22). The Americans in the south, for their part, found their situation even more complicated and troublesome. Much of this difficulty arose because, as they had desired, the Americans controlled the capital of Seoul, the major stage and prize of political contestation. From the perspective of Korean political actors vying for influence in Seoul, the American occupation would constitute the dominant factor. The two occupations, in turn, used this intra-Korean strife to further secure their own favored political outcomes in their respective zones.

This complex dynamic became apparent almost immediately, especially after the announcement by the superpowers in late December of 1945 of a five-year trusteeship over Korea, an idea originating from Allied summits during the war. This promptly triggered vociferous opposition from just about everyone in the country. The communists, though, quickly changed their stance to support the trusteeship, and thus began the most conspicuous, though not necessarily the most important, source of division among Korean political interests in the south. Henceforth the right wing solidified itself around opposition to the trusteeship, which became a convenient bogeyman for excluding and suppressing leftist opponents, who could readily be tarred for taking a treasonous stance. The United States Army Military Government in Korea (USAMGIK), with its own set of concerns about the left, assisted this effort, maintaining its role as primarily an enforcer of anti-communism and cultivator of conservative, pro-American political forces despite their disagreements over trusteeship. The declassified military intelligence documents from the very beginning of the southern occupation demonstrate clearly the premises, suspicions, and ignorance that colored American perceptions of Korean actors. And various stripes of right-nationalist Korean interests were keen to goad the occupiers into reckless actions.

IMPLANTING THE SOUTHERN SYSTEM

Anti-communist autocracy, then, became the hallmark and bulwark of the American military government, and of South Korean political rule, for another forty years. The southern system took hold, however, not only by matching the American occupiers' inclinations—including, ultimately, the acceptance of a separate southern state if necessary—but also by eliminating rival political forces. The communists and other leftists were dealt with most harshly (see below). Even moderates, however, who pursued a coalitional solution to the great challenge of establishing a unified government amidst rival superpower occupations, faced constant harassment and pressure. Syngman Rhee and Gim Gu, the two right-nationalists with the largest followings, maneuvered to block any outcome that might incorporate moderates in a power-sharing arrangement. The most conspicuous victim of this dynamic was Yeo Unhyeong, the widely revered leader who had led the earliest post-liberation governing order in the summer of 1945. Yeo was assassinated in July of 1947, just as he appeared as the only viable alternative to the far right. The rightists had recognized this, and they eliminated Yeo from the scene. As it turned out, with him died any chance for non-extremists to survive in this volatile political atmosphere.

The American occupation, too, did its part in ensuring the victory of the immoderate right wing. One of the first major steps taken by the American leadership after marching into Seoul in the fall of 1945 was to declare illegitimate the people's committees in the south, absurdly suspecting this vast collection of disparate groups as uniformly left-revolutionary. Afterwards, USAMGIK paved the way for the triumph of the right, not by intervening in the disputes among political leaders as much as by clamping down on any organized activity the occupation deemed too close to communism. Beginning in the spring of 1946, the American military and rightist constabulary forces incarcerated thousands of leftist activists and killed hundreds of them. This intractable American orientation was sufficient to prohibit leftists from vying for any realistic influence in Seoul or the rest of the south. As for its dealings with the Soviet occupation through the occasional gatherings of the Joint Commission, which sought to construct a unified governing mechanism, USAMGIK, like its Soviet counterpart, was never prepared to countenance any Korean government that smacked of the opposing occupation. After yet another failure to come to terms in the spring of 1947, it became clear that the deadlock had only tightened. Thereafter the Americans sought to shift responsibility to the newly-created United Nations while promoting the formation of a provisional governing council in the south. Headed by Syngman Rhee, this council further purged leftists and combined various militias and paramilitary groups into a policing force that would carry out an often brutal elimination of political opponents. As for the UN, it declared its first priority to be the holding of a UN-sponsored election for a new Korean government. Given that the Soviets refused to participate in this effort, in effect the elections would establish a government for only southern Korea.

The United Nations forged ahead with these plans even after being denied entry into the northern occupation zone in early 1948. And so, over increasingly vocal resistance, on May 10, 1948, elections were held to choose representatives for the National Assembly, the first concrete step toward establishing a separate southern state. By all accounts, the people showed great enthusiasm, as voters waited patiently in long lines for this new privilege of electing their political leaders. Those so chosen gathered in Seoul at the end of May and selected Syngman Rhee as the Assembly's speaker, then voted promptly to implement a presidential system over a parliamentary one—clearly a reflection of Rhee's increasing hold on power. On June 20, the Assembly elected Rhee the new president, establishing a pattern for indirect presidential elections frequently used later in South Korea to maintain dictatorial rule. Indeed, despite the outwardly liberal constitution of the new Republic of Korea, what was inaugurated on August 15, 1948—the third anniversary of liberation—was a South Korean state that would use its dogged claims of jurisdiction over all of Korea to justify repression. (The separate North Korean government, formally established a few weeks later, would be no different.)

Little wonder, then, that throughout the post-liberation period in the south, anti-state and anti-imperialist sentiment grew, as people became aware that freedom from Japanese colonialism was leading to neither independence nor national unity. The discontent was further fueled by rampant inflation, unemployment, and poverty in the first year of the occupation. This in turn fed the swelling labor movement led by leftists, and in the fall of 1946 a massive general strike that began in the southern industrial city of Daegu shook the nascent southern system. The resulting crackdown by police and military forces resulted in the deaths of hundreds of strikers, policemen, and officials. The other major group of southern dissenters were the so-called *ppalchisan* ("partisans"), communist guerrillas who, while under constant siege, still managed to wage resistance campaigns, particularly after the separate southern elections were announced. They also appear to have instigated the eruption of an uprising on Jeju Island off the southwest coast in April of 1948, as protests against the southern elections turned into a major insurrection by hundreds of combatants. The response by the south's paramilitary forces, though, was excessive, sweeping, and horrific, as whole villages were wiped out indiscriminately and tens of thousands of innocent bystanders were killed. Later, in the fall of 1948, some members of these government militia forces themselves rose up in Yeosu and Suncheon on the south-central coast. The rebels, quickly joined by communist guerrillas holding out in the surrounding mountains, managed to capture several towns before being chased back to the hills by the military. As with the Jeju Island massacre, the government response was brutal, and over half of the captured instigators, numbering in the hundreds, were summarily executed by firing squad.

The Yeosu-Suncheon Rebellion would be the originating backdrop for the acclaimed multi-volume novel (and later, film), *The Taebaek Mountains*, which depicted people already caught up in the ideological polarization, political violence, and terrible recriminations that would soon mark the Korean War itself.

A TROUBLING HISTORICAL SHADOW

Lodged between the long colonial ordeal and the Korean War that solidified national division, the abbreviated liberation space has chronically tugged at contemporary South Koreans' sense of self, an uncomfortable reminder of what might have been. What if the Allies had left the country alone following the end of the Second World War? What if the Americans had supported the moderate elements that sought a coalitional solution to the political divisions? What if Yeo Unhyeong, or even the assassinated rightists Gim Gu and Song Jinu, had lived? And, what if decolonization had been sincerely pursued, when it appeared that most people considered this the most pressing issue?

Beyond political autonomy, so the thinking goes, true decolonization would have addressed above all the injustices and severe hierarchies of the late colonial period, hence overturning the economic and political privileges associated with Japanese colonialism. The American military government, ever wary of Soviet influence and communist ascendance, cracked down on the people's committees and left in place the police and high officials of the colonial system as a way of ensuring stability. In turn, rightists such as Syngman Rhee and Gim Gu found the American preoccupation with communism a convenient facilitator of their own political aims. The landed and business interests, though sometimes in contentious relations with Rhee, would have been the targets of any purge of late colonial elites, along with the police and high bureaucracy, and hence these groups in the end had to throw in their lot with him. And in turn, Rhee helped to salvage their privileges in late 1948, when he implemented the National Security Law, the all-purpose tool of the state's suppression of political opposition down to the present day. In the summer of 1949, a sweeping land reform to address the economic inequities from the colonial period (achieved in northern Korea in early 1946) was finally promulgated, suggesting that the landed elites were in danger of losing their most entrenched advantages. But soon, Rhee, under the pretext of anti-communism, dissolved the year-long criminal court investigating the most notorious pro-Japanese collaborators.

The historical narratives of responsibility for both national division and the Korean War are thus dramatically complicated by the reality of multiple fissures among Koreans and the unsavory behavior of many influential actors. In the search for what went wrong, the overarching impact of the superpower occupations, of course, cannot be discounted, but ultimately the actions of Koreans themselves must be, and recently have been, the focus of attention. Even if southern Korea in the liberation space was not really on a path toward a social revolution, what did happen in the southern zone has cast a troubling historical shadow over South Korean state and society: the uneasy examples of ready complicity with another foreign occupier, the brutal suppression of political opponents and innocent bystanders alike, and the preservation of late-colonial sociopolitical privileges, the vestiges of which remain powerful today.

21 The Korean War

CHRONOLOGY

1948 summer	Formal establishment of the states of South Korea and North Korea
1948–49	Training and fighting of North Korean troops in the Chinese civil war
1950 January	US Secretary of State's declaration of the American defense perimeter
1950 June 25	Outbreak of the Korean War as Northern army crosses the border
1950 September	Landing of American forces in Incheon
1950 October	Chinese intervention in the Korean War on behalf of the North
1951 July	Commencement of peace talks
1953 March	Death of Soviet leader Joseph Stalin
1953 July 27	Armistice to end fighting

THE CHINESE ENTRANCE INTO THE KOREAN WAR, 1950

In late October of 1950, hundreds of thousands of Chinese soldiers began crossing the Yalu River to flood the battlefront of the Korean War. This brought about a startling turn in the conflict, which by the closing months of 1950 had been approaching a decisive victory by the US-led United Nations forces. The Chinese soldiers, along with their North Korean allies, quickly pushed the front down to the middle of the peninsula, where the Korean War had started a half-year earlier, and where it would be waged for another two-and-a-half years, with tremendous bloodshed, until the Armistice of July 27, 1953. By then, Chinese intervention had been integral to the Korean War as well as to the emerging Cold War order that engulfed the Korean peninsula, and indeed the entire East Asian region.

The Chinese military had intervened in peninsular affairs on multiple occasions throughout history. In the late nineteenth century alone, the

Chinese thrice helped put down Korean rebellions—first an insurrection by a group of Korean soldiers in 1882, and then in 1884, when radical enlightenment activists attempted a coup. Finally, in 1894, Chinese troops arrived to assist the ailing Joseon government in quelling the massive Donghak Uprising, a move that would launch the 1894–5 Sino-Japanese War and bring an end to China's preeminent standing in Korea. In earlier Chinese interventions, the stakes were even higher: the Ming dynasty's assistance in saving Korea from the Japanese invasions of the late sixteenth century; and the Tang dynasty's alliance with Silla to conquer the two other kingdoms on the peninsula in the seventh century, which led to the first unified Korean polity. The lone Chinese military intrusion of the twentieth century, that of October 1950, would also play a crucial role in the founding of a Korean state, but this time, in the context of the emerging Cold War, the beneficiary was not Korea as a whole, but rather a part.

CIVIL WARS AMIDST THE COLD WAR

The Korean War that began in 1950 is commonly cited as the first "hot war" of the Cold War, the global confrontation between the capitalist and communist blocs that dominated the second half of the twentieth century and still leaves Korea divided today. One could argue, however, that this label should apply to an even earlier conflict, the Chinese civil war of 1945–49 between the communists, with the backing of the Soviet Union, and the nationalists, who were supported by the United States. Having cooperated for the common anti-Japanese cause during World War II, the rival Chinese parties almost immediately turned their guns on each other after the defeat of Japan in 1945, and after four years, the communists under Mao Zedong drove Chiang Kai-shek's nationalists to Taiwan. The nascent polity of North Korea even played a small role. Kim Il Sung's ties to China from his youth and his bonds with fellow communists led to a contingent of North Korean troops training under, and fighting for, the Chinese communists. This relationship, which was later highlighted by both sides, might have provided valuable experience in forging a crack North Korean fighting unit.

The forces behind Korea's own civil war originated in the colonial period and intensified in the occupation and division of the peninsula immediately following liberation in 1945, which led to the establishment of separate states in 1948 (Chapter 20). This rendered the conflagration unleashed in 1950 almost an inevitability. The South Korean president,

Syngman Rhee, himself agitated for a forcible reunification, and his soldiers along the increasingly fortified border came close several times to
sparking a full confrontation, with North Korean troops returning the
hostility in kind with their own provocations. Such skirmishes reflected
the bitter conflicts that had arisen out of an array of interests in the
post-liberation years. As in China, however, while one must not lose sight
of the profound divisions among Koreans that resulted in the civil war,
the larger geopolitical context framed the outbreak and progress of the
conflict.

The decision by Kim Il Sung, the North's leader, to launch the Korean
War in fact required adherence to the pecking order of the communist
bloc. De-classified archives and other sources have revealed his dogged
efforts to gain permission and assurance of support from the heads of
the Soviet Union and China. For this, Kim played the two leaders, Josef
Stalin and Mao Zedong, off each other. Stalin first had to consent to
Mao's returning thousands of North Korean troops left over from the
Chinese civil war. Kim then found it easier to convince Mao that the
North Koreans should proceed with a communist-led military reunification of the fatherland, just as Mao had done. Mao, though wary of
American involvement, even offered Kim Chinese military assistance,
but Kim Il Sung was convinced that such help would not be necessary, so
quickly and decisively would the North Koreans overwhelm their southern counterparts. Plus, American Secretary of State Dean Acheson had
flatly stated in early 1950 that South Korea lay outside the US defense
perimeter, suggesting strongly that the Americans likely would not get
involved. Stalin, while committing only strategic and material assistance
from the Soviet Union, gave the final go-ahead in April 1950 for Kim to
pursue militarily his desperately sought unification.

6–25

Until recently, "Six-Two-Five" (*Yug-i-o*) was the simple, powerful term
for the Korean War among South Koreans, in the same way that "Nine-
Eleven" suffices for Americans in reference to their signal moment in
recent history. What now is more commonly referred to as simply "The
Korean War" in South Korea and the "Fatherland Liberation War" in
North Korea began at dawn on June 25, 1950, when the (North) Korean
People's Army launched a full-frontal assault over the border at the
thirty-eighth parallel. Despite the saber-rattling on both sides that had
been going on for months, this attack came as a major surprise. The

South's lack of preparation showed clearly in the Northern army's easy rampage to Seoul, which it captured within a couple of days, trailing just behind the massive flight of refugees streaming southward. Koreans throughout their history had experienced these sudden invasions that turned their world upside down, but never from their own national brethren. There was no advantage of local knowledge in fending off the intruders this time.

Indeed, as the Northern army chased the refugees and the Southern forces and quickly captured most of South Korea within a few weeks, it was joined by the leftist guerrillas holding out in the mountains, as well as by communist sympathizers hiding within South Korean society. Together they instituted a swift revolutionary change in the occupied territories. Administration was reorganized according to the Northern model, land and other properties were confiscated and redistributed, and prominent local leaders, intellectuals, and businessmen were arrested, quickly tried, and often killed, while others were simply taken up north. For its part, the Southern army, assisted in part by American forces, took little care to differentiate possible northern collaborators from regular citizens as it committed atrocities on its southward retreat. Most horrific perhaps was the fate of thousands of spuriously accused leftists and other political prisoners who had been undergoing the Southern government's anti-communist reeducation program. Still considered unreliable and not valuable enough to care for or transport, they were simply rounded up and shot, their bodies thrown into mass graves. So began the cycle of recriminations and reprisals that would victimize countless innocent people and constitute one of the many great tragedies of the Korean War. This brutal cleansing of opposing or simply suspicious elements set the stage for reciprocity once the tide of the war changed and towns were reoccupied by the opposing side. The people of Seoul, which the North Koreans claimed to have "liberated" in June 1950 and went on to change hands four times in the first half-year of the Korean War, would bear some of the most awful retributions in this truly vicious cycle.

The first major turning point of the war took place while the "Pusan [Busan] Perimeter," the roughly forty-mile radius around the southeastern port city, held off the North Korean siege long enough for the United Nations to organize an American-led recapturing of the South. In September of 1950, through the famous "Incheon Landing" just to the southwest of Seoul, the American forces, led by General Douglas MacArthur, attacked the North Koreans on the backside as UN reinforcements were sent into the south. This in effect squeezed the Northern forces with a pincer movement. The retreat of the Northern army up the peninsula thereafter was almost as swift as its sweep down the peninsula a few months earlier. The combined US-ROK forces quickly recaptured Seoul and within a few weeks had chased the People's Army out of Pyongyang as well. In their flight northward, the North Koreans made sure to destroy both the property and persons that might assist the Southern forces. These horrific sights failed to deter the American military commanders' push up the peninsula, all the way to the border area with China, in their determination to take a complete and quick victory, which, by late 1950, seemed well in hand.

CHINESE INTERVENTION, THE STALEMATE, AND NATIONAL MEMORIES

It was not as if the American army were completely blind to the potential intervention by the Chinese People's Liberation Army on behalf of the North Koreans, as the Chinese had issued warnings, and as reconnaissance flights had showed Chinese troops assembling close to the border. Apparently, however, the American commander, General MacArthur, believed the Chinese would never engage American might. (There remains speculation that MacArthur might actually have sought to provoke a wider confrontation as a way of overturning the communist victory in China. If so, he badly miscalculated both the formidable military challenge presented by China as well as the degree of support he would enjoy back in Washington.) When the Chinese did indeed enter the fray, the sheer scale and suddenness of their intervention delivered a stunning blow, as hundreds of thousands of Chinese troops chased the joint US–ROK forces back down the peninsula. Only after the joint Chinese–North Korean forces recaptured Pyongyang, then briefly even Seoul, did the UN forces put a halt to this southward advance and press the front back to just north of the Southern capital, where it would remain for the next two-and-a-half years.

The ensuing stalemate from early 1951 to mid-1953 refers to the lack of major movement of the battlefront itself, which shifted little until the Armistice of July 1953 and ultimately left the country divided along the same thirty-eighth parallel where the war had started. Such was the setting for the American film and TV series *M*A*S*H*, which actually used the Korean War as a substitute backdrop for issues arising from the Vietnam War. This in turn reflects the strange place that the Korean conflict, the so-called "forgotten war," long held in the American mindset, overshadowed by both the preceding World War II of the romanticized "greatest generation" and the subsequent Vietnam War that sowed such bitter social discord. On the other hand, the Korean War has remained popular in American publishing, whose works focus on the gritty details of individual battles, the relationship between major figures such as MacArthur and President Truman, and the military and geopolitical strategies. Particularly intriguing has been the issue of why and how the main global combatants, the United States and China, could not reach agreement to end the war even though both sides clearly sought this as early as the summer of 1951, when formal peace talks commenced in Panmunjom. Among the major stumbling blocks, perhaps the most difficult was the problem of repatriating prisoners of war, as many of the thousands of Chinese and North Korean prisoners held in camps, such as the enormous site on Geoje Island south of Busan, refused to return to their originating country. Until Stalin's death in March of 1953 finally opened the way toward a settlement, the difficulties of resolving this and other thorny political issues dragged out the conflict.

The notion of a stalemate, however, should not lead one to consider the final two years of the war a respite, for the relentless combat of this period continued perhaps the most inexcusably disastrous feature of the Korean War: the utter destruction of the population and landscape, with ultimately little to nothing accomplished other than millions of deaths and a bitterness and mistrust singed into the memory of all actors. To North Koreans, the war, especially during the "stalemate," brought the relentless barrage of American bombs, napalm, and other carriers of genocidal devastation that drove the people into literally an underground existence, as they built elaborate tunnel networks to escape the aerial bombardment. By the summer of 1953 in North Korea, the infrastructures of modern life had been destroyed, agriculture had been decimated, reservoirs and damns had been bombed useless, and few major buildings remained standing. This is the memory of the war that the North Korean regime has sustained and incited as a reminder of American brutality, and thereby also as a reinforcement of its own legitimacy.

In South Korea, memories of the Korean War have hardly been as uniform or straightforward, and in fact they continue to reflect and spawn strong ideological and social divisions. Despite the findings of a "truth and reconciliation commission" in the opening years of the twenty-first century that laid bare the atrocities committed during the war, reconciliation has been hard to achieve, mostly due to the fundamental divide over the historical legitimacy of the South Korean state. To those who view South Korean history more triumphantly, the Korean War represented the moment of great heroism and sacrifice for the sake of preserving the South's independence from communism and of integrating into the American-led global order. To those South Koreans who view the American role in their history more soberly, the Korean War preserved something else: national division, dependence on international powers, and a series of anti-communist South Korean dictatorships generated, legitimated, and sustained by national division and the Cold War.

Finally, to the Chinese, the Korean War is remembered as the conflict in which Chinese "volunteers" bravely kept American imperialism at bay. Today, the sacrifice of thousands of these soldiers prompts the grief of Chinese tourists who visit the site of a major battle in the South Korean border town of Cheorwon, which displays open-air artifacts from the war as a reminder of South Koreans' sacrifices and need for vigilance (see Image 21). In North Korea, the hyper-nationalist historical narrative has since deleted China's contributions toward preserving the country during the Korean War, just as Chinese assistance in fending off the Japanese invasion of the sixteenth century has been officially forgotten. But the replay of historical motifs is striking. As it had done throughout the

Image 21 *The shelled-out headquarters of the South Korean Communist Party from the Korean War, left intact in Cheorwon, South Korea, near the border with North Korea. (Author's photo.)*

course of Korean history, Chinese participation in the Korean War once again helped determine Korea's standing in the larger East Asian regional order. China's participation in the Korean War likewise symbolized the peninsula's distinctively modern entanglements, and Korea remains one of the few places on the globe where the Cold War persists. Indeed, while the stage has changed dramatically, the primary geopolitical actors in the early twenty-first century affecting the peninsula are the same as those that converged there for the Korean War: the United States and China. And given the strong but contrasting ties today between China and both Koreas, Chinese actions likely will affect significantly the ultimate fate of Korea in the near future, just as they did in 1950, and just as they have done throughout much of Korean history.

22 Early North Korea

CHRONOLOGY

1945 August	First Soviet incursions into northern Korea; liberation from Japanese colonial rule
1945 September	Soviet Central Administration established; Jo Mansik asked to head a governing body
1945 October	Kim Il Sung introduced by Soviet occupation to crowds in Pyongyang
1945 November	Massacre of Christian nationalists in Sinuiju
1946 spring	Initiation of comprehensive land reform in the northern occupation zone
1946 November	Elections for the interim northern legislature
1947	Establishment of the Korean People's Army
1948 September	Formal establishment of the Democratic People's Republic of Korea
1950–53	Korean War
1955 December	Kim Il Sung's "Juche speech"
1956	Failed attempt to oust Kim by Soviet-Korean communists
1957	Beginning of the *Cheollima* industrialization campaign
1962	Purge of novelist and leading propagandist Han Seorya
1968	North Korean seizure of the *USS Pueblo*

KIM IL SUNG'S "JUCHE" SPEECH, 1955

To an audience of propaganda officials of the North Korean Communist Party, Kim Il Sung delivered a speech in late December of 1955 that introduced the notion of "Juche," the ideal of self-reliance that would eventually become the country's ruling ideology. Kim's emphasis, as it would be for the *Juche* concept itself, lay in forging a distinctively Korean path to socialism through a focus on national customs and conditions. The mistakes made thus far in North Korea, he claimed, stemmed from an excessive dependence on external models, particularly those of the Soviet Union. Not coincidentally, this speech came amid a purge of Kim's political rivals, including those Soviet-Korean communists who had come to the country as Soviet occupation advisors. Indeed, despite the outward appeals for achieving "peaceful reunification" by presenting a stellar model of Korean socialism in the North, this speech and its political context pointed directly to the solidification of Kim's political power. It encapsulated the core elements in the politics, economy, and culture of the early northern system and became the basis for the dominion of *Juche* as North Korea's ideological justification for Kim's absolute rule.

By the early 1960s, Kim Il Sung stood as the undisputed source of political authority, and the country had embarked on a heavy industrialization campaign that sped the North past its southern counterpart in economic development. Furthermore, the reordering of society into categories that reflected this political and economic collectivization, a process that had begun in the post-liberation period, was by now well in place. Kim's speech in 1955 outlining the basic principles of *Juche*, which nourished the idea of self-reliance with a fierce nativism and wariness of the outside world, also demonstrated his regime's preoccupation with history—history as knowledge, but also as an ideological tool. As it turned out, this obsession with historical orthodoxy constituted a cover as well as a corrective for dependence.

LIBERATION SPACE NORTH KOREA

There remains considerable debate about the Soviet impact on northern Korea during the post-liberation period from 1945 to 1950, when the North Korean "revolution" took hold. The more that previously classified Soviet documents have become accessible, however, the more it appears that Soviet influence was paramount and indeed decisive in determining the political outcome in the northern occupation zone. This should be expected, but such a revelation goes completely against the North Korean historical orthodoxy and challenges historical scholarship, including that based on captured documents from the Korean War, that forwards a dominant role for domestic forces in shaping the early northern system. The stakes are as high as they are for South Korea (Chapter 20), for this issue gets to the heart of North Korea's national character, historical legitimacy, and purported autonomy, touted by *Juche* ideology as the foundation of North Korean existence.

The Soviet occupation, however, faced almost as much difficulty in bringing about its desired outcome in North Korea as the Americans did in the southern occupation zone. Like the Americans, the Soviets, who entered Korea as combatants a week before the end of the Pacific War on August 15, 1945, were utterly ignorant of their new territory and unprepared to manage it. The Soviet Central Administration (SCA), the makeshift governing organization of the Red Army in Korea, stumbled onto a complex scene, with a diverse population characterized by ideological differences that overlapped with socioeconomic, religious, and geographical ones. The regional variations in northern Korea, deeply rooted in history and shaped considerably by the colonial experience, showed that while the northeastern region had conditions conducive to communist growth, the northwestern part of the country—where Pyongyang lay—was a stronghold of right-wing Korean nationalism.

The nationalists in this area tended to be landed, with a strong business ethos, and Christian. All of these strains were embodied in the most respected and well-known figure in the north, Jo Mansik, a Presbyterian elder who had steadfastly resisted colonial assimilation and mobilization efforts. He was, in this sense, the northern zone's counterpart to Yeo Unhyeong, the left-moderate who commanded a great following in the south before his assassination in 1947. Jo was not killed until 1950, but the SCA, after turning originally to him in September of 1945 to head a Soviet-friendly, ostensibly coalitional governing body, found him recalcitrant in opposing communism and any hint of national division. He was arrested by 1946, but the Soviet occupation's difficulties with him reflected the hostilities in northern Korea that had developed between Protestant nationalists and Soviet or communist elements. An early outbreak of violence in this struggle took place in November of 1945 in the border city of Sinuiju, on the Yalu River, when a Christian protest against Soviet occupation policies sparked a massacre of dozens.

One of the great ironies of North Korea is that Kim Il Sung, this country's dominant communist figure, came from a typical Protestant household in Pyongyang. The Soviet occupation officials' fateful decision, in October of 1945, to promote Kim as the prospective Korean leader came only after their failure to win over Jo Mansik, whose anti-communism stemmed from his religiously-inspired nationalism. Unlike Jo, Kim wielded little influence over the populace, despite his being known to some as a famed guerrilla leader from the 1930s who had managed to escape the Japanese hunt for him. After four years of living quietly in the Soviet Union from 1941 to 1945, the period when his son, Jong Il (Gim Jeongil), was born in Siberia, Kim accompanied the Soviet army's entrance into his home city in late September 1945. In a large mid-October rally in Pyongyang staged to celebrate the Soviet occupation, Kim was introduced to a cheering crowd as one of several featured Korean leaders, including Jo Mansik. But through cunning, ruthlessness, charisma, considerable political skill, and a lot of luck, Kim gradually won enough confidence from the Soviet authorities to take, step-by-step, the reigns of the native political system in northern Korea.

Henceforth it became difficult to separate Kim Il Sung from the fate of the northern communist party, for the two grew together in stature and authority under Soviet auspices. Beginning at the end of 1945, the Soviets gradually placed Kim in the leading party positions and provisional governing structures, which took increasing responsibility over administration in the north. The northern communist party eventually superseded the Seoul-based party in the southern zone, and the election for an interim northern legislature in November of 1946 was a classic Soviet-style, single-candidate ballot. By late 1947, a separate northern regime, backed by a powerful People's Army, was effectively in place, along with the usual accoutrements of a Stalinist state. Even Kim's personality cult was on early display in the grand celebrations in Pyongyang on August 15, 1947, the second anniversary of liberation, which featured large portraits of him being paraded about. In a scene that would become familiar later, film footage of this event shows Kim, flanked by Soviet officials, contentedly overlooking the adulatory spectacle, much of which is devoted to hailing him, along with Stalin.

One must be careful, however, before dismissing Kim Il Sung and the communist party as creatures solely of Soviet favor. By most indications, there was substantial popular support for the actions taken by the northern political authorities, at least initially, and Koreans themselves directed key components of what became a true social revolution—systematic, indeed totalizing, in scope and ambition. By the first half of 1946, a comprehensive land reform stripped large landowners and others deemed social enemies, such as former colonial officials, of their property and redistributed it to the peasantry. The thorough reorientation of the economy, culture, and daily life followed suit, as people, particularly those outside the capital and beyond the Soviet occupation authorities, practiced self-governance, organization, and communal interaction in ways that disregarded previous social identities. All of this made life in the north uncomfortable, if not dangerous, for landlords, businessmen, professionals, and former colonial officials. To the northern leaders, the mass exodus of these social elites southward to the American occupation zone represented good riddance, allowing the northern regime to pursue decolonization and consolidate power with relatively little competition (and bloodshed). What remained was a northern society and culture primed for shaping by a determined communist party controlling an ambitious, and in many ways typical, communist state. The strength and military prowess of this state, in particular, were on display in June of 1950, when it launched the Korean War (Chapter 21).

THE FORMATIVE FIFTIES

North Korea's recovery from the complete devastation of the Korean War began immediately, and with a flourish: an effort not only to rebuild, but to reconstruct society from the ground up, quite literally, through political integration, ideological discipline, cultural uniformity, and accelerated industrialization under state command. However, while the post-Korean War 1950s represented the most formative period of North Korean history, this process did not start from scratch, despite the decimated landscape. A strong foundation for the developments of the 1950s had been laid earlier, the most critical element of which was Kim Il Sung's political ascendance.

Kim had garnered the Soviet and Chinese go-ahead to launch the Korean War, for which he acted as the North's chief military commander. And as was the case in South Korea with Syngman Rhee, the Korean War served ultimately to solidify Kim Il Sung's grip on political power. But also like Rhee, Kim found himself still facing challenges to his absolute rule, which the December 1955 address to the communist party's propaganda officials attempted to overcome. This so-called "Juche speech" indeed emphasized self-reliance, autonomy, nativism, and absolute national unity—the pillars of the comprehensive *Juche* ideology that later came to be identified with North Korea. In a tacit rebuke of the North's war effort, Kim claimed that the overt dependence on foreign models and ideas, including even the international communist movement itself, had hindered North Korea's progress. And hence the party workers must turn to a focus on Korean customs and conditions arising from the country's distinctive historical experience. "Only when we educate our people in the history of their own struggle and traditions can we stimulate their national pride and arouse the broad masses to revolutionary struggle," he exhorted. Later, the North Korean regime deemed such a mentality the core spirit of *Juche*—an overarching approach, more than a term, that considered Korean realities before "mechanically copying" external forms.

Just as revealing, the flip side of this Korea-first theme in the December 1955 speech was a diatribe against some internal political forces, whom Kim accused of toadyism. Indeed he called out the guilty parties by name, including Bak Heonyeong, who had been executed just a few days earlier on charges of being an American spy. Bak had been the leader of the domestic Korean communist movement at the time of liberation, but he soon found himself in the wrong occupation zone, that of the south. Following his move to the northern sector in 1947, he gained some appointments to high posts, but ultimately his fate mirrored that of the domestic communists themselves—that is, he lost out in the intra-communist struggle for power. By the mid-1950s, Kim Il Sung actually found the greatest challengers to his own faction, the former guerrillas from Manchuria, to be not the domestic communists but rather the Soviet-Koreans, who stood as embarrassing reminders of his own dependence on the Soviet Union. These Soviet-Koreans attempted, in fact, to oust Kim in 1956 through a targeted campaign of open criticism and appeals to the Soviet leadership, but Kim gathered enough support to outmaneuver and eliminate them from the scene. This might have been a signal moment in North Korean history, a potential turning point that was not to be. The last rival group remaining toward the end of the 1950s, the Chinese-based Korean communists, also met their end.

These purges of Kim's political opponents, then, required shifting from a Soviet-sponsored North Korean state to one of greater autonomy. But aside from the ousted figures themselves, Soviet influence was still preeminent; indeed the methods of eliminating political undesirables— from the show trials to the trumped up accusations of espionage, anti-party activity, and "factionalism"—displayed the ongoing reliance on the Soviet template. North Korea in fact moved toward a firmer Stalinism just as many other communist states, led by the Soviet Union itself, began to repudiate it following Nikita Khrushchev's famous speech in early 1956 denouncing the Stalin personality cult. The North Koreans also owed a considerable debt to Mao Zedong, the Chinese communist leader who espoused a paternalistic, even Confucian, dictatorship as the way to maximize his following. Indeed Kim Il Sung appropriated from Mao many ideas related to cultivating a blend of nationalism, communism, and personality cult.

These strands of foreign influence were also on prominent display in the great effort, called "Cheollima" (named after a legendary flying horse of Korean folklore), to collectivize and industrialize the North Korean economy beginning in the late 1950s. The nationalization of industry, along with other economic measures such as currency reform, had begun in the years preceding the Korean War through the exploitation of colonial period infrastructure, especially in hydroelectric generation and mining. The *Cheollima* campaign completed this process and launched a mammoth effort focused on heavy industries, such as construction, steel, and agricultural and military machinery. It required—and gained, it appears—a mammoth mobilization of labor, which resulted in a substantial increase in North Korea's economic output and, in turn, living standards. The campaign was contemporaneous with and similar to the doomed agricultural collectivization effort in Mao's China, the Great Leap Forward, but it avoided China's mass starvation—mostly because North Korea's agricultural mobilization was limited in scale and scope. Still, the foreign connections continued to play a central role: the promulgation of Soviet-style fixed-period development plans; the contributions of Soviet, Soviet-Korean, and Chinese experts; the Chinese troops stationed in North Korea until 1958 for help with security and reconstruction; and the ongoing economic aid coming from China and especially the Soviet Union that allowed, by accounts, North Korea's economic growth to outpace that of South Korea from the late 1950s through the 1960s.

Such a collective fervor for reconstruction manifested itself in cultural mobilization as well, as culture became politicized into a form promoting nativism and the Kim Il Sung-led state. This process, too, had already appeared in the post-liberation period, as music, theater, literature, paintings and sculptures, and cinema became immersed in revolutionary state making. As in communist societies elsewhere—and ironically, given the Marxist emphasis on the material basis for historical development—ideological and cultural training was perceived as paramount in fortifying mass support for the system. Divergence into "frivolous" or "empty" expression, the coded terms for art that failed to strive for "socialist realism," came under attack in the 1950s. Aesthetics had to service ideology. Leftist artists and intellectuals who had moved to or stayed in North Korea as a progressive haven for decolonization soon found themselves at the mercy of political developments, none more potent than the ongoing concentration of authority in one man and his party. The novelist credited with devising Kim Il Sung's personality cult, Han Seorya, became the most powerful figure in North Korean literary circles, himself leading many of the 1950s witch hunts of suspect writers. But tellingly Han, too, eventually fell victim to the whims of politics and was purged in 1962, never to be heard from again.

JUCHE, HISTORY, AND LEGITIMACY

Perhaps the most dramatic and enduring ideological outcome of this intense political concentration and mass mobilization came in the shaping of a new historical perspective. As Kim indicated in his 1955 speech, the most urgent task for propaganda workers—and presumably for society at large—was to focus on the core lessons of Korean history. As elaborated upon later but clearly present already in the 1950s, the self-reliance constituting the core of *Juche* ideology could not be divorced from a strong consciousness of Korea's historical experience, in particular the calamities caused by foreign intervention.

The Pueblo Incident

To put a cap on the economic recovery, social stability, and political consolidation achieved by the mid-1960s, in the summer of 1966 North Korea's national football team stunned the world by defeating heavily favored Italy in a World Cup match. As if this triumphant event emboldened the North Korean regime, over the next three years it aggressively challenged its sworn enemies, the United States and South Korea, through a series of incidents that together appeared as resumption of unfinished business from the Korean War. The most notable such provocation was the so-called Pueblo Incident, in reference to the North's capture of the American naval intelligence vessel USS *Pueblo* in early 1968. Just a couple of days before this event, on January 21, 1968, a group of thirty North Korean commandos had attempted a raid on the South Korean presidential compound, resulting in the deaths of nearly all the assassins and scores of South Koreans. Apparently, however, news of this event had not reached the *Pueblo*'s officers, who continued their surveillance off the peninsula's east coast in what the United States considered international waters. Speedy North Korean boats, claiming American infringement on North Korean territory, attacked the *Pueblo*, boarded the ship, and took into custody its crew of over eighty. After months of negotiations behind the scenes that resulted in a formal apology from the United States for having entered North Korean waters, the crew was released. Immediately thereafter, upon learning of the abuse and torture that the sailors had endured in captivity, the American government retracted its apology. But the damage had been done.

The Pueblo Incident was followed by a hunt for North Korean soldiers who had landed on the east coast of South Korea in the fall of 1968. In the spring of 1969, North Korean fighter jets shot down an American naval surveillance plane, killing a crew of over thirty. To the United States and South Korea, these incidents presented proof of the need to maintain vigilance; to North Korea, they reinforced the chronic sense of threat from American imperialism as well as from its South Korean "puppet." Today the USS *Pueblo*, presented as a tourist attraction while docked on the banks of the Daedong River in Pyongyang, continues to serve the interests of the North Korean regime's legitimation narrative, just as it had done in 1968.

Image 22 *The captured ship* USS Pueblo *on display on the banks of the Daedong River, Pyongyang, 2003. (Courtesy of Tae Gyun Park.)*

The fabrication of historical details to shape this grand narrative began in the post-liberation period and gained momentum through the propaganda activities of intellectuals like Han Seorya. All of Korean history eventually came to be seen as an unrelenting struggle against harmful external forces and exploitative internal elements, such as those Koreans who had collaborated with the Japanese colonialists. In service to Kim Il Sung's political ascent, his colonial period struggles against the Japanese in Manchuria underwent transparent inflation, even gaining credit for having achieved Korea's liberation in 1945. Indeed, in the

1950s, as the North Korean regime's legitimacy became more firmly hitched to Kim's credentials as an independence fighter, his official biography gave him another boost, this time hailing him for having defeated the Americans in the Korean War as well. In his speeches Kim lashed out at the United States for having launched the war, seeking world conquest, and desiring to "enslave" the Korean people. For evidence, he noted, one needed only to look at what had happened to South Korea since liberation. The clear message in this emerging North Korean historical orthodoxy was that only a great historical figure—namely, Kim Il Sung himself—could rally the people to learn from their historical experiences. It was a story that equated Kim with nothing less than the fate of Korean civilization itself.

The historical irony was compelling and, given North Korea's turn toward nativist isolationism, tragic, as this narrative stemmed from efforts to hide Kim's dependence on, as much as to tout his resistance to, outside forces. The Soviet occupation put him in power in the first place, and then China's intervention in the Korean War preserved the nascent North Korean state itself. The lofty *Juche* rhetoric of fierce autonomy and nativism that accompanied the North's turn toward isolationism, then, compensated for the fact that North Korea the country, and Kim Il Sung the leader, began with and were sustained by external assistance.

23 1960s South Korea

CHRONOLOGY

1960 March	Rhee government rigs election for vice president; protests in Masan
1960 April 19	Outbreak of student demonstrations and violent crackdowns
1960 April 26	Resignation of Syngman Rhee
1960 June	Establishment of the Second Republic, a parliamentary system of government
1961 May 16	*Coup d'état* engineered by Major General Park Chung Hee
1961–63	Rule by the Supreme National Reconstruction Committee, headed by Park
1962	Promulgation of the First Five-Year Economic Development Plan
1963 September	Election of Park as president, start of the Third Republic
1964 March	Student protests against prospective normalization of relations with Japan
1965 May	Dispatch of the first contingent of South Korean troops to Vietnam
1965 June	Signing of the normalization treaty with Japan
1967 May	Reelection of Park; establishment of Pohang Iron and Steel Company and Guro Industrial Park
1969	Mass protests against a constitutional amendment that would allow a third presidential term for Park

DEMONSTRATIONS AGAINST THE NORMALIZATION OF RELATIONS WITH JAPAN, 1964

In the spring of 1964, as throngs of young people in some other parts of the globe were enraptured by Beatlemania, their counterparts in South Korea filled the streets for something quite different. With news that the South Korean government was close to reaching an agreement to formally reestablish diplomatic ties with Japan, Korean students erupted in protest. To them, the shameful period of Japanese colonial rule, especially the horrors of wartime mobilization, remained a contemporary event. They could not fathom why the South Korean government, under the direction of President Park Chung Hee, would even consider such a thing. Their demonstrations reached a crescendo in June of 1964, when tens of thousands of university students disrupted campus life throughout the country and invited a government crackdown as well as the imposition of a state of emergency. Such a struggle between students and state power would act as defining moments for much of the 1960s, just as they did around the world.

It turned out that Park Chung Hee had authorized secret negotiations for this agreement with Japan not long after he came to power through a military coup on May 16, 1961. Park considered the normalization of relations, in particular the capital investment and technology transfer that it would bring, a cornerstone of his plan to modernize the nation's economy. Historical judgment has largely looked favorably upon the "miraculous" economic development that marked the second half of the twentieth century in South Korea, and the 1960s, under Park's direction, is considered its take-off period. But as the student protests and other forms of resistance indicated, the particular pattern of economic growth institutionalized in the 1960s—driven by the combination of anti-communist ruling ideology, military government, and big business—came at a high cost. These challenges, too, would characterize the 1960s, and indeed, much of the subsequent history of South Korea.

DICTATORSHIP, DEMOCRACY, AND REVOLUTIONS

Student demonstrators, in fact, had acted as the catalyst behind the major event that opened this decade. When Syngman Rhee, whose presidency over the First Republic descended into despotism and rampant corruption in the post-Korean War 1950s, attempted to steal another election in the spring of 1960, the unrest that followed led to his overthrow. The occasion this time was his regime's blatant rigging of the polls for vice president, with massive fraud such as ballot stuffing conducted in the open. Rhee was perhaps emboldened by the fact that his own electoral opponent for the presidency had died shortly before the election— the second Rhee opponent to die, with the previous challenger from the 1956 election, Jo Bongam, having been executed for treason in 1959. The anti-Rhee protests of 1960 gained momentum initially along the south coast, and with the discovery of the body of a student protestor killed by a tear gas canister in the city of Masan, students in Seoul rose up, only to be met with a brutal crackdown themselves. On April 19, 1960, this led to an eruption of student demonstrations throughout the country, with the most furious clashes coming in the capital and reaching a scale of mass unrest not seen since the immediate post-liberation period. Hundreds of protestors were killed before Rhee, under pressure from a wide range of political and social sectors, including university professors, agreed to step down and go into exile in Hawaii (where he died in 1965). Even at the time, this series of events was referred to as a "revolution," for it brought down a dictatorial system and displayed the power of concerted popular action.

What followed the April Student Revolution was Korea's first experiment in full-fledged democracy. The pronouncement in June 1960 of the Second Republic, a parliamentary system with the president serving a ceremonial role, unleashed creative energies and accompanied a spike in civic cooperation and volunteerism, along with a dose of optimism. Chang Myon (Jang Myeon), a former vice president who was defeated in the sham March election, was selected as the prime minister, and he ruled through a coalition of mostly conservative elites who had grown weary of the Rhee dictatorship. In addition to the eradication of blatant corruption at the top of the government, some major policy shifts took place under Chang's leadership, including the extension of electoral democracy to the provinces. In December 1960, for the first time in Korean local elections—which did not reappear until the 1990s—people went to the polls to directly choose provincial governors and the mayor of Seoul. This, too, constituted a revolutionary step.

Naturally, with the loosening of the state's grip came the allowances for people to protest their conditions even more freely, which intensified political polarization. Large-scale unrest starting in late 1960 also reflected a worsening economy, especially high unemployment, although the situation had actually improved compared to the end of the Rhee period. The Chang Myon government responded by implementing more public works programs, including the construction of a nationwide transportation infrastructure. Such episodes represented the natural growing pains attendant to the beginnings of electoral democracy, and they did not necessarily constitute a threat to the nascent system. But what might have tipped the scales toward endangering this order were student demonstrations in early May of 1961 calling for immediate reunification with North Korea. Such a step, the students claimed, represented the true spirit of the April Student Revolution, and they announced plans for a march to the border. A segment of the army, having long planned an overthrow of what it deemed a corrupt political and military system, used this as an opportunity to take action. On May 16, 1961, troops under the command of Major General Park Chung Hee occupied government offices and immediately pronounced another revolution that emphasized first and foremost anti-communist vigilance. This represented the third "revolution" in thirteen months, and another shift in the historical arch of struggle between students and dictatorships in South Korea.

PARK CHUNG HEE

No person is more closely associated with South Korean history than Park Chung Hee (Bak Jeonghui), the apex political figure for almost two decades, from 1961 to his death in 1979. For good and bad, in the pervasive historical perspective, he is inseparably linked to the combination of authoritarian state making, industrialization, and the politics of national division amid the Cold War that characterized the modern transformation of South Korea. He stands as both the symbol and agent, then, for a particular path toward modernization that prioritized material growth over political liberalization, and militarized regimentation over civic engagement. In the geopolitical arena, Park helped cement an American-led East Asian order through South Korea's participation in the Vietnam War, a cornerstone of his anti-communist industrialization drive. Thus his life and thought, as well as his regime and the sociopolitical system that it instituted in the 1960s, reflect well the complexities of Korea's modern experience as a whole and continue to arouse passionate debate.

Born into a poor rural family in the south-central part of the peninsula in 1917, Park experienced first-hand the decay of the countryside, a theme that would preoccupy him in office. Gifted and ambitious—his hero as a boy was Napoleon—he took advantage of opportunities made available by Japanese colonialism. Following a stint as a school teacher in his native region, in the early 1940s he became one of the young Koreans selected to receive training at a Japanese military school in Manchuria. There, and later as a cadet in the Japanese Military Academy in Tokyo, he imbibed the lessons of the rapid modernization of Japan, in particular the military's preeminence in the Japanese approach to governing. As with many of his compatriots who came of age in the late colonial period, his affinity for Japan, or at least the Japanese model, did not subside, even after liberation. He also became somewhat of an idealist, which perhaps explains why, following graduation from the new South Korean Military Academy in 1946, he secretly joined the South Korean Workers'

Party, following in the footsteps of his older brother, a communist activist. This proved a risky move indeed, when, as part of the government forces sent to quell the Yeosu-Suncheon Rebellion of 1948 (Chapter 20), Park was instead arrested, with his life being spared only through the intervention of some high military officials, including an American. For the Korean War and the rest of the 1950s, Park retreated to the South Korean army, keeping a low profile due to his leftist past, gradually ascending the ranks and cultivating high-ranking patrons, ties to certain army factions, and a following among officers that would prove decisive later.

Although he spent most of the 1960s as a civilian president, his approach to rule throughout the decade was militaristic, from the way he gained power through a coup to the regimentation of politics, society, and economy set in motion by his military junta. The junta took form as the Military Revolutionary Committee and then the Supreme Council for National Reconstruction from 1961 to 1963. This "revolutionary" government in 1961 immediately set out to clean up the streets by eliminating blight and seedy social elements, rounding up and putting to work street kids, vagrants, and even gangsters. To maintain surveillance and control over perceived threats, particularly opposition political figures, Park also established the notorious Korean Central Intelligence Agency (KCIA), the internal security apparatus of the military government, at the time of the coup in 1961. For most people, however, "reconstruction" became the all-encompassing word on their lips, a shorthand for the comprehensive changes that would require destruction as much as construction: elimination of the old ways of thinking that led to corruption and decay, of the legacy of Korea's sad history that had produced weakness and tragedy, and of the impoverishment that made the country an easy target for communism. As it had under Syngman Rhee's regime, hostility to communism became a mainstay of Park's claims to legitimacy and method of rule. In the latter part of the 1960s, sensationalistic incursions by North Korean commandos and spies (Chapter 22) further stoked the government's anti-communist campaign.

Such a heavily martial bent in the polity and society, and even in the economy and culture, actually complicates any general assessment of 1960s politics. Although one is inclined simply to label the entirety of Park's rule from 1961 to 1979 as an era of "military dictatorship," in the 1960s, at least, it looked more like a militarist order seeking dictatorship. While many among his cabinet and top advisors came from the military, Park had to shed his officer's uniform to run in the 1963 election for the civilian presidency, which he narrowly won. And while his reelection in

1967 was a more comfortable affair (over the same opponent, interestingly), throughout the 1960s Park had to deal with constraints imposed by the formalities of a republican system, including opposition from national assembly members, civic activists, workers, and especially students. Nevertheless, he eventually pushed through most of his agenda, particularly the manner by which the country would achieve economic growth.

ECONOMIC TAKEOFF

Park made clear that his highest priority was to modernize the country through industrialization. For the most part, the economy made great strides, although it took the entirety of the decade, and there were periodic shortages of basic goods. Borrowing an approach found in communist states, ironically, Park deployed the model of the "five-year plan" for economic development, with clear-cut goals and blueprints for pursuing a growth strategy managed by state bureaucrats. His junta promulgated the first Five-Year Plan in 1962, the same year that it also selected, as a special industrial development zone, the city of Ulsan on the southeastern coast, which would become the base of the Hyundai Corporation's manufacturing juggernaut. By the end of 1966, the final year of the plan, there were indeed signs of major infrastructural and urban growth, as well as of the drive for exports gaining full force. One of the most tangible changes had appeared in 1964, when some areas in the country began to enjoy around-the-clock electricity provision, which engendered a dramatic lifestyle change by expanding the scope of nighttime activity. Indeed, especially in the urban areas, conditions continued to improve, and people's perspectives, especially those of the youth, widened with greater exposure to foreign cultural and material products.

The second Five-Year Plan, beginning in 1967, more explicitly targeted export-oriented growth as the primary goal, which would lay the foundation, in turn, for a shift toward heavy industry. That year the government finalized plans to establish a nationally-owned steel venture, the Pohang Iron and Steel Company, or POSCO. POSCO became incorporated the next year and went on to supply the major industries of shipbuilding, auto manufacturing, and construction through which South Korea became an industrial power. 1967 also witnessed the creation of a special export manufacturing zone in southwestern Seoul, the famed Guro Industrial Park. With its concentration of toiling workers producing everything from shoes and clothes to machinery, the Guro Industrial Park eventually turned into a symbol of the sacrifices made by the labor force.

South Korean workers, exploited by the state and big business for the comparative advantage of cheap labor, suffered conditions not unlike what their counterparts did throughout the modern world, and in many ways their experiences revived patterns established earlier in the colonial period (Chapter 17). There were, however, some distinctive features of the South Korean work force arising from the circumstances of the post-liberation era. First was South Korea's subordinate position in the Cold War, which accounted for the type of goods the country produced within the East Asian regional trading system and, eventually, for the legions of soldiers sent to Vietnam. This furthermore resulted in the emergence of economies attached to the American military bases in South Korea, including a substantial population of sex workers who seemed to replicate the country's larger dependence. Second, female workers, both those in the sweat shops and those in the "service" industries such as prostitution and domestic work, constituted an even more essential component of the labor force beginning in the 1960s. For the most part, however, their careers were limited by customary expectations and a militarized regimentation of society that promoted procreation and domesticity over vocational training or sustainable work. Finally, the accelerated economic development of this decade drew from, and justified, the centrality of anti-communism as the ideological antidote to national division, which in turn facilitated authoritarian state practices that kept the workers in line. Many South Korean laborers resisted this heavy-handed state control and even won significant concessions through collective action. But hounded by suppression and pressured by calls for national sacrifice, they had to fall in line with the emerging industrialization drive. Their contributions, bolstered by their dogged pursuit of education and training, made workers the most indispensable element of South Korea's "economic miracle."

The biggest beneficiaries, however, of state-led, export-oriented industrialization were the family-owned conglomerate corporations, the so-called *chaebol* (*jaebeol*), a mostly pejorative term meaning "financial clique." Some of the best known of these conglomerates today, such as Samsung and LG (Lucky Goldstar), started as small enterprises in the colonial period, while others, such as Hyundai, began shortly after liberation. By the 1960s, the South Korean government selected well-performing companies for targeted export-oriented production, rewarding them with cheap and big loans, easy licenses, tax benefits, and state guidance. The result was the astonishing growth of many of these firms into the "octopus"-like entities that came to dominate the South Korean economy. The families that controlled the conglomerates came to be followed as national celebrities, though not always flatteringly, and the tycoons who began these enterprises won listing in the pantheon of national heroes.

Hyundai presented a prime example. Begun by Chung Ju-Yung (Jeong Juyeong), a man from the east coast of what is now North Korea, as a transport service supplying the American military, Hyundai became perhaps the most celebrated beneficiary of government largesse in the 1960s. Hyundai's first major industry, construction, jump-started its rise through the procurement of contracts in Southeast Asia in the mid-1960s, while at home it won major infrastructure projects, including construction of the national artery, the Seoul–Pusan Expressway, completed in 1970. Its second major industry, automobile manufacturing, began in 1967 with an agreement to build a Ford model in its plant in Ulsan. By the 1970s, Hyundai would produce and export its own car, the Pony, and by the 1980s it would penetrate the largest auto market in the world, the United States. Hyundai eventually expanded into shipbuilding, for which it became a global leader, as well as cement, chemicals, and even electronics. Today, like the other well-known *chaebol*, Hyundai is commonly seen as a standard-bearer for South Korean industrial prowess, and even for South Korea itself.

A final major factor in the 1960s economic takeoff, though not as easily discerned, can be deemed "association with America." The United States affected the South Korean economy in several ways. Its dozens of military bases and tens of thousands of soldiers stationed around the country injected capital into the consumer economy and, as noted above, gave rise to specialty occupations and businesses servicing them. Furthermore, the Americans' direct aid to the South Korean government in the form of grants and loans provided the regime great leverage, through its control over lending practices of major banks, in getting industry and labor to comply with state-directed development. There was also the considerable impact of American soft power—the widespread influence of American ideals, popular music, fashion, movies, and entertainers, some of whom, like Louis Armstrong, actually performed in South Korea. This influence helped set trends and increase demand for American products, both cultural and material.

A more pronounced effect came from South Korea's participation in the Vietnam War, which, beginning with over 17,000 troops sent in 1965, came to form the second largest foreign contingent after the Americans. As with the Japanese investment of capital and technology following the 1965 normalization treaty, the total economic impact of

South Korea's involvement in the Vietnam War is difficult to measure, but it was likely enormous: In addition to gaining favorable treatment and direct aid from the US government, South Korea became a major supplier of American military provisions, which added further to the national coffers supporting export-oriented industrial growth. And would-be Korean entrepreneurs, many as soldiers, flooded Vietnam, with some making a small fortune, others sending more modest amounts back home, and still others using their Vietnam experience as the basis for businesses and careers after their return. To many younger South Koreans, in fact, the image of Vietnam as a great opportunity for adventure and money making tended to overshadow any sense of danger and alleviate the anxiety.

YOUTH AND ANGST

Although both the Vietnam War and the normalization of relations with Japan played significant roles in South Korea's economic push and global integration in the 1960s, youth culture displayed a contrasting response to the two ventures. While many of the South Korean elite who had come of age in and benefited from the colonial period, like Park Chung Hee, might have viewed the prospect of reconciliation with Japan more pragmatically, university students and others, especially younger Koreans, fiercely resisted this as a betrayal of the nation. Park made his first official visit to Japan in November of 1961, just half a year after seizing power, and his advisors soon engaged in secret negotiations to reestablish formal diplomatic ties and attract an infusion of Japanese know-how and capital, much of it through reparations for colonial rule. When word spread in March of 1964 that the two governments were on the verge of an agreement, students filled the streets, engaging in clashes with riot police and even entering into protest fasts. By June, over ten thousand student demonstrators had risen up, inviting the promulgation of a state of emergency in Seoul. The spirit of rebellion was further fueled by a hit film released that year, "Barefooted Youth"—Korea's answer to "Rebel Without a Cause"—which portrayed the uneasy and directionless existence of a younger generation falling victim to the constraints of customs and authority. Whether so intended or not by the filmmaker, Gim Gideok, this movie was taken as tacit support for the protesting students. In the end, the delay in finalizing this treaty did not last long, and by June of 1965 the treaty was signed, followed by easy approval in the government-controlled National Assembly later in the fall. The heavy-handed ratification process compelled the mass resignation of opposition politicians and the eruption of more student protests, which the government suppressed through a military occupation of college campuses.

These demonstrations against the Normalization Treaty with Japan represented both the confluence and conflicts of economic, political, and cultural forces that drove the spirited decade of the 1960s. While the state, big business, and geopolitics moved the country in one direction, less powerful sectors of society, embodied especially in the students, pushed back, or at least demanded a reorientation of priorities and a reconsideration of consequences. This dynamic reappeared in 1969, as politicians and students rose up to block the prospective constitutional amendment that would allow Park Chung Hee to run for a third consecutive presidential term. Once again, universities were shut down and opposition political figures were stifled as the amendment, like the Normalization Treaty, was rammed through the National Assembly before being approved in a national referendum. With this, the turbulent 1960s came to a close, setting the stage for the somber 1970s.

24 Culture and Politics in 1970s South Korea

CHRONOLOGY

1970 April	Proclamation of the New Village Movement by Park Chung Hee
1970 May	Publication of Gim Jiha's narrative poem, "Five Bandits"; Gim's arrest
1970 November	Protest through self-immolation by young labor organizer Jeon Taeil
1971	Reelection of Park Chung Hee to third consecutive presidential term
1972 summer	Joint declaration of reconciliation by the two Koreas
1972 October	Suspension of constitution, establishment of the *Yusin* constitutional dictatorship
1973	Global oil shocks; kidnapping of opposition politician Kim Dae Jung
1974 August	Assassination of Park's wife, Yuk Yeongsu
1975 April	Quick execution of eight alleged dissidents following high court denial of appeal
1975 May	Promulgation of Emergency Measure No. 9 prohibiting all expressions of dissent
1977	Achievement of $10 billion in value of South Korean exports
1979 October	Assassination of Park Chung Hee, end of Yusin system

PUBLICATION OF GIM JIHA'S "FIVE BANDITS," 1970

Gim Jiha, a budding poet laden with personal travails from the 1960s, published one of his earliest major works in 1970, and was promptly arrested. His alleged crime, and that of his publishers, was violation of the Anti-Communist Law, although the poem in question, "Five Bandits," made no mention of support for North Korea or communism. It simply satirized the gross inequalities in South Korean society due to corruption, though in an unmistakably condemnatory and mocking fashion. For continuing to protest the political and economic injustices of the South Korean autocracy, Gim Jiha spent most of the 1970s in jail, even receiving a death sentence in 1974. Gim was not alone in openly criticizing contemporary South Korean society and politics, for the primary thrust of cultural expression in this period carried a political undertone, particularly in response to the heightening of repression itself. But Gim Jiha, through his connections and impact, can be considered a fitting representative of the 1970s, the memory of which continues to be colored by the term "Yusin" in reference to the constitutional dictatorship forcibly implemented in 1972.

Those who arose to counter and call attention to the abuses of the Yusin system included writers like Gim, artists, musicians, publishers, journalists, lawyers, and religious leaders, in addition to the students and laborers who maintained their core role. Indeed the 1970s witnessed the emergence of many major historical figures who would dominate lasting perceptions of South Korean history, especially in the arenas of politics and culture. Whether explicitly or not, the most notable cultural developments of this decade, which reflected and affected broader historical currents to an extent unseen since the colonial period, were tinged with politics.

THE YUSIN DECADE

Not everything in 1970s South Korea was shaped by the Yusin system; it just seemed that way. Even the remarkable economic growth through export-led industrialization and domination by conglomerate companies appeared as a handmaiden to the dictatorship. As is the case eventually with most autocrats, Park Chung Hee became convinced of his indispensability and conflated his power with the people's welfare, although the country—partly due to the success of his policies, ironically—was very different in the early 1970s than it had been a decade earlier. Nevertheless, in October 1972 Park imposed the so-called *Yusin* ("revitalization") constitution, which prohibited political dissent and in effect rendered him president for life (which turned out to be true). The official justification for this move—which amounted to his second *coup d'état*, this time of a system that he was already heading—was to strengthen the path toward reunification. Forced into a response to the Sino-American *détente* in 1972 that had cast doubt on great power commitments, the two Koreas had achieved some stunning breakthroughs in reconciliation talks, at least publicly, earlier in the summer that year. But the new dictatorship clearly came amid signs of growing dissatisfaction with Park's rule, as reflected in his less-than-convincing reelection in the 1971 presidential race. And soon after the inauguration of the Yusin system, the global oil shocks beginning in 1973 and the killing of his wife by an assassin in 1974 added further to Park's siege mentality. By the fall of 1979, amid unmistakable indications of widespread, impassioned opposition to the dictatorship, Yusin came to an end with that of Park's own life at the hands of his own internal police apparatus. By then, the Yusin system had intensified the militarized approach to rule of the 1960s to suppress all forms of dissent through a constitutional dictatorship that bordered on absolutism.

Such an ostensible comfort zone of total power provided Park the capacity to push through a state-led revamping of the countryside as well. The New Village Movement (*Sae maeul undong*), which in some ways emulated the North's *Cheollima* campaign in the 1950s, began in 1970 through a personal directive from Park. The "New Village Movement" quickly became the general catch-phrase for all efforts to improve the countryside and was even applied to an overarching spirit of reform that the government encouraged in urban and industrial areas as well. The mobilization of state resources focused first on improving the rural communities' infrastructure and appearance—removing, for example, the blight of thatched roofs, for which Park was said to have had a particular disdain. By the middle of the 1970s, the New Village Movement became a comprehensive effort, driven by a systematic, large bureaucracy that directed money, labor, and expertise to mechanization, irrigation, road construction, electricity, and the provision of consumer items. The goal was to improve agricultural output, to be sure, but also to raise living standards in the countryside. Some historians view the New Village Movement, which continued in revised form into the 1990s, as having been more of a political ploy to divert excess materials, such as cement, and thereby tamp down any potential restiveness in the rural populace. But without a doubt the material welfare of Koreans in rural areas improved dramatically. Alas, this did little to stem the steady stream of migration out of the countryside, and in fact might have accelerated it.

The movement of people to the cities and factories fueled the explosive growth of metropolitan areas, especially in and around Seoul, as well as of the major conglomerates, the family-controlled enterprises that expanded through the government-guided export drive. These firms propelled the next stage of South Korea's industrialization drive to heavy industry and high technology. Companies like Samsung Electronics and LG produced a bevy of consumer products such as televisions and microwave ovens, while Hyundai and Daewoo manufactured big-ticket items such as automobiles and supertankers designed primarily for export. Such enterprises also facilitated the mobilization of expertise and workers, in the tens of thousands, for large-scale construction projects overseas, especially the Middle East, to build power plants, water treatment facilities, roads, bridges, and big buildings. Such efforts resulted in the achievement, with great fanfare, of the $10 billion mark in the annual value of South Korean exports in 1977, an extraordinarily feat given that, at the beginning of the decade, the figure was barely $1 billion.

Needless to say, the clearing of such economic benchmarks reflected and induced major changes in everyday life, especially for people in urban centers. There, a robust consumer culture arose, spurred by the increasing supply of goods and buying power as well as by the extension of communications and transportation networks. In the first half of the 1970s, South Koreans witnessed the opening of the Seoul–Pusan Expressway and other major highways, the launch of the first subway line in Seoul, and the sizable expansion of the capital city to many areas south of the Han River. Not everyone, however, was benefiting from these advances. The agitation of the growing working class, which manned the factories and provided services that made these developments possible, continued to remind everyone of the underbelly of rapid industrialization: gross inequality, persistent poverty, oppression, and exploitative, even dangerous, working conditions. Tellingly, the Yusin decade had begun with one of the most memorable moments in South Korean history, one that compelled attention to the plight of laborers: In late 1970, a young man named Jeon Taeil, who had attempted without success to improve the conditions of his fellow workers in a typical sweatshop, committed ritual suicide by setting himself on fire while brandishing a book of labor laws that the government had failed to enforce.

LITERARY RESISTANCE

Gim Jiha sought to speak for such downtrodden victims of South Korean society, and in later works such as "Cry of the People," he invoked the memory of Jeon's self-immolation in his calls for action. As for the work that thrust Gim into the public spotlight, "Five Bandits" (*Ojeok*) was published in the May 1970 issue of the journal *Sasanggye* ("World of ideas"), then soon again in the organ of the main opposition political party. The government immediately shut down both publications and arrested their editors and publishers. Gim Jiha himself was booked on charges of violating the Anti-Communist Law, a generic tool for silencing political opposition. Gim likely knew what would happen—he even anticipated his arrest in the balladic poem's preamble—for he bore the battle scars of struggle against the anti-communist system. As a college student he had participated in the demonstrations to overthrow Syngman Rhee in 1960, helped lead the reunification campaigns that had prompted Major General Park Chung Hee to seize power in 1961, and joined the huge student protests against the Normalization Treaty with Japan in 1964 (Chapter 23). He had spent most of the latter part of the 1960s trying to fend off both severe illness and government surveillance, a pattern that would also characterize his life in the 1970s. Indeed he spent most of the decade either in jail or under house arrest, even being briefly sentenced to death in 1974 after being nabbed in a sweep of activists and students on fabricated charges of sedition. When this happened again the following year, he was fortunate to escape with his life, for eight others were quickly executed following sentencing in a kangaroo court. His resilience in the face of hardship, including torture, inspired a persistent, concerted movement to win his freedom that became a *cause célèbre* in literary and intellectual circles far beyond Korea. Gim Jiha served, then, as the counterpart to Park Chung Hee as the symbol of 1970s South Korea, and it had all begun with a brilliant, biting poem.

"Five Bandits"—a title in unveiled reference to the "Five Traitors of 1905" (*Eulsa ojeok*) who had signed the protectorate treaty leading to the Japanese takeover (Chapter 16)—is a narrative poem suffused with the lyrical elements of local dialect and the singing quality of shamanistic rituals. Its story revolves around a contest between five bandits—a contest in corruption, that is, among representatives of the five most privileged and powerful groups of people in South Korean society at the time: tycoons of conglomerates, national assemblymen, high-ranking bureaucrats, generals, and cabinet ministers. Each of these five bandits takes turns to outdo the other in debauchery, ostentatious wealth, and venality, and before the poem ends with heavenly retribution, a sixth class of miscreant emerges, a clueless detective who ends up joining rather than apprehending the bandits. The message could not be clearer: The system itself suffered from a comprehensive miscarriage of social justice that divided the populace into the parasitic and exploited. And while Park Chung Hee himself escapes direct mention, "Five Bandits" unmistakably targets him. In the poem's accounting of the five bandits' contest, for example, they joyously recall that they had originally gathered "ten years ago" to begin their collective efforts to rob the people. The bandits' affinity for Japanese ways and brutality, and the fact that one of the five bandits is actually a general, all point to Park. Gim also makes no attempt to hide his own personal connection: The poem's poor, suffering peasant who makes an appeal to the detective has come to Seoul from Gim's home region of Jeolla province.

While not so brazen in their condemnation of the South Korean system, other great writers of the 1970s, too, came to be marked by a pervasive social consciousness in their works. One was Ko Un (Go Eun), who led a campaign in the literary world to bring about Gim Jiha's release from jail and himself was arrested for his political activities. Like Gim originally from Jeolla province, Ko Un had spent his twenties as a Buddhist monk, and this religious sensibility infused his perspective on social injustice and the means to overcome it. His breakthrough work came in 1974 with a narrative poem, "To Munui Village," which described and decried the desolate winter landscape in a rural area, and took the snow as a cover for and symbol of death. A social consciousness is only hinted at here, but in later poems Ko exuded a clearer anti-government voice. In "Arrows" (1977), for example, Ko calls on those fighting for democracy to let go of all of their possessions, accomplishments, and even "happiness" for the singular purpose of "becoming arrows and advancing with all our might" toward a bloody struggle. Ko would later establish himself as Korea's most revered contemporary poet through his epic narrative verse, especially the "Genealogy of Ten Thousand Lives" (*Maninbo*) that recounts his imagined encounters with people both contemporary and historical. His most stirring expressions, though, came in the cauldron of the 1970s.

Many of the great South Korean novelists also made their mark in this decade. Interestingly, three of the most renowned—and not only as authors of anti-establishment, social commentary fiction—all made their literary debuts in the same year, 1970, as the publication of "Five Bandits." Hwang Seogyeong, considered by some Korea's greatest contemporary novelist, entered the literary scene in 1970 with a short story of the Korean War as the backdrop (Hwang had just returned from a tour of duty in the Vietnam War). But his big splash came the following year with "Kkaekji." "Kkaekji," roughly translated as "strange land far from home" in reference to the story's focus on struggling factory laborers who had migrated from the countryside, established Hwang as the foremost practitioner of what came to be called "people's literature," or *minjung munhak*. In later works, Hwang would display a remarkable versatility in topics and settings, but always through a concern with the stifled voices of the oppressed. 1970 also was the year Jo Jeongnae debuted with the first in a string of novels that discerned the impact of modern Koreans' historical experiences on their current circumstances. Jo would later expand his literary canvas in the 1980s and 1990s as a prolific producer of the multi-volume historical novel. The best known such work was *The Taebaek Mountains*, which featured the connection between historical and contemporary conditions by dramatizing the conflicts that led to the Korean War from a more balanced rather than the conventional anti-communist perspective. Finally, the 1970s witnessed the flowering of literature by female novelists, and none more prominent than Bak Wanseo, who debuted with a novel published in 1970, *The Naked Tree*. In later works such as *A Hobbling Afternoon*, Bak combined a probing rumination on Korea's historical experiences, especially that of national division, with a critique, through a distinctly female sensibility, of the emerging middle-class existence.

A final author who embodied this charged world of 1970s literature was Bak Gyeongni, a towering figure who combined Bak Wanseo's prioritization of the female voice with Hwang Seogyeong's attention to the underclass within Jo Jeongnae's sweeping historical flow. Though she was already well established, it was through the serialized unveiling of her masterpiece, *Land (Toji)*, in the 1970s that Bak Gyeongni—coincidentally, Gim Jiha's mother-in-law—came to be perhaps the nation's representative literary voice. An epic at once sprawling and intimate, *Land* traces a family over several generations as its members, and the community around them, adjust to dramatic developments on the south coast of the peninsula from the late nineteenth to the mid-twentieth centuries. In using this family's story as an allegory for the turbulent experience of modern Korea itself, Bak calls attention to the mighty accumulation of quotidian changes through a focus on the lives and perspectives of the main female characters. *Land* thus epitomized the scratchy realm of literary production in the 1970s, when almost everything, whether intended or not, seemed to allude to the ominous restlessness of the times.

MASS CULTURE UNDER THE YUSIN

During the darkest days of the Yusin period, beginning around 1974, expression became suppressed to an extent that would be unfathomable to younger South Koreans today, and in fact was not far removed from the conditions up in North Korea. Indeed the Emergency Measures issued by the Park regime criminalized all manner of actions, and by the time Emergency Measure Number 9 came around in the spring of 1975, the government proclaimed sweeping powers to arrest people summarily for any expression or behavior deemed anti-state. The atmosphere of intimidation also stemmed from the regime's efforts to prevent any potential outbursts of anti-government sentiment in broadcasting, film, music, and publishing. But these areas also reflected the expanding channels of social interaction and access to information through the dissemination of technological advances. Television viewing, for example, became widespread, and while government censorship kept programming fairly tame, television's capacity to act as a mirror of society kept it a potentially subversive element.

The start of South Korea's television age

In 1969 just over 200,000 television sets were in operation in South Korea. Ten years later, the number was almost six million, meaning that in the 1970s the number of televisions in use increased nearly thirty-fold, from penetrating 6 percent of households to nearly 80. Many South Koreans recall the 1980s as the heyday of television, particularly through its service as a medium for tearful reunion telethons for families separated by the Korean War, but it was the Yusin period that witnessed the emergence of now-familiar patterns of television broadcasting and viewing. In this decade, for example, the Korean Broadcasting System (KBS) went from being a government broadcaster to a public company much like the British Broadcasting Corporation, and another, MBC, founded in 1969, became a private national network and competitive alternative to KBS.

In terms of programming, however, broadcasters faced definite limits from the Yusin censors. Furthermore, in this age of black and white TV (color would come in the 1980s), the government restricted not only television's content but also its style, issuing a decree in the mid-1970s, for example, prohibiting the appearance of male personalities with long hair. Programming was mostly limited to censored news, soap operas, variety shows, educational programs, sports, and foreign, especially American, entertainment shows. Even the amount of broadcasting was curtailed, shutting down in the afternoon and late-night. (Twenty-four-hour programming was only introduced in the new century.) Still, television

→

had a major impact in the 1970s, especially with soap operas that hooked large audiences and became a cultural phenomenon. Such programs drew condemnation from social critics for their alleged portrayal of frivolous, decadent, and immoral lifestyles, but clearly, at a certain level, these shows provided a much-need escape from the atmosphere of political tension.

Not everything, though, could be so tightly controlled as to prevent the injection of untidy politics. A shocking example came on August 15, 1974. As often was the case for the national holiday celebrating liberation from Japanese colonial rule (August 15, 1945), the anniversary was to be marked by a major occasion, this time the formal opening of the first subway line in Seoul. The day started, as usual, with an address by the president to an assembled audience in a public hall, carried live on television. Very few people could have foreseen what happened next: As President Park Chung Hee was delivering his speech, a man came running down the aisle firing a gun in the direction of the stage. The assassin, ostensibly aiming for Park, instead hit the first lady, Yuk Yeongsu. After she was carried away to the hospital, where she would pass away, and the commotion died down a bit, an equally remarkable thing happened: Park continued with his speech! Perhaps nothing better captured Park and the spookiness of Yusin—as anyone watching television could see.

Government repression also aroused dissent in mass culture that otherwise might not have formed. One example of this came in popular music, which had earlier become a ubiquitous entertainment medium. In the 1970s, the Koreans' ingrained affinity for socialization through music turned some popular songs into collective expressions of anti-government sentiment. The ballad "Morning Dew," released in 1971 by the singer Yang Hee-Un (Yang Huieun), for example, resonated with its lyrical tribute to inner strength and determination in the face of hardship. Young people caught in the constraints of the dictatorship found in this message a stirring call to resistance, and when the Yusin regime caught onto this possibility and banned the work, "Morning Dew" only grew in popularity and eventually became the anthemic "movement song" for a generation. The ballad's composer, folk singer Kim Min-ki (Gim Mingi), became a champion of the anti-Yusin artists' movement and continued to churn out protest music.

The realm of publishing also grew into a potent voice of opposition in the 1970s. In addition to *Sasanggye*, the magazine founded by renowned activist Jang Junha that published "Five Bandits," other intellectual journals, political organs, and newspapers served as forums for provocative analysis and criticism of Yusin. In response to increasing repression, journalists banded together to fight for legal protections of press freedom and, through their writings and research, to uncover the hidden structures of political and intellectual domination exercised by the state. Among literary journals with an activist bent, most notable was perhaps *Creation and Criticism* (*Changjak gwa bipyeong*), a publication begun by academic Paik Nak-Chung (Baek Nakcheong) with modest aims in the 1960s but which, by the 1970s, had become an indispensable player in the public discourse. While continuing to remain wary of censors, *Creation and Criticism* published seminal works of literature, literary scholarship, and social commentary, and hence became an arbiter of not only great literature but also of political debate. Finally, the maturation of the "Hangul generation"—the first South Koreans raised in the postcolonial practice of disseminating information printed primarily in the Korean alphabet, or Hangul (*hangeul*)—also contributed greatly to the growth of publishing.

The higher literacy rate and publication activity were likely related to another phenomenon in mass culture that came to define the Yusin decade, the social standing and influence of organized religion. While dramatic religious growth was a story that continued throughout the twentieth century, not since the 1910s had religions and the religious establishment exerted such a pronounced impact on society and polity as in the 1970s. As noted above, Buddhism inspired the social criticism of Ko Un, and the same could be said for Catholicism's role in the work and actions of Gim Jiha. Indeed much of Gim's Catholic inspiration came from his being mentored by Bishop Ji Haksun, who in the 1970s stood at the forefront of the Catholic Church's steadfast opposition to the Yusin system, suffering arrests and beatings but unbending in his criticism. The same could be said for the Catholic politician Kim Dae Jung (Gim Daejung), who, like Gim Jiha, was raised in the city of Mokpo on the southwestern coast. Kim Dae Jung had been the opponent who nearly pulled off the miraculous victory over Park Chung Hee in the 1971 presidential election. For this offense and his continuing opposition to the regime—much of it inspired by his Catholic faith—Kim was kidnapped while in Japan by South Korean agents and came close to being shoved into the sea before international pressure forced Park to relent. It is little wonder,

then, that the Catholic clergy in South Korea developed a stout reputation for social justice that endures to this day.

The same does not necessarily apply to Protestantism, which—
despite, or perhaps because of, its enormous growth in followers—
remained mostly an anti-communist and pro-government stalwart. But
there were many exceptions, including major schools and denominations
of progressive activism and scores of eminent clergymen such as Mun
Ikhwan, a Presbyterian minister who headed organizations that fiercely
resisted the Yusin dictatorship, for which he was arrested and constantly harassed. Probably the most acclaimed Protestant figure of this
period, though, was a Quaker, Ham Seokheon. Unlike many of his fellow
Protestants originally from the north, who were driven by their hostility
to communism, Ham sought to influence public opinion on major issues
such as reunification through a focused push against dictatorship. Ham,
already well-established as a renowned activist from the colonial period,
began publishing a monthly in 1970, *Ssial ui sori*, which perhaps can best
be translated as "Voices of the people." This journal became the mouth-
piece for Ham's calls for ecumenism, non-violent resistance, and human
rights, cementing his moniker as the "Gandhi of Korea." Ham became,
then, a symbol of the long journey toward democratization in modern
Korea, a breakthrough in the 1980s that would not have been possible
without the trials of the 1970s.

The historical impact of the Yusin decade, however, hardly disap-
peared with the transition toward an electoral democracy in 1987. Indeed
Yusin returned with a vengeance in the early twenty-first century, when
Park's daughter, Park Geun-hye, twice ran for president. The younger
Park, who ironically lost both her parents to Yusin political violence,
rode a cresting wave of nostalgia for her father, mixed considerably with
sympathy for her, to a slim electoral victory in 2012. Once in power,
Park Geun-hye, though officially recognizing the excesses of the 1970s
political repression, indeed cultivated the sense of a reviving Yusin, by
embracing the interests of the business oligarchy and practicing forms
of secrecy, hierarchy, and domination that seemed, to many, at odds with
a liberal democracy. Most intriguingly, Park focused on shaping public
memory: In 2015, the 50th anniversary of her father's reestablishment
of diplomatic relations with Japan, her administration arrived at a settlement of the "comfort women" dispute with Japan over responsibility for
the latter's World War II military prostitution system. And earlier that
year, her ruling party announced a renationalization of secondary school
history textbooks. Both efforts joined the ongoing campaign to overturn
the roundly negative perception of her father's rule, especially Yusin, by

stoking the impression that his autocratic ways had constituted a necessary sacrifice for the nation to become a wealthy democracy. Stunningly, joining her in this venture was Gim Jiha himself, who in his old age did a complete about-face, not only to express political support for Park, but even to denigrate progressive activists. This was but the latest eerie twist to the legacy of the Yusin period.

25 Monumental Life in North Korea

CHRONOLOGY

1972	Erection of a colossal bronze statue of Kim Il Sung in Pyongyang
1980	Formal introduction of Kim Jong Il as North Korea's next leader
1982	Opening of the Tower of the Juche Idea, Arch of Triumph, and Great Study Hall of the People
1987	Beginning of construction of the Ryugyong Hotel
1992	Halting of construction of the Ryugyong Hotel
1994	Confrontation with the United States over the nuclear program; death of Kim Il Sung
1995–97	Floods and famine; stirrings of unauthorized market activity
2000	Summit between Kim Jong Il and South Korean President Kim Dae Jung
2008	Resumption of construction of Ryugyong Hotel
2011	Death of Kim Jong Il, transfer of leadership to son Kim Jong Un
2012	Failed launch of a North Korean rocket on April 12, the 100th anniversary of Kim Il Sung's birth

GROUNDBREAKING FOR THE RYUGYONG HOTEL, 1987

The construction of Pyongyang's Ryugyong Hotel, a massive, pyramid-shaped building over 100 stories and 300 meters tall, began in 1987 amid the ongoing battle for prestige in advance of the Seoul Summer Olympics the following year. The North Korean regime believed this mammoth edifice would symbolize the advancement, power, and pride of North Korea. But after construction was halted in 1992, which left the building an empty shell for over fifteen years thereafter, the Ryugyong Hotel became a national monument for all the wrong reasons. Like North Korea itself, and especially its regime, the structure originated in visions of grandeur, depended on foreign assistance, was built on the backs of the suffering masses, and stalled in the face of cold reality. In 2008 construction of this colossus restarted. What remained unclear was whether it would ever function as originally intended, endure more as a symbol of the decay, mystery, and tragedy of North Korean history, or perhaps reflect the stunning changes of the early twenty-first century.

THE HISTORICAL CHALLENGE

Anyone attempting to understand North Korea faces a host of obstacles, beginning with the difficulties of accessing reliable information about this notoriously secretive land. This problem is compounded when pursuing a historical examination, for the temptation is to focus on North Korea as an immediate, present object of concern. We tend to ask about current conditions without wondering how they might have gotten that way, and to view North Korea through the country's relationship to the outside world instead of as a product of unique, mostly internal historical circumstances. Still, the dearth of unfiltered information has not stopped the emergence of a major prognostication industry on North Korea, particularly on the prospects of its survival in current form. In the West, and particularly the United States, the demand for knowledge has stemmed from the chronic fear of the North Korean nuclear program and from concerns over the welfare of the North Korean people. Among South Koreans, a more tangible awareness of their ethnic brethren has come through sporadic joint development ventures and official North Korean media content, the value of which has been limited due to its monotony and transparent propaganda.

The attempt to decipher the realities of North Korean society and history, then, must rely on accounts from the growing ranks of defectors and refugees, as well as on reports from foreign governments, aid agencies, and the occasional visitors. But in all instances, the picture that emerges from both the official and unofficial sources should serve to demystify North Korea and its people, and to move beyond caricatures and the easy condemnation of its ruling system. The other major historical challenge is to treat North Korea on its own terms and to integrate it into Korean history, overcoming the temptation to dismiss the country as somehow an aberration. Only then can we can attempt a sincere understanding of North Korea's development within the broader historical context—not just that of the recent or modern periods, but of Korean civilization a whole. We can thus find strong parallels to premodern patterns, which are essential to understanding North Korea's own past and present, and come closer to solving that most daunting of all historical questions about modern Korea: How did North and South Korea diverge so dramatically out of common origins?

HISTORICAL PATH, 1970s TO 2010s

Notwithstanding these lessons, it is difficult to avoid a consciousness of South Korea when tracing the North's history, and vice-versa, for in part the eventual radical split in the two states' developments stemmed from their strenuous efforts to contrast themselves with each other. For both, the rivalry drove their self-perceptions and actions. By the turn of the 1970s, both countries had completed their post-Korean War recoveries and established the sturdy foundations of industrialization and military autocracy. Whereas South Korea continued to undergo comprehensive change thereafter, however, in the North the post-war progress hit a wall, and politically the leadership revealed a disturbing recidivism, a retreat into primal forms and values. It was as if North Korean leaders had nothing to do, and nowhere to go, but to reassure themselves of their specialness. The echo chamber, however, resulted in an ongoing tragedy of modern Korean history.

Like many countries, North Korea squandered its relative plentitude in natural resources, such as hydroelectric capacity and coal. The industrialization of the 1960s and 1970s made possible many advances in material comfort, especially in the urban areas, where citizens enjoyed modern amenities. Even in the agricultural sector, where growth from collectivized farming appears to have been inconsistent, production was sustained sufficiently to allow the country even to export grains into the 1980s. The following decade, however, was one of unremitting economic catastrophe, beginning with the collapse of the Soviet Union and the end of the Cold War, and hence the halt to cheap fuel and other subsidies. This was soon compounded by the disastrous floods of the mid- and late-1990s, which resulted in a famine that likely killed more than half a million people (with some estimates reaching two million) and robbed the country of an entire generation to malnourishment. North Korea, then, entered the twenty-first century a basket case, with its people suffering from severe food shortages, lack of power and heating, and general misery. How much of this downfall can be attributed to natural disasters, and how much to deficiencies in the political and economic system itself, became a moot point, for the system was responsible for placing the people in such a vulnerable position in the first place.

The opening decade of the twenty-first century witnessed somewhat of a recovery. Efforts to attract foreign investment in the tourism and manufacturing sectors resulted in, for example, the construction of the Gaeseong Industrial Complex, which hosted dozens of South Korean firms employing thousands of North Korean workers. The most pronounced changes, however, resulted from internal dynamics, particularly the famine itself. As people scrambled desperately to meet basic needs, private markets sprouted around the country, resulting in a fundamental shift in the way of life for many North Koreans. Outside of Pyongyang and a few other strategic locales, even the domineering state dissipated, as restrictions controlling people's activities and movements weakened amidst a growing ethos of everyone, including lower-level officials, fending for herself. Perhaps most startling in this regard was the overturning of the gender hierarchy in areas where unofficial economic activity thrived. Women, less bound in the collectivized economy to keep up appearances at dysfunctional jobs, became the entrepreneurs and market vendors heading the new economic sectors. Outside the military and the government, then, North Korea became in some ways a female-driven capitalist society, at least at the informal level. Bribes and unofficial transactions lubricated the flow of goods and people across the country and, significantly, over the Chinese border. At the turn of the twenty-first century, North Koreans began crossing into China in the tens of thousands as economic refugees and opportunists, blending into the long-established Korean population along the Sino-Korean border and living in the shadows. This rising tide of migrants suggested, then, that liberalization, however considerable, failed to overcome widespread privation—or more likely, that the economic conditions continued to be dramatically uneven across the country.

According to visitors' accounts, the people of the showcase capital city of Pyongyang, which functioned as a giant Potemkin village, appeared anything but impoverished. This simple reality offered a reminder of how this self-identifying socialist paradise depended on starkly unequal access to privileges and resources. While the revolution of the immediate post-liberation years had permanently overturned the pre-1945 order, as time passed tight control over social interaction led to a startling regression to the premodern Korean patterns of hereditary hierarchy. Ancestry, in short, became paramount and, as in the dynastic eras of the past, much of the purity of one's blood was measured in accordance with the political circumstances of the regime's founding. Below the royal family, the Kims, the aristocratic elite were the party leaders whose ties to Kim Il Sung extended back to the Manchurian guerrilla days. After the descendants of party cadres, bureaucrats, and military brass, North Koreans with peasant backgrounds came to occupy the commoner middle class. A despised or stigmatized population, meanwhile, was comprised of descendants of political criminals, people originating in the south, and colonial-era elites and landlords. A bureaucracy that investigated lineage backgrounds for determining entrance into universities, the communist party, elite occupations, and even prospective marriages maintained this bizarre transplantation of traditional life.

Such a social hierarchy reflected, of course, the distribution of political power as well. But as time passed, evidence surfaced that the regime, despite its outward appearance, stopped far short of operating as a monolith, particularly after the death of Kim Il Sung in 1994 following half a century of rule. Even before this staggering event, military units, party leaders, individual bureaucracies, and local agencies appear to have established their own power bases that, for funding, relied on corruption, black marketeering, illicit international operations, and enterprises such as in food production. The divisions and rivalries between these power centers might have played a role in the circumstances surrounding Kim Il Sung's death and resurfaced following the 2011 passing of his son Kim Jong Il.

Kim Jong Il, formally introduced as the successor to his father in 1980 while in his late thirties, in fact always relied on his association with the army. His preferred official title as the military's supreme commander was bestowed upon him just three years before his father's death, and after his assumption of power he was commonly referred to as "The General" despite having no military background. And the public proclamation of a "Military First" state policy beginning in the 1990s appeared as a tactic to ensure the support of this formidable institution. Indeed, despite his ostensibly unquestioned supremacy, Kim Jong Il never enjoyed the same aura of command as his father, for legitimacy was always based on the recognition of the latter's personal heroics.

Kim Jong Il's own successor, his third son Kim Jong Un, also faced challenges in establishing personal rule and even resorted to sudden purges of high ranking officials, including his uncle in 2013, to secure his fledgling authority. Even more daunting for the grandson was to maintain the Kim dynasty's delicate balances. Its constant struggles to prop up the economy while holding onto power led to a recurring pattern in foreign relations behavior: Periodic provocations, such as nuclear weapons tests, rocket launches, or artillery attacks on South Korea, would draw enough international concern to gain the necessary external aid to tide the regime over until the next provocation.

While people outside of North Korea prioritized such an impact on the world in attempting to understand the country, more illuminating was the question of how external forces or, more precisely, the perception of these forces, determined the internal workings of North Korea. On the one hand, of course, the regime exercised stringent control over the people's exposure to external realities, for it depended on the belief, within the country, of North Korea's relative superiority. Here, ignorance was a powerful tool. On the other hand, the regime found foreign threats useful in reinforcing the foundations of its rule. The everlasting Korean enmity for Japan was stoked whenever necessary, for example, given that it provided the basis of Kim Il Sung's historical claims, and hence the Kim family's hold on legitimacy.

The United States, too, readily served as a bogeyman for constant vigilance, based on the populace's grim memories of the Korean War and occasional skirmishes with the US military thereafter (Chapter 22). In the mid-1990s, this chronic hostility suddenly triggered a crisis, following the American detection of North Korean activities to reprocess nuclear fuel. The response of the North Korean regime to international demands for inspections was to withdraw from the Nuclear Non-Proliferation Treaty and to intensify the public vilification of American intent. Just as tensions in the summer of 1994 seemed to have reached a point of imminent military confrontation, former American President Jimmy Carter traveled to Pyongyang and came away with an accord, which was eventually signed later in the year as the Agreed Framework. The Agreed Framework's requirement of inspections of North Korean nuclear facilities in exchange for fuel and food aid, however, failed to permanently halt the nuclear program, mostly due to the regime's attempts to stall indefinitely while extracting as many concessions as possible. But the Americans shared the blame. Indeed North Korea's relentless push to develop nuclear weapons was historically fated to prick and preoccupy the United States, for the genuine fears of American interventionism drove much of its nuclear ambitions. American political leaders who engaged in juvenile name-calling of North Korean leaders while remaining painfully ignorant of these larger circumstances only exacerbated the North's fears and thereby strengthened the effects of the regime's propaganda for internal consumption.

And finally, South Korea, the so-called American puppet, was steadily condemned as a prime example of shameful foreign domination, despite the occasional breakthroughs in reconciliation such as the 2000 summit in Pyongyang with South Korea's president, Kim Dae Jung. What outsiders called North Korea's isolation, then, was touted internally rather as a manifestation of the country's fierce autonomy. Following the famine and economic collapse of the latter half of the 1990s, however, the country had to open up sufficiently to entice foreign capital and know-how. Even Internet and cell phone traffic was made available to a privileged few. But the wariness of the slippery slope potentially leading to the collapse of the system itself remained, and this delicate balance between too much exposure and too much hardship suffered ever greater stresses with the onset of the new leadership in the 2010s.

MONUMENTAL LIFE

One begins to understand, then, the paramount significance of keeping up the impression of North Korean superiority within the country, and hence also the extraordinary lengths undertaken to enforce this narrative. This accounts for the unsettling monumentality of life in North Korea that hardened in the closing decades of the twentieth century: the mind-numbing proliferation of over-the-top propaganda, gigantic memorials and construction projects, and ever-stupendous claims about the country and regime. In a classic case of overcompensation, such grandiosity and myth-making that lay at the heart of North Korean existence, in which everything was said to be "perfect," seemed to intensify the more it diverged from reality. North Korea, and in particular Pyongyang, turned into not only an Orwellian society, but an uncannily precise realization of Orwell's vision in the novel *1984*. All the elements were there, including the viral surveillance, the double-talk and absolute control of information, the relentless vigilance and incapacity to turn off the propaganda, the erasure and fabrication of history, the ritualized hatred of a bogeyman enemy, the submission of the self into the mass, brutal punishment for nonconformity and political crimes, and, of course, Big Brother.

The cult of personality quickly reached absurd proportions and eventually went beyond the scale of other totalitarian regimes in its attribution of extraordinary powers to both the father and son, but especially the latter, Kim Jong Il, who was not only showered with adulation but credited with superhuman skill. There is evidence that the younger Kim viewed this narrative, much of which he probably crafted himself, more soberly, and repeated the explanation of other North Korean officials in rare moments of candor: The lessons of Korean history, especially in the modern period, required resolute regimentation in order to preserve national independence and dignity, and a heroic leader was necessary to induce and properly channel this energy. Tellingly, however, the personality cult in North Korea, as well as political rule itself, also took on a hereditary nature, an understandably rare occasion for communist regimes subscribing officially to an ideology, socialism, with pretenses to perfect rationality. While some commentators detected an unmistakably Christian tenor in the droning public worship of the father–son tandem, the most common and plausible explanation was to observe simply that the North Korean ruling system revived the Korean kingship. In addition to preserving power within a given family, the Kim dynasty tapped into a basic longing for stability, national pride, and autonomy (however imaginary), as well as for a singular leader whose authority was expressed in familial overtones.

But this kind of mythology required constant reinforcement, especially as reality intruded upon it. Hence the erection of enormous monuments celebrating the system, its ideology, and especially its leader. The round-numbered anniversaries of Kim Il Sung's birthday of April 15, 1912 (incidentally, the day of the sinking of the *Titanic*) seem to have generated the most memorable memorials. In 1972, on the occasion of his sixtieth birthday, a 20-meter bronze statue of Kim's most majestic pose was unveiled close to the banks of the Daedong River. His seventieth birthday in 1982 brought forth a staggering trio of monuments that dominated the visitor's impression of the city: the Arch of Triumph, a little taller and wider than the one in Paris after which it was styled, in celebration of Kim's leadership of the Workers Party; the Tower of the Juche Idea, a paean to the official ruling ideology of self-reliance that was simply called "Kim Il Sung-ism," so transparently did it serve to rationalize the Kim monarchy; and the splendid Grand Study House of the People, a public library that stood as the largest building anywhere in the traditional Korean architectural style.

It was hoped that the Ryugyong Hotel (see Image 25) would be completed in time for the next super-great birthday celebration, Kim Il Sung's eightieth in April 1992. Groundbreaking for this one-of-a-kind building, towering over 100 stories, took place in 1987, at the height of the feverish competition over which Korea could outdo the other ahead of the 1988 Seoul Summer Olympics. In addition to planting a bomb in 1987 that destroyed a South Korean airliner with over a hundred souls on board, the Northern regime prepared to host the World Youth Festival in 1989, for which the world's largest stadium, with a seating capacity of 150,000, was actually completed. The Ryugyong

Hotel, however, ran into troubles, and construction stopped midway in 1992 due to astronomical costs and, as widely suspected, problems in the building's structural integrity. Thereafter it remained an unsightly skeleton, a 300-meter hollow pyramid of concrete. Visitors to Pyongyang remarked, though almost never flatteringly, on its unavoidable presence, visible from just about everywhere in the city. Some observers described it as "hideous" or "monstrous," while one American magazine dubbed it "the world's worst building." Others, however, found the super structure a tremendous curiosity and remarked on its distinctive shape with three extended wings, each grounded by a smaller pyramid at the base. The hotel, then, appeared to mimic the layout of the Egyptian pyramids of Giza, although many commented that it looked like a giant rocket ship ready to launch. After a fifteen-year dormancy, construction on the hotel was revived in 2008, this time targeting for completion, at least of the facade, April 12, 2012, the one hundredth anniversary of Kim Il Sung's birth. As it turned out, however, on that day, it was actually the (failed) launch of a North Korean rocket that drew the most attention, at least from the outside world.

Image 25 *Ryugyong Hotel in Pyongyang, 2003. (Courtesy of Tae Gyun Park.)*

The Ryugyong Hotel, then, turned into an unwitting symbol of North Korea itself, given the megalomaniacal ambitions that marked its construction, as well as its struggles under economic bankruptcy and disabling stagnation, waiting only for collapse itself. And as with North Korea's historical development and ultimately its survival, the Ryugyong Hotel project became a matter of utter will, dedication, delusion, and mobilization for the sake of preserving a fantasy: Given the overarching primacy of formality in the ruling *Juche* ideology, correspondence to reality was less significant than the collective will to forge an ideal. Furthermore, like the ruling system that built it, the hotel became at once omnipresent but impenetrable, an empty shell incapable of functioning for actual people and a testament to misplaced priorities (and funds). And somewhat like the regime itself, the hotel, which remained uninhabited despite its external makeover, was overtaken by the historical forces that eventually drove the North Korean people to take matters into their own hands following the devastating famine at the close of the twentieth century.

As noted above, gauging how the people of North Korea actually led their lives remained a challenge, as so much that foreign visitors observed was carefully staged and limited to the gleaming capital. But the available evidence, particularly from the thousands of migrants to South Korea in the new century, suggested major difficulties and widespread hardship. In the 1970s and 1980s, a modicum of economic development and political stability had produced enough to eat as well as a modern lifestyle, at least for Pyongyang and the larger cities, not terribly different from that of other communist societies. People pursued their routines of work and family life, followed long-established modes of social interaction, enjoyed leisure and play, engaged in romance, and in keeping with traditional Korean passions, often went picnicking, singing, and dancing. They also partook in centrally-guided mass culture by consuming grand theatrical, musical, and filmic productions, such as "Sea of Blood," an epic opera about colonial resistance reputedly composed by Kim Il Sung himself, and traditional folk stories such as the "Tale of Chunhyang".

With the collapse of the Soviet Union and the famine of the 1990s, however, came deprivation and resignation, and an intensified dulling of the senses from the relentless monotony and hardship. Any move toward reform would have needed help from the privileged minority with the most to lose in any dramatic change: the elites of the army and Communist Party, who grew dependent on the system of permanent exploitation and radical difference between the haves and have-nots. For the rest of the country's people, existence might have been occasionally satisfactory but debilitatingly hollow—intellectually, psychologically, and spiritually—especially as they struggled to remain alive amid the horrors of the famine. The dramatic transformation of economic life that ensued in the opening years of the twenty-first century did little, it appears, to relax the limitations over the people's thoughts and expressions beyond service to the Kim cult, or to liberate them from the overpowering fear, backed by a network of gulags, through which the state controlled them.

Above all, then, North Korea became a historical tragedy, and "tragic" ultimately rang truer than the other adjectives that immediately came to mind: weird, unknowable, evil. While those labels were readily applied to the regime, the greater concern could only be the North Korean people, victimized by the disastrous turns taken by their country's history. An investigation into the manner by which the regime came to hold such destructive sway over the populace must be balanced by an inquiry into how the people came to find themselves in such a position in the first place. Here a consideration of the greater historical context is inescapable. One cannot deny that the obsessive fear of external domination was rooted in the painful memories of the colonial period, the post-liberation occupation, and the devastation of the Korean War. One also cannot deny the allure of a fierce nationalism for North Koreans—indeed, Koreans as a whole—given their historical experience. The Soviet occupation determined the Cold War orientation of the North's political system, but understandably a charismatic strongman appealing to fear and touting himself as the savior from foreign intervention found resonance. The effects of the colonial experience, furthermore, were not just oppositional: The colonial state's militaristic and industrializing mobilization of the populace provided a model and foundation for such a system to continue functioning after liberation. And the reception of traditional forms of monarchical authority, paternalistic leadership, and hereditary social hierarchy also made perfect sense.

In short, North Korea was an unmistakably direct product of its history, including the history that it had in common with South Korea before 1945. That these two states and societies eventually diverged so drastically as time passed suggested not that North Korean history was somehow an aberration, but rather that the two Koreas served as counter-factual examples for each other: each a logical, if perhaps extreme, outcome of a shared past.

26 South Korean Democratization

CHRONOLOGY

1979 October	Assassination of Park Chung Hee
1979 December	*Coup d'état* engineered by Chun Doo-hwan
1980 May	The Gwangju Uprising
1987 June	Mass pro-democracy demonstrations in Seoul; "June Declaration" of direct presidential elections
1987 December	Election of President Roh Tae-woo
1988	Summer Olympics in Seoul
1992	Election of President Kim Young Sam
1997	Economic crisis; election of President Kim Dae Jung

THE JUNE DECLARATION, 1987

Tear gas again filled the streets of downtown Seoul and other major cities in June of 1987, just as it had so often in recent South Korean history in response to civil unrest. This time, however, the number, determination, and makeup of the demonstrators portended something on another level altogether. Anger and frustration against the Chun Doo-hwan dictatorship among the students and workers had been a given for many years, but in June they were joined by increasing numbers of white-collar workers, representing the burgeoning middle class. These soon swelled the ranks of the protestors to upwards of a million people throughout the country. They called for the immediate revocation of plans, just announced, to hand over the presidency to Chun's designated successor, Roh Tae-woo, which had appeared as clear intent to continue the dictatorship in defiance of the popular will. Chun was inclined to proceed with a harsh crackdown on the demonstrations that would have brought chaos and great bloodshed. What stopped him was the reality that such a move, coming on the eve of the Seoul Olympics to be held the following year, would garner little support from the bureaucracy, his American allies, or even the military. Roh then acceded to demands for a direct presidential election on June 29th, 1987.

The "June Declaration" that announced this change signaled the formal transition to the democratic governing system, the Sixth Republic, that remains in place today. But to suggest that democratization itself began in 1987 would erroneously diminish the long and painful struggle of South Koreans against the forces of both political and economic domination—a struggle that, as in 1960, even attained formal success occasionally. Narratives of the political history of South Korea have, understandably, tended to focus on state actors, structural factors such as industrialization and the rise of a middle class, or geopolitical circumstances, including the ending of the Cold War, in accounting for the timing and nature of democratization. But counter-narratives view democratization as the central feature of South Korean history. Many who hold this view also consider the process as ongoing, indeed under constant threat, and that 1987 constituted more the culmination of long-standing popular yearning and sacrifice for democracy than a conclusive, durable triumph.

THE PRELUDE: GWANGJU, MAY 1980

One could argue, in fact, that the single most important event in South Korean democratization did not happen in 1987, but rather in 1980: the Gwangju Uprising, normally called simply "5–18" in reference to the date, May 18, of its beginning. The incapacity to account for this bloody episode denied the South Korean regime of the 1980s any lasting legitimacy. Likewise, the memory of Gwangju drove the intensifying struggle against dictatorship until it burst forth irrepressibly in the spring of 1987. It is safe to say that, without Gwangju, the breakthrough to formal democracy would probably have taken much longer, if at all.

The Gwangju Uprising itself stood as an outcome of resistance efforts in the 1970s against the "Yusin" system that Park Chung Hee instituted in 1972 to stifle all dissent and keep himself permanently in power (Chapter 24). As the end of the decade approached, a tense national atmosphere formed from the combination of many factors: Park's inaccessibility and siege mentality, which steadily deepened following the assassination of his wife in 1974; a deteriorating economy hit by the worldwide oil shocks; a heightened crackdown on dissidents of all stripes and on opposition politicians who had gained a plurality in the December 1978 National Assembly elections; and the escalation of popular protests. On October 26, 1979, in the midst of the largest mass unrest to date exploding in the southern coastal cities of Busan and Masan, Park was assassinated at a dinner gathering by, ironically, the head of the Korean Central Intelligence Agency, the internal security apparatus that had muzzled political dissent throughout his reign. During his trial, this man, Gim Jaegyu, insisted that he had been motivated by a desire for democracy.

Following their initial shock, the Korean people, too, could justifiably expect, after almost two decades of Park's rule, an opportunity finally to establish a fully democratic order. As with the period following the overthrow of Syngman Rhee in 1960, the national mood entered an expectant stage with the cancellation of Park's state of emergency, the release of political prisoners, and the selection of a temporary new president, Choe Gyuha. The man appointed to lead the investigation into Park's assassination, General Chun Doo-hwan (Jeon Duhwan), however, had other ideas. On December 12, 1979, Chun engineered a coup by arresting the country's top military commander. Henceforth, despite the nominal political authority vested in President Choe, it was Chun's group of officers, which included General Roh Tae-woo, who held real power. The awakening to this reality fueled the "Seoul Spring" of 1980, when laborers and students staged large demonstrations calling for an end to Chun's control, a lifting of martial law, and a concerted effort to establish a functioning democracy. The peak of these demonstrations came on May 15, when a hundred thousand mostly student protestors gathered in the plaza of Seoul Station. They retreated the following day to their classrooms, but another crisis would emerge on May 17 with the extension of martial law to the entire country, the shutdown of campuses, and the arrest of opposition leader Kim Dae Jung. Chun was solidifying his grip on power.

The Gwangju Uprising that erupted the next day, on May 18, 1980, started in a familiar way, with students gathered at the gate of a university for a rally. But the shockingly brutal response by the government troops—in this case, paratroopers sent down to quell any such disturbances—sparked the intensification of the conflict from a student protest to a civil uprising involving a considerable portion of the region's citizenry. Over the years scholars and other observers have cited many factors that might have contributed to the stunning phenomenon of crack troops, trained to fight North Korean soldiers, unleashing their fury on the very citizens whom they were supposed to protect: the suspicion fed by misinformation on the presence of North Korean agitators; regional antipathy toward Jeolla province, where Gwangju lay; and even the drugging of the paratroopers. Whatever the precise combination of causes, the result, after ten days of the uprising, was a total of more than two hundred citizens killed, many more hundreds injured, and a deep wound in the national soul that would take decades to heal. The city of Gwangju itself functioned as an autonomous, almost pristinely primal collectivity following the retreat by government troops from the city center on the fourth day. When the soldiers returned to retake the Provincial Hall building at dawn on May 27, many of these citizens, knowing full well their fate, chose to take up arms against the troops in a final act of defiance.

These victims of the Gwangju Uprising were not aiming for a hallowed place in the annals of Korean history, but rather expressing outrage and insisting on their dignity in the face of brutality. The citizens of Gwangju, however, came largely to embrace the popular judgment that their sacrifices represented an indispensable element in the process of democratization. In fact, in the larger scheme of things, the Gwangju Uprising took on even greater historical significance: as the explosive climax of the buildup of wrenching divisions in South Korean society; and as the origin of many other defining features of South Korean politics and society thereafter, including radicalization, regionalism, anti-Americanism, and, of course, democracy. It was, then, truly a watershed event, and if popular culture and public memory were any indication, the Gwangju Uprising remained a source of fascination and contemplation. Researchers, civic activists, novels, television dramas, feature films, and documentaries over the next three decades continued to explore its multi-faceted significance.

THE DEMOCRACY GENERATION

The most pronounced and durable impact of Gwangju, however, was felt by the first generation to come of age following the uprising. To these young Koreans, news about what happened in Gwangju leaked out via the thriving underground networks of first-hand written accounts, art work, photos, and even video footage smuggled into the country from foreign news outlets. Chun's consolidation of power through the Gwangju bloodbath rendered the validity of his regime null and void, but it was enough to instill an atmosphere of official silence about what really happened during the so-called "Gwangju incident." The excesses of this systematic repression pushed these activists into a revolutionary reconsideration of South Korean society as a product of the twentieth century's structures of capitalist imperialism, including the US alliance. Some even went so far as to idealize contemporary North Korea as having boldly resisted such forces. Above all, however, the intellectuals, students, workers, and others were driven by the memory of Gwangju, which they used also as the chief rallying cry for overthrowing the Chun regime in the 1980s.

These activists also employed Gwangju as the springboard for further refinement of the *minjung*, or "people's" movement that pervaded the anti-government resistance circles in the 1970s and 1980s. This was a movement in the sense not of a coherent organization, but rather of a powerfully enveloping mood that framed the perspective on Korean politics, culture, foreign relations, and, in particular, national history and division. From the *minjung* perspective, the people had been stripped of their primacy in recent Korean history by authoritarian and corrupt government, big business, and foreign powers that all conspired to divide the masses and suppress their will. The *minjung* movement sought to regain the people's autonomy and subjectivity by expressing itself not only in anti-government activity, but also in popular culture, patterns of public life, and academic inquiry. The primary practitioners, furthermore, were those who came of age in this era, mostly as university students.

In the 1990s, when the *minjung* movement faded, these people would be referred to as the "386 generation" (a play on the name of a well-known computer chip): those who were in their 30s, went to college in the 1980s, and were born in the 1960s. By the middle of the twentieth century's final decade, members of the 386 generation could look back on their formidable influence in the 1980s, when they represented both the vanguard and the shock troops behind the democratization movement. In subsequently entering the workforce and the comforts of middle-class domesticity, they found themselves concerned with matters other than politics, but their intense struggles for democratization would maintain a grip on their outlook. Indeed, when many of them, in their late thirties and forties, reached the top circles of political power in the opening years of the new century, they showed that issues of historical justice remained uppermost in their concerns.

THE 1987 DECLARATION AND ITS AFTERMATH

However essential this group of young people was to the democratization cause, the breakthrough of 1987 would not have occurred without the massive show of support from the growing middle class, which now included many graduates of the democratization struggle. To understand this phenomenon, we must return to the core problem of the Chun Doohwan regime: its utter lack of legitimacy. Following his consolidation of power from late 1979 to late 1980, Chun instituted a rule that largely continued the 1970s *Yusin* patterns of state surveillance, violent suppression of dissent, absurd personality cults, and the cultivation of family-run conglomerates as the dominant players in the economy, though now with less direct state oversight. Stunningly, the US and other major governments recognized his government soon after it began and, for a while at least, economic growth continued apace. While these developments might have helped procure the rights to host the 1988 Summer Olympics, they could do little to garner recognition from the South Korean populace. As an atmosphere of corruption and brutality emerged around the Chun junta, the bitter memories of 1980 brought forth an entrenchment of resistance to his rule.

This sentiment went far beyond the semi-permanent base of anti-government activists, as civil society, comprised of organizations and behaviors in opposition to the state, matured out of the foundation laid by the 1960s and 1970s resistance movements. Indeed, when the long-reigning dictator of the Philippines, Ferdinand Marcos, was overthrown by a popular uprising in 1986, South Koreans felt emboldened to take steps that would bring forth an end to their own humiliating condition of chronic dictatorship. Not surprisingly, then, protests erupted when, contrary to the expectations of most people, Chun Doo-hwan announced on June 10 of 1987 that the end of his "term" later that year would be followed by a parliamentary, not popular, election for the next president. This blatant move was designed to ensure that his hand-picked successor, Roh Tae-woo, would take office, but it also triggered an immediate outpouring of anger that spilled into the streets and begat the largest mass protests in South Korean history, with upwards of a million demonstrators throughout the country (see Image 26). The students who initiated these efforts had little idea that they would soon be joined by salary workers, managers, housewives, and others. Unlike in the past, when political dissent remained the purview of students, religious leaders, and labor activists, this time the middle class flooded the streets and expressed their support for the protests in numerous other ways as well. The Chun regime had grossly overestimated the degree to which the people would succumb to the latest machinations of dictatorship. As revealed later, the regime also miscalculated its support from the military and bureaucracy for a potential crackdown on these demonstrations. A catastrophe surely would have ensued, marring the much-anticipated hosting of the Summer Olympics in Seoul the following year. So feared also the American ambassador to South Korea, who in a private meeting with Chun relayed his government's strong warning that no violent moves should be made to force the demonstrators off the streets.

Image 26 *Clash between protestors and police in the city of Gwangju, June 26, 1987. (Courtesy of Noonbit Publishers.)*

The final, major actor to intervene in order to avert disaster was the man picked as Chun's successor, Roh Tae-woo. Roh understood that any severe crackdown would gravely stain his own government, just as Gwangju had marked Chun's. With Chun's grudging consent, Roh issued a declaration on June 29, 1987, calling for a direct presidential election and a new constitutional system that would make permanent an entire range of democratic reforms. This did not quell the spirit of revolt, however, as a massive wave of strikes and other labor actions arose immediately afterwards in the late summer of 1987, which served as a reminder that democratization would have to go far beyond formal constitutional changes. As if to underscore this sobering reality, Roh Tae-woo placed himself as the presidential candidate from the ruling party in the upcoming election. Given the public's widespread distaste for Chun's stewardship, Roh should not have anticipated electoral success, but the two leading political figures in the democratic resistance since the 1970s,

Kim Dae Jung and Kim Young Sam, failed to reach a compromise to field a single opposition candidate. The result, to the dismay of so many who had waged the struggle against authoritarianism, was the election of Roh with a plurality of less than 40 percent of the ballot, as the Kims split the opposition vote.

Kim Young Sam and Kim Dae Jung would eventually get their turn at the coveted prize of the presidency in the 1990s, with each new president, and each new peaceful transfer of power, further solidifying the democratic political culture. As for Roh, he made no attempts to reverse the democratization process, although he did little to enhance it either. Most of his attention and accomplishments came in foreign affairs, for which he benefited from international developments such as the collapse of the Cold War and China's growing assertiveness on the world stage. Riding these major currents of geopolitics, Roh pursued his "Nordpolitik" strategy of establishing diplomatic relations with China, the Soviet Union (soon Russia), and other communist states, which also led to the further isolation of North Korea. Kim Young Sam's election in 1992, which came about after he literally joined hands with Roh in order to procure conservative support, nevertheless occasioned the further establishment of legal and institutional structures preventing a return to dictatorship. Indeed his administration represented the first popularly elected civilian presidency since the early 1960s, following three decades of rule by military leaders. And the election of his successor in 1997, Kim Dae Jung, constituted the first peaceful transfer of power to the opposition candidate in South Korean history.

Both Kim presidencies, while beset by corruption surrounding the president's confidants and family members, also advanced national healing from the battle scars of democratization. Kim Young Sam's administration, in fact, revisited Gwangju, this time to officially vindicate the citizenry and launch a prosecutorial investigation into the circumstances, from October 1979 to May 1980, that had led to the massacre. As a result, South Korean citizens soon stood transfixed at the stunning sight of the two main aggressors in these events, Chun and Roh, being tried and found guilty for their illegal grab for power over this period, as well as for the astronomical slush funds they had accumulated as presidents. Their respective sentences of death and life imprisonment were eventually commuted, and Kim Dae Jung, as the new president in 1998, formally pardoned them for the sake of achieving national reconciliation amidst an economic crisis. That the South Korean people successfully weathered this storm spoke volumes about the health and reparative capacity of their nascent democracy, which was marked by an explosive growth of civic organizations dedicated to strengthening and extending the culture of fairness, transparency, and accountability.

Still, retrospectives on this achievement have taken unanticipated turns since the turn of the twenty-first century, with some observers even calling into question whether democratization truly took place. This has reflected mostly the languid pace of change in realizing greater economic equality, as well as the rise of conservative political forces and historical interpretations that have both denied and embraced core features of the democratization narrative. While acknowledging the wrongdoings of the Chun dictatorship, for example, a triumphalist view of South Korean history has come to argue that economic development, rather than the anti-government struggle itself, constituted the most important factor in the breakthrough to democracy in 1987. Indeed, this perspective sees the entirety of modern Korean history as a linear progression toward the achievement of a prosperous democracy, and thus everything that preceded this accomplishment eventually contributed toward it. On the other side, progressive historians and commentators have come to lament what they see as the shortcomings, ultimately, of the formal transition to a democratic order, which fell short of overturning the concentration of economic and social power held by privileged groups. For them, democratization, while a noble effort, remained incomplete and will likely stay that way as long as larger structural forces, such as national division and South Korea's diplomatic, military, and economic dependence on the United States, hold sway.

27 South Korea in the Twenty-First Century

CHRONOLOGY

1997	Asian financial crisis in South Korea
1997 December	Election of President Kim Dae Jung
1998	Inauguration of Kim's "Sunshine Policy" of engagement with North Korea
2000	Summit between Kim Dae Jung and North Korean leader Kim Jong Il
2002	Co-hosting of the World Cup Finals; election of President Roh Moo-hyun
2007	Election of President Lee Myung-bak
2009	Suicide of former president Roh Moo-hyun; death of Kim Dae Jung
2012	Election of President Park Geun-hye
2014	Sewol ferry disaster

QUARTERFINAL MATCH VERSUS SPAIN, 2002

As South Koreans entered the new century they were trying to overcome the so-called "IMF period," which had begun when the economy fell into a foreign exchange crisis in 1997 and had to be rescued by a colossal loan from the International Monetary Fund (IMF). But following the election of longtime dissident Kim Dae Jung as president later that year, citizens had rallied to recover from this shock. Not only did the government repay the IMF loan ahead of schedule, but the weathering of this crisis, together with the 2000 summit between Kim Dae Jung and Kim Jong Il of North Korea, instilled a widespread sense of a new era: South Korea had matured past the growing pains of rapid industrialization and social transformation, dictatorship and democratization, and even the Cold War. Behaviors and technologies, often devised by Korean companies, that exploited the endless possibilities of the Internet and the mobile phone turned South Korean society almost overnight into a futuristic urban space where identities could be readily mixed and reinvented. Mass culture also reflected this newfound confidence and determination, establishing the basis for the "Korean wave" (*hallyu*) in pop culture that swept through Asia in the new century.

The 2002 World Cup Finals, hosted jointly by South Korea and Japan, served as a potent symbol of this new era. The unanticipated success of the national team on the field corresponded to the citizenry's extraordinary energy in demonstrating collective support, as seen in the throngs gathered in the streets for viewing parties whenever the team played. The peak in the mass euphoria might have come with South Korea's stunning victory, in an overtime shootout, over Spain in late June 2002, which sent the upstart Koreans to a wildly improbable berth in the semifinals. Indeed, the ecstasy of the entire World Cup month served as the emblem of a continuing "coming out party" of sorts. The new century allowed South Koreans to start anew, and to enter a postindustrial age that coincided with rapid social and cultural changes. Little could they have foreseen, then, that this sense of renewal would not sweep away all the troubling vestiges of the past, and that they would therefore face continuing challenges in forging a good society worthy of the country's increasing prominence in the world.

ECONOMIC GROWTH: A RECONSIDERATION

Even before the financial crisis of 1997–98, throughout the 1990s South Koreans had a creeping sense that not all had gone well with the extraordinarily rapid economic growth they had traversed over the previous three decades. Perhaps the pace had been too quick, or that government oversight had not matched its policy ambitions, but whatever the causes, the construct of the economic miracle began to come apart at the seams. The roads were constantly clogged by too many cars on too little space, and even relatively simple structures seemed unstable. In 1993 a rail line collapsed over an illegal tunnel project in Busan, killing scores of people, and the next year, a section of one of the major bridges spanning the Han River in Seoul gave way, plunging several to their deaths. In the spring and summer of 1995 came the biggest such disasters: an explosion at a subway construction site in the city of Daegu that killed over a hundred, and the sudden collapse of the Sampung Department Store in Seoul, which took the lives of over five hundred shoppers and workers. In the latter case, it turned out that the shoddy construction pursued on the cheap by a would-be tycoon had been permitted to pass, through bribes, by government inspectors. Such unethical collusion led Koreans to wonder aloud whether, in the relentless pursuit of development, they had lost their soul. Such national handwringing and reflection had a long history, and in fact had intensified following the Gwangju uprising of 1980, but now it seemed as if the country was being bombarded with material evidence for this sense of malaise.

The worsening mood continued through the final year of the Kim Young Sam presidency in 1997, with the revelations of corruption surrounding his son only magnifying his administration's unpopularity. The final blow to Kim's reputation hit in late summer of 1997, in the midst of the presidential election campaign for his successor. What began as a precipitous depreciation of currencies through a speculative run in Southeast Asia soon hit South Korea, which suffered, like these other countries, from runaway growth and foreign debt that left it vulnerable to fluctuations in the currency markets. More ominously, the spreading financial crisis in Asia exposed a South Korean economy with serious structural problems, such as mountains of underperforming loans—many government-sponsored—to enormous conglomerates that had taken this unending supply of easy credit to expand without restraint. Like the roads, bridges, and buildings of the preceding years, the edifice of the South Korean financial and economic system came down like a house of cards. This resulted in the rapid depreciation of the Korean *won*, a dive in the stock markets, and worst of all for the populace, the bankruptcy of thousands of firms both big and small. The collapse and downsizing of companies and the massive wave of layoffs struck the people like a punch in the stomach, victimizing workers both blue and white collar alike. The social dislocation and bitter despondency that ensued were exacerbated by the national humiliation suffered, from the South Korean perspective, at the hands of the IMF. The IMF rescued the South Korean government from insolvency by arranging a $57 billion bailout, but only according to its formula of austerity coupled with structural reforms. Prevailing views still refer to this crisis as the "IMF period," as if the lords of world capitalism were more responsible for a problem that South Koreans appear to have brought onto themselves.

In licking their wounds, however, South Koreans soon demonstrated that the worst of times could also bring out the best in people. They found the bitter medicine of restructuring and sacrifice in every major sector of the economy—from the conglomerates and state-controlled banks to labor unions—a bit easier to swallow by their sense of national cohesion. This collective consciousness suffused the social fabric, made visible in everything from telethons to locally organized campaigns to help laid off workers and contribute to the repayment of the IMF loan. The stunning sight of South Koreans bringing their jewelry, family heirlooms, and wads of cash to the collection centers pointed to the power of national identity, as well as perhaps to the thoughtful reflection on their recent history that began well before the financial collapse. In the midst of the most serious crisis to hit the South Korean economy since the Korean War, the people demonstrated a resolve to lay the foundation for national rebirth.

The IMF loan was repaid far ahead of schedule, and the reforms demanded by the IMF, while imposing austerity measures that might have exacerbated economic polarization and maintained the power of the major conglomerates, facilitated the transition to a postindustrial economy. This economy would be built largely on information technologies that turned South Korea into the most wired country in the world. Some of the same technological, social, and cultural factors also converged to transform South Korea quickly into one of the most wire-*less* countries as well, with much of social interaction coming to be centered on the mobile phone. Such a revival corresponded, in the political arena, also to a fundamentally different approach to the relationship with North Korea. The "Sunshine Policy" of President Kim Dae Jung, who won election in late 1997 with the slimmest of victory margins and promptly shepherded the country through the economic crisis, sought to engage the North through a focus on reconciliation and assistance. This shift led to the historical summit meeting in Pyongyang in the summer of 2000 between Kim Dae Jung and Kim Jong Il. It was discovered later that this agreement had included a massive, secret payment to the Northern regime, a revelation that tainted the historical judgment on these efforts as well as on Kim Dae Jung's Nobel Peace Prize that year. But despite these setbacks, symbolically the summit signaled the transformation of South Korea as it reemerged from the financial crisis to face the new century.

WOMEN AND FAMILY: SEISMIC SHIFTS

One of the areas that underwent the most striking shifts involved the social and familial standing of women. The suddenness and scale of changes along these lines said more about the relatively slow pace of progress in gender relations before the 1990s, especially in the broader areas of customs and family law. In fact, until the closing decade of the twentieth century, family law had remained the legal realm that had most successfully resisted de-Confucianization, despite the many and rapid developments in political rule and socioeconomic conditions over the modern era. But the industrialization, urbanization, and democratization of the late twentieth century compelled the legal system to account, finally, for very different circumstances. The 1990s witnessed a major series of family law reforms that provided greater rights and authority to women. These included the possibility for women to succeed a descent line as family head, the legal recognition of children born out of wedlock, and equal rights for divorced women in child custody and property disputes. But as the strengthening voices of women's organizations made clear, these steps only partially addressed the realities of family life for females, and through these groups' influence another major set of legal reforms was passed in the middle of the 2000s. These provisions attacked the last major vestige of traditional family law, that of the household registration system, which had given overwhelming authority to the male "head of household" to determine the identity and rights of family members. These reforms also abolished the centuries-long prohibition of marriage between two people of the same patrilineal "clan" identity, eliminated the six-month delay before divorced women could remarry, allowed children of divorced parents to take the surname of the mother or stepfather, and legally recognized the relationship between divorced mothers and their biological children.

As these moves suggested, the increasing incidence of divorce stood out as one of the most conspicuous phenomena in South Korean society. In fact, within a decade after the legal reforms of the mid-1990s, South Korea became marked by one of the highest divorce rates in the world, which was probably not unrelated to other extraordinary changes: a precipitous drop in the birth rate, and an equally stark increase in the number of women who either did not get married or declined to have children after marriage. While traditionalists decried these developments and saw the legal reforms as only exacerbating the problem, many citizens perceived such outcomes as a reflection of social realities and as a release for women from the unequal burdens of Confucian family customs. Furthermore, these developments, so went the argument, represented only a portion of the larger phenomenon of Korean women belatedly gaining the freedom to pursue interests, careers, and family arrangements long enjoyed by modern Korean men. (The capstone to this trend came in 2015 with the overturning of the prohibition on adultery, which seemed astoundingly outdated but actually had been instituted in the 1950s in order to abolish institutionalized concubinage, for the sake of women's rights.)

The seemingly sudden emergence of prominent women in many social realms—with big business a conspicuous exception—seemed to support such growing sentiments and legal changes. Beginning in the late 1990s, but especially in the opening years of the new century, South Korean women took high-profile, leadership positions in academia, broadcasting, and politics and government. The latter realm included the first female prime minister, in 2006, and later the first woman president, in 2012. Interestingly, Korean women also made a major splash in sports. Long having succeeded in international competition in archery and Taekwondo—offshoots of well-established traditional sports—and, of all things, short-track speed skating, Korean women, in the most striking development of all, began to dominate international golf. Starting with the breakout of Pak Se Ri in 1998 through her victories in two major championships, Korean women flooded the upper ranks of professional golf. Given South Korea's short history in this sport, the number of top Korean players and their victories was staggering.

Popular culture, too, reflected the rapidly changing standing of women in South Korea. Much of the mass culture industry was driven by female consumers, although the portrayal of Korean women in films and television dramas often depicted a shallow preoccupation with material interests, especially among urbanites. But these dramatizations also showed the contradictions that tugged at the South Korean female: economic limitations as well as consumerist freedom, familial duties as well as individual desires, social controls as well as opportunities. What the portrayals and consumption patterns of popular culture had in common was their reflection of a very different world for South Korean women in the new century. The perennially popular television historical dramas also reflected these changing circumstances. In revisiting familiar historical figures and imagining others, these dramas showed a strikingly *modern* Korean female in settings dating back centuries or even millennia: intelligent, savvy characters determined to overcome life's limitations instead of being consumed by social constraints or fatalism. Perhaps most representative in this regard was "Jewel in the Palace" (*Daejanggeum*), about a sixteenth-century woman who began as a palace servant and, through her wit, skills, and perseverance, rose to the position of royal physician and chef. This television series became an international hit, attesting both to the sophistication of the Korean entertainment industry behind the "Korean wave" that washed over foreign shores, as well as to the wide-ranging appeal of contemporary changes affecting Korean women.

TOWARD A NEW ERA

While perhaps most conspicuous in their impact on women, the dramatic and rapid socioeconomic developments pervaded the country as a whole, which became increasingly driven by the lifestyles and interests of the younger generations. The generational divides of the new century proved influential, as the so-called Generation X of twenty-somethings, as well as the 386-generation in their thirties and forties (Chapter 26), together displayed a decidedly different perspective on a wide range of issues. The Gen-X youth, with their unprecedented spending power and cultural influence, often set the trends not only in consumer behavior, but also in the expansive realms of politics, civic movements, and collective consciousness. Largely unbound by conventional imperatives, they proved deft in negotiating disparate cultural norms, social behaviors, and identities. They were much more cosmopolitan than their elders, as South Korea's Internet revolution placed the world at their fingertips, and as they were increasingly composed of people from various ethnic backgrounds. Indeed, the continuing rapid influx of migrants from other parts of Asia came to constitute a major component of the evolving character of South Korea in the new century. Their social impact—from marriage patterns and government services to consumer culture—increased to the extent that the entire notion of Koreanness demanded reassessment.

Such an eagerness to reconsider long-standing norms accounted for much of the extraordinary displays during the 2002 co-hosting of the World Cup Finals. The unofficial fan club of the national team called itself the "Red Devils," and red shirts and sundry paraphernalia emblazoned with "Be the Reds" and other phrases in awkward English could be seen everywhere. The sentiment spread that this choice of nickname and slogan defied the association of the color red with North Koreans and communists from the days of anti-communist authoritarianism. If so, South Korean youth were appropriating the symbols of the past to craft a new identity, even national identity, that moved well beyond the Cold War confrontation and forged a greater awareness of Korea's ties to the larger world. As the national team—managed, significantly, by a Dutch coach—performed far beyond expectations, and as the streets filled with larger swarms of people eager to partake in the euphoria, it became clear that these gatherings were about much more than watching football together; they were about the overwhelming desire to experience directly a new mode of social connection as it was being invented.

After South Korea, a heavy underdog, beat Portugal to advance to the round of sixteen, the crowds grew even bigger for the next game against Italy, another perennial power. At the start of this game, the Red Devils constructed a gigantic sign on one end of the stadium reading "Again 1966." This referred to the last time an Asian team shocked the football world with a win over an established World Cup nation: North Korea's victory over Italy in 1966. As if on cue, the South Korean team achieved a hard-fought, stunning overtime win over the exhausted Italians. For the next game, the quarterfinal match against Spain, what seemed like a phenomenon that could not get any bigger did exactly that, as now millions of Koreans filled city plazas, parks, and other designated areas to channel their collective spirit to the national team. The game ended in regulation time with a scoreless tie, but the Koreans had escaped some close calls and seemed, finally, overmatched. When the extra period achieved no resolution, however, the game entered the penalty kick shootout stage, when psychology was said to be more decisive than skill. Playing in front of a raucous home crowd in the city of Gwangju, the South Korean team proved this aphorism true, as the captain, Hong Myung-Bo, booted the ball past the Spanish goalkeeper for the game-winner. This moment, magically captured in a famous photo of Hong gliding across the pitch with his arms outstretched in celebration, would represent the high point in the annals of Korean football, for South Korea would fall to Germany in the semi-final match, then lose again in the third-place match against Turkey. But the national team had taken the country on a rapturous journey over a four-week span, a symbolic capstone to South Korea's revival from the depths of despair just five years earlier.

THE PENDULUM OF SOUTH KOREAN POLITICS

It is likely that the youth-led excitement of the 2002 World Cup also played a role in the election of Roh Moo-hyun as the next president later that year. Roh, the "liberal" candidate who came almost out of nowhere to earn the ruling party's nomination, had faced long odds of winning. The people had grown weary of Kim Dae Jung's administration, which was mired in corruption scandals, and the opposing candidate from the conservative party was a highly-respected, well-known figure. But, in addition to overwhelming support from the younger generations, who were cultivated through an innovative Internet-centered campaign, Roh rode a wave of anti-American sentiment in 2002. When two school girls were accidentally run over by an American military vehicle in the spring, fierce protests and large-scale candlelight vigils arose to demand punishment of the soldiers involved. Even before this incident, one of Roh's central campaign platforms had been a reconsideration of the American alliance, including greater assertiveness of South Korea's autonomy and interests. That such a pledge enjoyed widespread support spoke to the way anti-Americanism, a very complex phenomenon that developed from many factors, continued to resonate among many South Koreans. Still, it was never known with any degree of probability that Roh would win, and when he did, the country witnessed the first transfer of power from one liberal administration to another.

Once in office Roh became the standard-bearer of the 386-generation's ideals and interests, even though he himself did not belong to this generation, and his broad appeal to younger, progressive Koreans generated a passionate following. In his governing approach, however, Roh, an inordinately introspective and intelligent man, also came across often as arrogant and aloof to both his political foes and the conservative media, which constantly hounded him. This ensured that many of his signature reform efforts, which on the whole were targeted at greater socioeconomic equality and the rectification of historical imbalances, would not succeed. He was even impeached for abuse of power before an election by the opposition-led National Assembly in 2004, though this transparently political move was soon overturned by the Constitutional Court. His biggest failure, perhaps, was the defeat of his efforts to move the administrative capital away from Seoul in order to relieve congestion and hyper-centralization, a step later taken anyway. And almost inevitably, it seemed, his presidency lost its public support, coming to an end amid a general sense of unease from stagnant job growth and, ironically, increasing bifurcation of the population according to wealth.

The next president, Lee Myung-bak, promised bold steps to provide "relief" from the policies pushed by ten years of liberal rule when he won the election in 2007. He called for a reassessment of the Sunshine Policy toward North Korea and a reaffirmation of close ties to the United States. And he vowed to achieve rates of economic growth that would harken back to the Park Chung Hee era. His signature campaign, the Four Major Rivers Project, in fact displayed the same approach to tackling problems by building and reshaping big things—his nickname was "The Bulldozer"—that he had deployed in his previous jobs as head of Hyundai Construction and mayor of Seoul. The latter experience, the perceived success of which became the basis for his political support on the national stage, had included the rehabilitation of downtown Seoul's dormant Cheonggye Stream, which became a well-received tourist attraction. The Four Rivers Project, then, constituted an exponential enlargement of this basic blueprint for state management of natural resources, touting restoration, beautification, and higher quality of life along the riverbanks while also strengthening the infrastructures for water conservation and flood prevention. These claims were vociferously disputed by a wide range of opposing civic forces, however, who all decried the heavy-handed, undemocratic manner by which Lee devised, got parliamentary approval for, and carried out a venture that took such a heavy financial and environmental toll. Although it was mostly completed, at a cost of nearly $20 billion, by the time he left office in early 2013, the project's larger impact remained unclear.

Otherwise, the most notable event during Lee's administration involved his predecessor: the shocking suicide of Roh Moo-hyun in May 2009 amidst intensifying investigations into suspicions of bribery during his presidency. And as if by fate, the other main pillar of recent liberal politics, former president Kim Dae Jung, passed away three months later. Main-line progressives found themselves suddenly without their two most prominent voices, which left them weakened in opposing Lee Myung-bak's administration and in articulating a compelling rationale for their existence, particularly in the face of smaller parties further to the left. The liberals' precarious public standing as a group of mostly opposition figures only deepened with the close defeat, in the 2012 presidential election, of their candidate, Moon Jae-in. Moon had been one of the closest aides to Roh Moo-hyun, whose popularity spiked after his death, and ran on a platform promising to restore Roh's governing approach and philosophy.

Moon's opponent from the conservative party was Park Geun-hye, the daughter of former president Park Chung Hee. This fact alone had allowed her to shoot up the ranks of the political establishment at the turn of the twenty-first century. In 2007, Park barely lost her party's primary election to the eventual president-elect, Lee Myung-bak, but on her second try in 2012, she won both the nomination and the presidential election. From early on in her presidency, however, it appeared that, more than as a distinctive voice, she served as a vehicle for broader political forces wanting to mobilize the nostalgia for her father among older generations. She and her handlers revived the twin pillars of her father's developmentalist drive, long after South Korea had achieved development—namely a fierce anti-communist rhetoric and policy vis-a-vis North Korea, and a reprisal of the state's patronage of big business. To be sure, these had been core orientations of also her predecessor, Lee

Myung-bak, but Lee had entered office with abundant executive experience in both government and enterprise. Park had only her name.

The sense that Park was unprepared and overwhelmed in her duties escalated precipitously with the most tragic event in South Korea in a generation: the sinking of the Sewol ferry on April 16, 2014 off the southwest coast that took over 300 lives, mostly high school students on an outing. As it turned out, they had been abandoned not only by the ship's captain, but by the system as a whole, a venal mix of regulators and company bosses who allowed such a dangerous vessel to operate. Even more stunning, however, was the utterly inept government response in the critical hours immediately after the ship began to capsize, when it was still substantially above the water. Helicopters showing live video could hover over the scene, but no rescue craft of sufficient capacity, in the air or the water, could take action. South Koreans watching this unfold on television found, incredibly, that nothing more was being done by emergency response agencies, and that the president herself remained largely detached from the crisis, unable to do anything beyond expressing hopes for a rescue.

The fallout from this unbearably sad event amounted to a stunning realization that, despite all the progress that South Korea had made over the previous several decades, including formal democratization and economic restructuring, some disturbing remnants of the past remained, or had been revived. The collusion between government and industry helped shape a culture of indulgence and misbehavior on both sides, even regarding public safety, through a prioritization of speed and results over propriety and process. The workings of these factors in producing such a tragedy were depressingly similar to what had happened two decades earlier with the collapse of the Sampung Department Store. Despite the sense of renewal that marked the turn of the twenty-first century, then, the Sewol disaster of 2014 would become an emblem of the new era as much as the hosting of the World Cup in 2002 had been. It remained to be seen which of these two events would have a more lasting impact on both the country and its history.

Further Readings

GENERAL HISTORIES AND SOURCE COMPILATIONS

Clark, Donald N. *Korea in World History*. Association for Asian Studies, 2012.

Cumings, Bruce. *Korea's Place in the Sun: A Modern History*. W. W. Norton, 1997.

Eckert, Carter et al. *Korea Old and New: A History*. Harvard University Press, 1991.

Kim, Djun-Kil. *The History of Korea*. Greenwood Press, 2005.

Kim, Sun Joo and Jungwon Kim (trs). *Wrongful Deaths: Selected Inquest Records from Nineteenth-Century Korea*. University of Washington Press, 2013.

Lee, Ki-baek. *A New History of Korea*. Translated by Edward W. Wagner, with Edward J. Shultz. Harvard University Press, 1984.

Lee, Peter H. (ed.). *A History of Korean Literature*. Cambridge University Press, 2003.

Lee, Peter, Theodore DeBary, Yŏngho Ch'oe, and Hugh H. W. Kang (eds). *Sources of Korean Tradition, Vols 1–2*. Columbia University Press, 1996, 2000.

Peterson, Mark. *A Brief History of Korea*. Facts on File, 2010.

Pratt, Keith. *Everlasting Flower: A History of Korea*. Reaktion Books, 2007.

Pratt, Keith and Richard Rutt, with additional material by James Hoare. *Korea: A Historical and Cultural Dictionary*. Curzon, 1999.

Robinson, Michael E. *Korea's Twentieth-Century Odyssey*. University of Hawai'i Press, 2007.

Seth, Michael. *A History of Korea: From Antiquity to the Present*. Rowman & Littlefield Publishers, 2010.

Shin, Gi-Wook. *Ethnic Nationalism in Korea: Genealogy, Politics, And Legacy*. Stanford University Press, 2006.

Shin, Michael D. (ed.). *Korean History in Maps—From Prehistory to the Twenty-First Century*. Cambridge University Press, 2014.

Wells, Kenneth M. *Korea: Outline of a Civilisation*. Brill, 2015.

1 GOGURYEO AND ANCIENT KOREA

Barnes, Gina. *State Formation in Korea: Historical and Archaeological Perspectives*. Routledge Curzon, 2001.

Byington, Mark (ed.). *Early Korea: Reconsidering Early Korean History Through Archaeology*. University of Hawai'i Press, 2008.

Jeon, Ho-tae. *Koguryo: The Origin of Korean Power and Pride*. Seoul: Northeast Asia History Foundation, 2007.

Kim Pusik. *The Koguryŏ Annals of the Samguk Sagi*. Translated by Edward J. Shultz and Hugh Kang. Seoul: The Academy of Korean Studies Press, 2011.

National Museum of Korea. *Goguryeo Tomb Murals – Replicas in the National Museum of Korea*. National Museum of Korea, 2007.

Nelson, Sarah. *The Archaeology of Korea*. Cambridge University Press, 1993.

2 QUEEN SEONDEOK AND SILLA'S UNIFICATION OF KOREA

Best, Jonathan. *A History of the Early Korean Kingdom of Paekche, Together with an Annotated Translation of The Paekche Annals of the Samguk Sagi*. Harvard University Asia Center, 2007.

Kim Pusik. *The Silla Annals of the Samguk Sagi*. Translated by Edward Shultz and Hugh Kang. Academy of Korean Studies Press, 2012.

Lee, Kidong. "The Indigenous Religions of Silla: Their Diversity and Durability." *Korean Studies* 28 (2005): 49–74.

McBride, Richard D., II. "Pak Ch'anghwa and the *Hwarang segi* Manuscripts." *Journal of Korean Studies* 13:1 (Fall 2008): 57–88.

Mintz, Grafton (ed.). Translated by Tae-Hung Ha *Samguk Yusa: Legends and History of the Three Kingdoms of Ancient Korea*. Silla Pagoda, 2008.

Nha, Il-Seong. "Silla's Cheomseongdae." *Korea Journal* 41:4 (Winter 2001): 269–81.

Park, Hyun-Sook. "Baekje's Relationship with Japan in the 6th Century." *International Journal of Korean History* 11 (December 2007): 97–115.

3 UNIFIED SILLA

McBride, Richard D., II. *Domesticating the Dharma: Buddhist Cults and the Hwaom Synthesis in Silla Korea*. University of Hawai'i Press, 2007.

Reischauer, Edwin O. (tr.). *Ennin's Diary: The Record of a Pilgrimage to China in Search of the Law*. Ronald Press Co., 1955.

Reischauer, Edwin O. *Ennin's Travels in Tang China*. Ronald Press Co., 1955.

Wonhyo. *Cultivating Original Enlightenment: Wohnyo's Exposition of the Vajrasamadhi-Sutra (Kumgang Sammaegyong Non)*. Translated by Robert E. Buswell Jr. University of Hawai'i Press, 2007.

4   FOUNDING OF THE GORYEO DYNASTY

Breuker, Remco E. *Establishing a Pluralist Society in Medieval Korea, 918–1170*. Brill, 2010.

Duncan, John. "Koguryŏ in Koryŏ and Chosŏn Historical Memory." *Journal of Inner and East Asian Studies* 1 (2004).

Ledyard, Gari. "Yin and Yang in the China-Manchuria-Korea Triangle." In Morris Rossabi (ed.). *China Among Equals: The Middle Kingdom and Its Neighbors, 10th–14th Centuries*. Berkeley: University of California Press, 1983.

Ro, Myoung-ho. "Perception and Policy of the Koryŏ Ruling Class toward the People of Parhae." *Seoul Journal of Korean Studies* 13 (2000): 125–42.

Rogers, Michael C. "National Consciousness in Medieval Korea: The Impact of Liao and Chin on Koryŏ." In Morris Rossabi (ed.). *China Among Equals: The Middle Kingdom and Its Neighbors, 10th–14th Centuries*. University of California Press, 1983.

5   RELIGION AND REGIONALISM IN THE GORYEO ORDER

Breuker, Remco E. "Koryŏ as an Independent Realm: The Emperor's Clothes?" *Korean Studies* 27 (2004): 48–84.

Chinul. *The Korean Approach to Zen: The Collected Works of Chinul*. Translated by Robert E. Buswell. University of Hawai'i Press, 1983.

Lancaster, Lewis R., Kikun Suh, and Chai-shin Yu (eds). *Buddhism in Koryŏ: A Royal Religion*. Institute of East Asian Studies, UC-Berkeley, 1996.

Shultz, Edward J. "An Introduction to the *Samguk Sagi*." *Korean Studies* 28 (2005): 1–13.

Vermeersch, Sem. *The Power of the Buddhas: The Politics of Buddhism during the Koryŏ Dynasty (918–1392)*. Harvard University Asia Center, 2008.

6   THE MONGOL OVERLORD PERIOD

Robinson, David M. *Empire's Twilight: Northeast Asia under the Mongols*. Harvard Asia Center, 2009.

Shultz, Edward J. *Generals and Scholars: Military Rule in Medieval Korea*. University of Hawai'i Press, 2000.

Yun, Peter I. "Popularization of Mongol Language and Culture in the Late Koryo Period." *International Journal of Korean History* 10 (December 2006): 25–41.

7   GORYEO-JOSEON TRANSITION

Bary, Wm. Theodore de, and JaHyun Kim Haboush (eds). *The Rise of Neo-Confucianism in Korea*. Columbia University Press, 1986.

Ch'oe, Yong-ho. *The Civil Examinations and the Social Structure in Early Yi Dynasty Korea, 1392–1600*. Seoul: Korean Research Center, 1987.

Choi, Byonghyon (tr. and annotated). *The Annals of King T'aejo: Founder of Korea's Chosŏn Dynasty*. Harvard University Press, 2015.

Duncan, John B. *The Origins of the Chosŏn Dynasty*. University of Washington Press, 2000.

Wagner, Edward W. *The Literati Purges: Political Conflict in Early Yi Korea*. Harvard University Press, 1974.

8   CONFUCIANISM AND THE FAMILY IN THE EARLY JOSEON ERA

Chung, Edward Y. J. *The Korean Neo-Confucianism of Yi T'oegye and Yi Yulgok: A Reappraisal of the "Four-Seven Thesis" and Its Practical Implications for Self-Cultivation*. SUNY Press, 1995.

Deuchler, Martina. *The Confucian Transformation of Korea: A Study of Society and Ideology*. Harvard University, Council on East Asian Studies, 1992.

Lee, Hai-soon. *The Poetic World of Classic Korean Women Writers*. Translated by Won-Jae Hur. Ewha Womans University Press, 2005.

Ro, Young-chan. *The Korean Neo-Confucianism of Yi Yulgok*. SUNY Press, 1989.

Yi Hwang. *To Become a Sage: The Ten Diagrams on Sage Learning*. Translated by Michael C. Kalton. Columbia University Press, 1988.

9   THE GREAT INVASIONS, 1592–1636

Ha, Tae-hung (tr.), and Sohn Pow-key (ed.). *Imjin Changch'o: Admiral Yi Sun-sin's Memorials to Court*. Yonsei University Press, 1981.

Haboush, JaHyun Kim and Kenneth R. Robinson (eds and trs). *A Korean War Captive in Japan, 1597-1600—The Writings of Kang Hang*. Columbia University Press, 2013.

Ledyard, Gari. "Confucianism and War: The Korean Security Crisis of 1598." *The Journal of Korean Studies* 6 (1988–89): 81–119.

Lewis, James B. *Frontier Contact between Chosŏn Korea and Tokugawa Japan*. Routledge Curzon, 2003.

Swope, Kenneth M. *A Dragon's Head and a Serpent's Tail: Ming China and the First Great East Asian War, 1592–1598*. University of Oklahoma Press, 2009.

Yu Sŏng-nyong. *The Book of Corrections: Reflections on the National Crisis During the Japanese Invasion of Korea, 1592–1598*. Translated by Choi Byonghyon. Institute of East Asian Studies, UC-Berkeley, 2002.

10   IDEOLOGY, FAMILY, AND NATIONHOOD IN THE MID-JOSEON ERA

Chi, Sung-jong. "The Study of Social Status Groups in the Chosŏn Period." *The Review of Korean Studies* 4:2 (December 2001): 243–63.

Deuchler, Martina. *Under the Ancestors' Eyes—Kinship, Status, and Locality in Premodern Korea*. Harvard University Asia Center, 2015.

Duncan, John B. "Proto-nationalism in Premodern Korea." In Sang-Oak Lee and Duk-Soo Park (eds). *Perspectives on Korea*. Wild Peony, 1998.

Haboush, JaHyun Kim (ed.). *Epistolary Korea: Letters from the Communicative Space of the Chosŏn, 1392–1910*. Columbia University Press, 2009.

Haboush, JaHyun Kim and Martina Deuchler (eds). *Culture and the State in Late Chosŏn Korea*. Harvard University Asia Center, 1999.

Kim, Sun Joo. *Voice from the North: Resurrecting Regional Identity Through the Life and Work of Yi Sihang (1672–1736)*. Stanford University Press, 2013.

Park, Chan E. "Sukchong's Triangle: The Politics of Passion." *Korean Studies* 19 (1995): 83–103.

Park, Eugene Y. *Between Dreams and Reality: The Military Examination in Late Chosŏn Korea, 1600–1894*. Harvard University Asia Center, 2007.

Peterson, Mark. *Korean Adoption and Inheritance: Case Studies in the Creation of a Classic Confucian Society.* Cornell University East Asian Program, 1996.

Setton, Mark. "Factional Politics and Philosophical Development in the Late Chosŏn." *Journal of Korean Studies* 8 (1992): 37–79.

Song, Ki-joong. *The Study of Foreign Languages in the Chosŏn Dynasty.* Jimoondang, 2000.

11   INTELLECTUAL OPENING IN THE LATE EIGHTEENTH CENTURY

Chŏng Yagyong. *Admonitions on Governing the People—Manual for All Administrators.* Translated by Choi Byonghyon. University of California Press, 2010.

Eggert, Marion. "Dramatic Art and Performativity in Pak Chiwŏn's Travel Narrative," *Asiatische Studien: Zeitschrift der Schweizerischen Asiengesellschaft* 58 (2004).

Jun, Seong Ho, James B. Lewis, and Kang Han-Rog. "Korean Expansion and Decline from the Seventeenth to the Nineteenth Century: A View Suggested by Adam Smith." *Journal of Economic History* 68:1 (March 2008): 244–82.

Haboush, JaHyun Kim. *The Confucian Kingship in Korea: Yŏngjo and the Politics of Sagacity.* Columbia University Press, 2001.

Haboush, JaHyun Kim (ed. and tr.). *The Memoirs of Lady Hyegyong: The Autobiographical Writings of a Crown Princess of Eighteenth-Century Korea.* University of California Press, 1996.

Ledyard, Gari. "Hong Taeyong and His Peking Memoir." *Korean Studies* 6 (1982): 63–103.

Organization of Korean Historians. *Everyday Life in Joseon-Era Korea— Economy and Society.* Michael Shin, (ed.) Brill, 2014.

Pak Chiwŏn. *The Jehol Diary.* Translated and edited by Yang-Hi Choe-Wall. Leiden: Brill, 2010.

Palais, James. *Confucian Statecraft and Korean Institutions: Yu Hyŏngwŏn and Late Chosŏn Dynasty.* University of Washington Press, 1996.

Park Jiwon. *The Novels of Park Jiwon.* Translated by Emanuel Pastreich. Seoul National University Press, 2011.

Setton, Mark. *Chŏng Yagyong: Korea's Challenge to Orthodox Neo-Confucianism.* State University of New York Press, 1997.

12   POPULAR CULTURE IN THE LATE JOSEON ERA

Haboush, JaHyun Kim. "Rescoring the Universal in a Korean Mode: Eighteenth-Century Korean Culture." In Hongnam Kim (ed.). *Korean Arts of the Eighteenth Century: Splendor and Simplicity*. New York: The Asia Society Galleries, 1993.

Jungmann, Burglind. *Painters as Envoys: Korean Inspiration in Eighteenth-Century Japanese Nanga*. Princeton University Press, 2004.

Kim, Jisoo M. *The Emotions of Justice: Gender, Status, and Legal Performance in Choson Korea*. University of Washington Press, 2015.

Pettid, Michael J. "Sexual Identity in Chosŏn Period Literature: Humorous Accounts of Forbidden Passion." *The Review of Korean Studies* 4:1 (June 2001): 61–85.

Pihl, Marshall R. *The Korean Singer of Tales*. Council on East Asian Studies, 1994.

Shima, Mutsuhiko. "In Quest of Social Recognition: A Retrospective View on the Development of Korean Lineage Organization." *Harvard Journal of Asiatic Studies* 50:1 (June 1990): 87–129.

13   NINETEENTH-CENTURY UNREST

Chung, Chai-Sik. *A Korean Confucian Encounter with the Modern World: Yi Hang-No and the West*. Institute of East Asian Studies, UC-Berkeley, 1995.

Deuchler, Martina. *Confucian Gentlemen and Barbarian Envoys: The Opening of Korea, 1875–1885*. University of Washington Press, 1977.

Kallander, George. *Salvation through Dissent: Tonghak Heterodoxy and Early Modern Korea*. University of Hawai'i Press, 2013.

Karlsson, Anders. "Challenging the Dynasty: Popular Protest, *Chŏnggamnok* and the Ideology of the Hong Kyŏngnae Rebellion." *International Journal of Korean History* 2 (2001): 255–77.

Kim, Sun Joo. *Marginality and Subversion in Korea: The Hong Kyongnae Rebellion of 1812*. University of Washington Press, 2007.

Palais, James B. *Politics and Policy in Traditional Korea*. University of Washington Press, 1991.

14   1894, A FATEFUL YEAR

Eckert, Carter. "Korea's Transition to Modernity: A Will to Greatness." In Merle Goldman and Andrew Gordon (eds). *Historical Perspectives on Contemporary East Asia*, pp. 119–54. Harvard University Press, 2000.

Hwang, Kyung Moon. *Beyond Birth: Social Status in the Emergence of Modern Korea*. Harvard Asia Center, 2004.

Lew, Young Ick. "The Conservative Character of the 1894 Tonghak Peasant Uprising: A Reappraisal with Emphasis on Chŏn Pong-jun's Background and Motivation." *The Journal of Korean Studies* 7 (1990): 149–80.

Lew, Young Ick. "Yuan Shih-kai's Residency and the Korean Enlightenment Movement, 1885–94." *The Journal of Korean Studies* 5 (1984): 63–108.

Mutsu Munemitsu. *Kenkenroku: A Diplomatic Record of the Sino-Japanese War, 1894–95*. Edited and translated by Gordon Mark Berger. Princeton University Press, 1982.

15   THE GREAT KOREAN EMPIRE

Chandra, Vipan. *Imperialism, Resistance, and Reform in Late Nineteenth-Century Korea: Enlightenment and the Independence Club*. Institute of East Asian Studies, UC-Berkeley, 1988.

Hwang, Kyung Moon. *Rationalizing Korea: The Rise of the Modern State, 1894–1945*. University of California Press, 2015.

Kim, Christine J. "Politics and Pageantry in Protectorate Korea (1905–10): The Imperial Progresses of Sunjong." *The Journal of Asian Studies* 68:3 (2009): 835–59.

Larsen, Kirk W. *Tradition, Treaties, and Trade: Qing Imperialism and Chosŏn Korea, 1850–1910*. Harvard University Asia Center, 2008.

Park, Eugene Y. *A Family of No Prominence: The Descendants of Pak Tŏkhwa and the Birth of Modern Korea*. Stanford University Press, 2014.

Schmid, Andre. *Korea Between Empires, 1895–1919*. Columbia University Press, 2002.

Son, Min Suh. "Enlightenment and Electrification: The Introduction of Electric Light, Telegraph and Streetcars in Late 19th Century Korea." In Dong-no Kim, John Duncan, and Do-hyung Kim (eds). *Reform and Modernity in the Taehan Empire*. Jimoondang, 2006.

16   THE JAPANESE TAKEOVER, 1904–18

Dudden, Alexis. *Japan's Colonization of Korea: Discourse and Power*. University of Hawai'i Press, 2004.

Duus, Peter. *The Abacus and The Sword: The Japanese Penetration of Korea, 1895–1910*. University of California Press, 1995.

Finch, Michael. *Min Yŏng-hwan: A Political Biography*. University of Hawai'i Press, 2002.

Henry, Todd. *Assimilating Seoul: Japanese Rule and the Politics of Public Space in Colonial Korea, 1910–1945*. University of California Press, 2014.

Moon, Yumi. *Populist Collaborators: The Ilchinhoe and the Japanese Colonization of Korea, 1896–1910*. Cornell University Press, 2013.

Myers, Ramon H. and Mark R. Peattie (eds). *The Japanese Colonial Empire, 1895–1945*. Princeton University Press, 1984.

Rhee, Syngman. *The Spirit of Independence: A Primer on Korean Modernization and Reform*. University of Hawai'i Press, 2001.

Robinson, Michael. "National Identity and the Thought of Sin Ch'aeho: Sadaejuŭi and Chuch'e in History and Politics." *Journal of Korean Studies* 5 (1984): 121–42.

Uchida, Jun. *Brokers of Empire: Japanese Settler Colonialism in Korea, 1876–1945*. Harvard University Asia Center, 2011.

17   THE LONG 1920s

Hyun, Theresa. *Writing Women in Korea: Translation and Feminism in the Early Twentieth Century*. University of Hawai'i Press, 2004.

Kawashima, Ken. *The Proletarian Gamble: Korean Workers in Interwar Japan*. Duke University Press, 2009.

Kim, Janice. *To Live to Work: Factory Women in Colonial Korea, 1910–1945*. Stanford University Press, 2008.

Kim, Yung-Hee. "Creating New Paradigms of Womanhood in Modern Korean Literature: Na Hye-sŏk's 'Kyŏnghŭi.'" *Korean Studies* 26:1 (2002): 1–60.

Robinson, Michael. *Cultural Nationalism in Colonial Korea, 1920–1925*. University of Washington Press, 1988.

Wells, Kenneth. *New God, New Nation: Protestants and Self-Reconstruction Nationalism in Korea, 1896–1937*. University of Hawai'i Press, 1991.

Yoo, Theodore Jun. *The Politics of Gender in Colonial Korea: Education, Labor, and Health, 1910–1945*. University of California Press, 2008.

Young, Louise. *Japan's Total Empire: Manchuria and the Culture of Wartime Imperialism*. University of California Press, 1998.

18   NATION, CULTURE, AND EVERYDAY LIFE IN THE LATE COLONIAL PERIOD

Atkins, E. Taylor. *Primitive Selves: Koreana in the Japanese Colonial Gaze, 1910–1945*. University of California Press, 2010.

Caprio, Mark E. *Japanese Assimilation Policies in Colonial Korea, 1910–1945*. University of Washington Press, 2009.

Ch'ae Man-Sik. *Peace Under Heaven*. Translated by Chun Kyung-ja. M.E. Sharpe, 1993.

Eckert, Carter J. *Offspring of Empire: The Koch'ang Kims and the Colonial Origins of Korean Capitalism, 1876–1945*. University of Washington Press, 1991.

Em, Henry E. *The Great Enterprise: Sovereignty and Historiography in Modern Korea*. Duke University Press, 2013.

Kim, Chong-un and Bruce Fulton (eds and trs). *A Ready-Made Life: Early Masters of Korean Fiction*. University of Hawai'i Press, 1998.

Pai, Hyung Il. *Constructing "Korean" Origins: A Critical Review of Archaeology, Historiography, and Racial Myth in Korean State-Formation Theories*. Harvard University Asia Center, 2000.

Park, Soon-Won. *Colonial Industrialization and Labor in Korea: The Onoda Cement Factory*. Harvard University Asia Center, 1999.

Park, Sunyoung (ed. and tr.). *On the Eve of the Uprising and Other Stories from Colonial Korea*. Cornell East Asia Program, 2010.

Park, Sunyoung. *The Proletarian Wave: Literature and Leftist Culture in Colonial Korea, 1910–1945*. Harvard University Asia Center, 2015.

Shin, Gi-Wook Shin and Michael Robinson (eds). *Colonial Modernity in Korea*. Harvard University Asia Center, 1999.

Yom Sang-seop. *Three Generations*. Translated by Yu Young-nan. Archipelago Books, 2005.

19   WARTIME MOBILIZATION, 1938–45

Allen, Chizuko. "Northeast Asia Centered Around Korea: Ch'oe Namsŏn's View of History." *Journal of Asian Studies* 49 (1990): 787–806.

Eckert, Carter J. "Total War, Industrialization, and Social Change in Late Colonial Korea." In Peter Duus, R. H. Myers, and M. R. Peattie (eds). *The Japanese Wartime Empire, 1931–1945*. Princeton University Press, 1996.

Fujitani, Takashi. *Race for Empire: Koreans as Japanese and Japanese as Americans during World War II*. University of California Press, 2013.

Howard, Keith. *True Stories of the Korean Comfort Women*. Cassell, 1995.

Kang, Hildi. *Under the Black Umbrella: Voices from Colonial Korea, 1910–1945*. Cornell University Press, 2001.

Lee, Ann Sung-hi. *Yi Kwang-su and Modern Korean Literature: Mujong*. Cornell East Asia Program, 2005.

Palmer, Brandon. *Fighting for the Enemy: Koreans in Japan's War, 1937–1945*. University of Washington Press, 2013.

Park, Hyun Ok. *Two Dreams in One Bed: Empire, Social Life, and the Origins of the North Korean Revolution in Manchuria*. Duke University Press, 2005.

Shin, Gi-Wook. *Peasant Protest and Social Change in Colonial Korea*. University of Washington Press, 1996.

20   THE LIBERATION PERIOD, 1945–50

Cheong, Sung-hwa. *The Politics of Anti-Japanese Sentiment in Korea: Japanese-South Korea Relations Under American Occupation, 1945–1952*. Greenwood Press, 1991.

Clark, Donald N. *Living Dangerously in Korea: The Western Experience, 1900–1950*. Eastbridge, 2003.

Cumings, Bruce. *The Origins of the Korean War*, 2 vols. Princeton University Press, 1981, 1990.

Oh, Bonnie B. C. (ed.). *Korea under the American Military Government, 1945–1948*. Greenwood, 2002.

Weathersby, Kathryn. "Soviet Aims in Korea and the Origins of the Korean War, 1945–1950: New Evidence from Russian Archives." Working paper no. 8, Cold War International History Project. Woodrow Wilson Center, 1993.

21   THE KOREAN WAR

Appleman, Roy A. *Disaster in Korea: The Chinese Confront MacArthur*. Texas A & M University Press, 1989.

Bateman, Robert L. *No Gun Ri: A Military History of the Korean War Incident*. Stackpole Books, 2002.

Halberstam, David. *The Coldest Winter: America and the Korean War*. Hyperion, 2007.

Jaeger, Sheila Miyoshi. *Brothers at War: The Unending Conflict in Korea*. W.W. Norton, 2013.

Jin, Jingyi. "A Historical Review of the Return to Korea of Korean Soldiers in the Chinese Army." *Social Sciences in China* 27:4 (Winter 2006): 72–85.

Kim, Hak-joon. "The Korean War and China: The Sino-North Korean Relations Before the Chinese Intervention in the Korean War." *Journal of Social Sciences and Humanities* 59 (June 1984): 1–90.

Lee, Chae-Jin (ed.). *The Korean War: 40-Year Perspectives*. The Keck Center for International and Strategic Studies, 1991.

Stueck, William. *Rethinking the Korean War: A New Diplomatic and Strategic History*. Princeton University Press, 2002.

Tucker, Spencer C. *The Encyclopedia of the Korean War*, 3 vols. ABC-CLIO, 2010.

22 EARLY NORTH KOREA

Armstrong, Charles K. *The North Korean Revolution, 1945–1950*. Cornell University Press, 2003.

Armstrong, Charles K. *Tyranny of the Weak: North Korea and the World, 1950–1992*. Cornell University Press, 2013.

Cathcart, Adam, and Charles Kraus. "Peripheral Influence: The Sinuiju Student Incident of 1945 and the Impact of Soviet Occupation in North Korea." *The Journal of Korean Studies* 13:1 (Fall 2008): 1–28.

David-West, Alzo. "Marxism, Stalinism, and the Juche Speech of 1955: On the Theoretical De-Stalinization of North Korea." *The Review of Korean Studies* 10:3 (September 2007): 127–52.

Kim, Gwang-Oon. "The Making of the North Korean State." *The Journal of Korean Studies* 12:1 (Fall 2007): 15–42.

Kim, Suzy. *Everyday Life in the North Korean Revolution*. Cornell University Press, 2013.

Lankov, Andrei N. *Crisis in North Korea: The Failure of De-Stalinization, 1956*. University of Hawai'i Press, 2004.

Lankov, Andrei N. *From Stalin to Kim Il Sung: The Formation of North Korea, 1945–1960*. Rutgers University Press, 2002.

Myers, Brian R. *Han Sŏrya and North Korean Literature: The Failure of Socialist Realism in the DPRK*. Cornell East Asia Series, 1994.

Suh, Dae-Sook. *Kim Il Sung: The North Korean Leader*. Columbia University Press, 1995.

23   1960s SOUTH KOREA

Brazinsky, Gregg. *Nation Building in South Korea: Koreans, Americans, and the Making of a Democracy*. University of North Carolina Press, 2009.

Cha, Victor D. "Bridging the Gap: The Strategic Context of the 1965 Korea–Japan Normalization Treaty." *Korean Studies* 20 (1996): 123–60.

Han, Sungjoo. *The Failure of Democracy in South Korea*. University of California Press, 1974.

Kim, Charles. "Moral Imperatives: South Korean Studenthood and April 19th." *Journal of Asian Studies* 71.2 (2012): 399–422.

Kim, Byung-Kook, and Ezra Vogel (eds). *The Park Chung Hee Era: The Transformation of South Korea*. Harvard University Press, 2011.

Kirk, Donald. *Korean Dynasty: Hyundai and Chung Ju Yung*. M.E. Sharpe, 1997.

Lee, Jin-kyung. *Service Economies: Militarism, Sex Work, and Migrant Labor in South Korea*. University of Minnesota Press, 2010.

Moon, Katharine. *Sex Among Allies—Military Prostitution in U.S.-Korea Relations*. Columbia University Press, 1997.

Nam, Hwasook. *Building Ships, Building a Nation: Korea's Democratic Unionism under Park Chung Hee*. University of Washington Press, 2009.

Park Chung Hee. *Our Nation's Path: Ideology of Social Reconstruction*. Dong-a Publishing Company, 1969.

Steers, Richard M. *Made in Korea: Chung Ju Yung and the Rise of Hyundai*. Routledge, 1991.

24   CULTURE AND POLITICS IN 1970s SOUTH KOREA

Chang, Paul. *Protest Dialectics: State Repression and South Korea's Democracy Movement, 1970–1979*. Stanford University Press, 2015.

Kim, Chi-ha. *Cry of the People and Other Poems*. Autumn Press, 1974.

Kim, Chi-ha. *The Gold Crowned Jesus and Other Writings*. Orbis Books, 1978.

Kim, Eun Mee. *Big Business, Strong State: Collusion and Conflict in South Korean Developments, 1960–1990*. SUNY Press, 1997.

Kim, Hyung-A and Clark W. Sorensen (eds). *Reassessing the Park Chung Hee Era, 1961–1979: Development, Political Thought, Democracy, and Cultural Influence*. University of Washington Press, 2011.

Moon, Seungsook. *Militarized Modernity and Gendered Citizenship in South Korea*. Duke University Press, 2005.

Oberdorfer, Don. *The Two Koreas: A Contemporary History*. Basic Books, 2002.

Pak, Kyŏng-ni. *Land: A Novel*. Kegan Paul International, 1996.

Pihl, Marshall R., Bruce Fulton and Ju-Chan Fulton (trs). *Land of Exile: Contemporary Korean Fiction*. M.E. Sharpe, 1992.

25 MONUMENTAL LIFE IN NORTH KOREA

Chinoy, Mike. *Meltdown: The Inside Story of the North Korean Nuclear Crisis*. St. Martin's Griffin, 2009.

Cumings, Bruce. *North Korea: Another Country*. The New Press, 2004.

Demick, Barbara. *Nothing to Envy: Ordinary Lives in North Korea*. Spiegel & Grau, 2010.

Kihl, Young Whan and Hong Nack Kim (eds). *North Korea: The Politics of Regime Survival*. M.E. Sharpe, 2005.

Lankov, Andrei. *The Real North Korea: Life and Politics in the Failed Stalinist Utopia*. Oxford University Press, 2013.

Oh, Kongdan and Ralph C. Hassig. *North Korea through the Looking Glass*. Brookings Institution Press, 2000.

Quinones, C. Kenneth and Joseph Tragert. *The Complete Idiot's Guide to Understanding North Korea*. Alpha, 2004.

Ryang, Sonia (ed.). *North Korea: Toward a Better Understanding*. Lexington Books, 2008.

Yu, Chong-Ae. "The Rise and Demise of Industrial Agriculture in North Korea." *The Journal of Korean Studies* 12:1 (Fall 2007): 75–110.

26 SOUTH KOREAN DEMOCRATIZATION

Abelmann, Nancy. *Echoes of the Past, Epics of Dissent: A South Korean Social Movement*. University of California Press, 1996.

Kim, Sunhyuk. *The Politics of Democratization in Korea: The Role of Civil Society*. University of Pittsburgh Press, 2001.

Lee, Jae-Eui, Kap Su Seol, and Nick Mamatas. *Kwangju Diary: Beyond Death, Beyond the Darkness of the Age*. UCLA Asia Institute, 1999.

Lee, Namhee. *The Making of Minjung: Democracy and the Politics of Representation in South Korea*. Cornell University Press, 2009.

Shin, Gi-Wook and Kyung Moon Hwang (eds). *Contentious Kwangju: The May 18 Uprising in Korea's Past and Present*. Rowman & Littlefield, 2003.

27   SOUTH KOREA IN THE TWENTY-FIRST CENTURY

Abelmann, Nancy. *The Melodrama of Mobility: Women, Talk, and Class in Contemporary South Korea*. University of Hawai'i Press, 2003.

Huat, Chua Beng and Koichi Iwabuchi (eds). *East Asian Pop Culture: Analysing the Korean Wave*. Hong Kong University Press, 2008.

Kendall, Laurel (ed.). *Under Construction: The Gendering of Modernity, Class, and Consumption in the Republic of Korea*. University of Hawai'i Press, 2001.

Kim, Jasper. *Crisis and Change: South Korea in a Post-1997 New Era*. Ewha Womans University Press, 2006.

Kim, Kyung Hyun and Youngmin Choe (eds). *The Korean Popular Culture Reader*. Duke University Press, 2015.

Russell, Mark James. *Pop Goes Korea: Behind the Revolution in Movies, Music, and Internet Culture*. Stone Bridge Press, 2009.

Index